WEST AFRICAN TRADE
AND COAST SOCIETY

WEST AFRICAN HISTORY SERIES

General Editor: GERALD S. GRAHAM
Rhodes Professor of Imperial History, University of London

WEST AFRICAN TRADE AND COAST SOCIETY

A FAMILY STUDY

MARGARET PRIESTLEY

LONDON
OXFORD UNIVERSITY PRESS
IBADAN NAIROBI
1969

Oxford University Press, Ely House, London W.1

GLASGOW NEW YORK TORONTO MELBOURNE WELLINGTON
CAPE TOWN SALISBURY IBADAN NAIROBI LUSAKA ADDIS ABABA
BOMBAY CALCUTTA MADRAS KARACHI LAHORE DACCA
KUALA LUMPUR SINGAPORE HONG KONG TOKYO

Preparation and publication of this series
has been made possible by the generous
financial assistance of Overseas Newspapers
Group, Freetown, Lagos, London, and
West Indies

Printed in Great Britain by
Western Printing Services Ltd., Bristol

For
NEIL

CONTENTS

ILLUSTRATIONS

MAPS

ABBREVIATIONS

Public Record Office, London
(P.R.O.)

Adm. 1   Admiralty Records, Secretary's Department, Captains'
         Letters
B. 1   Records of the Court of Bankruptcy, Order Books
B. 4   Ibid., Registers of Commissions of Bankruptcy
B.T. 6   Board of Trade, Miscellanea
C.O. 267 Sierra Leone, Original Correspondence, Secretary of
         State
C.O. 388 Board of Trade (Commercial), Original Correspon-
         dence
P.C. 2   Records of Privy Council Office, Privy Council Office
         Registers
T. 70   Treasury Records, Records of African Companies

Ghana National Archives, Accra
(G.N.A.)

ADM. 1   Original Correspondence (distinguished from Adm. 1
         in the P.R.O. by the addition of 'G.N.A.' in each
         reference)
H.C.C.C. Records of the High Court, Cape Coast. These records
         are unclassified in the Archives except by accession
         number. In the present work, H.C.C.C. has been added
         to the accession number for ease of identification

Other

S.P.G.   Society for the Propagation of the Gospel ('C' Manu-
         scripts, West Africa, in the Society's Archives, London)
W.I.C.   Archives of the second Dutch West Indies Company
         in the State Archives, The Hague. (Consulted in the
         notes and transcripts of the Furley Collection, the Balme
         Library, University of Ghana)
Gen. Office Genealogical Office, Dublin Castle.

PREFACE

West African family history is a much neglected subject, although in 1947 Professor Raymond Firth drew attention to its potentialities in an article in *Africa* (volume XVII, number 3), and some years later Dr. Arthur Porter enlarged on the theme in his paper 'Family Histories and West African Social Development' (*Historians in Tropical Africa*, Salisbury, 1962). The present study aims at making a contribution to this field, focusing on the Brew family in the Fanti region of Ghana, and spanning more than one hundred and fifty years.

Many different personalities and facets of affairs are involved over this period of time, and it is hardly surprising that the data available should be somewhat uneven. Thus the life of the Irish trader, Richard Brew, can be depicted more fully than the lives of his African descendants, with the possible exception of James Hutton Brew and J. E. Casely Hayford. The lengthy research that was necessary to construct an account of the nineteenth-century Brews has precluded full concentration on these two active public figures. It must also be pointed out that the study seeks to relate the Brews to important themes in the history and development of Ghana; areas where current knowledge is inadequate, for example Fanti in the eighteenth century and the economic history of the coastal region in the nineteenth, are thereby thrown into prominence.

The archival work and interviewing on which this study is based were carried out in Ghana, Sierra Leone, England, and Ireland, and have resulted in a wide range of indebtedness. I am also most grateful to those friends and colleagues who provided references and read draft chapters, although the responsibility for deficiencies and errors remains my own.

Among the many people to whom thanks are due, I must especially mention Dr. J. W. de Graft Johnson of Cape Coast for his constant and invaluable assistance; also members of the Brew family and others in Ghana, notably Miss Victoria Brew, Mr. Mictor Collins Brew, Mr. Ernest Wood, Mrs. Ward Brew, Mr. James Hutton Brew, Nana R. K. Quansah, *Ohene* of Abura Dunkwa, the late Mr. J. E. Eminsang, Mr. P. J. Bartels and

Mr. D. M. Abadoo. Mrs. F. C. Appiah-Robertson kindly lent
a photograph of James Hutton Brew, and in Freetown, Mr.
S. H. F. Brew provided useful information.

Help of various kinds, which I greatly appreciate, has been
given by Professors Daryll Forde, J. D. Fage, P. D. Curtin,
D. F. McCall, G. W. Irwin and W. Minchinton; also by Mr.
Gerard Slevin, Thomas Hodgkin, Ivor Wilks, Edmund Collins,
Robin Mayhead, Paul Ozanne, Dr. S. Fisher, Mr. R. Ford,
Mr. R. Porter and Miss E. T. May. Mr. P. L. Carter generously
provided photographs of Anomabu from his own collection,
and Mr. Anthony Hyland kindly drew the sketch plan of the
Little Fort there. Mrs. Miriam Dean worked with patience and
insight through legal records in the Ghana National Archives,
and Mrs. J. Heimovaara and Mrs. R. Phillips gave assistance
with translations.

My thanks are due to Dr. David Kimble for allowing me to
use material and quote from his book, *A Political History of
Ghana, 1850–1928* (Oxford, 1963) in my chapter on James
Hutton Brew, and to the International African Institute for
permission to use material which I had already published in
their volume *The New Elites of Tropical Africa* (London, 1966).
Like all contributors to the 'West African History Series' I
have benefited throughout from the advice and wisdom of Professor G. S. Graham. Miss Audrey Bayley of Oxford University
Press later provided much assistance in technical matters.

To the staff of the Public Record Office, the Ghana National
Archives, the Balme Library, University of Ghana and the
Library of the Society of Genealogists, London, I owe a great
deal, as I do to the Chief Herald and staff of the Genealogical
Office, Dublin Castle. I am also indebted to the Establishment
Secretary, Government of Ghana and to the Director of the
Ghana Museum and Monuments Board.

It is a great pleasure to acknowledge the grant towards research expenses which was given by the Institute of African
Studies, University of Ghana. Subsequently I was most fortunate
in receiving a grant from the International African Institute
enabling me to devote a period to the full-time writing up of the
research, and I wish to record my appreciation to the Institute
for the opportunity to do this.

My last debt is a very extensive one indeed. It is to my husband, who not only typed the final draft and most of the preliminary ones, but prepared the Index and gave unfailing help and encouragement, despite the many other pressing demands on his time.

Evanston,   MARGARET PRIESTLEY
Illinois.
March 1969

INTRODUCTION

European contact with West Africa has a long history behind it. For five hundred years the techniques, attitudes, and values of an alien western culture have infiltrated African society, and yet have been successively modified by it. Distinguishing this Afro-European relationship is the fact that it was primarily commercial for four hundred years and colonial for less than a hundred—in the latter case from the second half of the nineteenth century. It was within a commercial framework, therefore, that social change first came to West Africa, and mainly through the agency of the slave trade. Not until the last century was there a metamorphosis that resulted in the gradual introduction of legitimate trade and ultimately of colonial status.

During the slave-trading era, however, variations must be noted in the degree and pace of westernization, arising out of the particular method of transacting trade. The main contrast lies between the areas in which Europeans settled in a trading capacity, and those where business was conducted from ships anchored off shore. The Gold Coast with its concentration of forts, fixed points for the diffusion of European influence through a commercial medium, is the best example of the former, and it is with this region, now the republic of Ghana, that the present study is concerned.

Recorded European contact with the Gold Coast dates from its discovery by the Portuguese in 1471 and their construction of Elmina fort in 1482; other nations followed suit, ultimately giving the coast its multinational trading character. By the second half of the eighteenth century a number of forts had been built, interspersed with the private commercial establishments of individual merchants. Settlements were in British, Dutch, and Danish hands, with the British predominant—a reflection of the world-wide supremacy they had come to enjoy in the sphere of trade and maritime power after their victory over the rival French.

The major British-occupied forts stood in territory controlled by the Fanti or coastal Akan; here, indigenous society both received and influenced the new forces. Social change was generated. Not the least important of its manifestations was the slow growth of a western-educated minority whose numbers increased in the nineteenth century under missionary impact. Nowhere on the Gold Coast were the western-educated to be more active than in Fanti, and nowhere can their origins be better traced. The Brews, a family of mixed descent, afford a good illustration of both aspects of the cultural process—European settlement originating in the circumstances of trade and the Fanti response to it, over a period of a hundred and fifty years, from the mid-eighteenth century to the early twentieth century.

PART ONE

The Interaction of Cultures

CHAPTER I

European Settlement

Britain's African trade during the eighteenth century formed part of the broad and increasingly specialized Atlantic network that linked her with the Guinea Coast and the New World.[1] From the standpoint of contemporary economic thinking, the trade with Africa was regarded as one thoroughly to be commended, both for its value in stimulating British exports[2] and shipping, and—most important—as a source of labour for the production of sugar, tobacco, cotton, and rum in the New World. A treatise published in London in 1772 gave the trade a leading place as 'the first principle and foundation of all the rest; the main spring of the machine, which sets every wheel in motion'. Based on the desirable exchange of manufactured goods for African 'gold, ivory, wax, dyeing woods and negroes', it was described as 'essentially necessary to the very being' of the New World colonies.[3] While allowance must be made for an element of special pleading and overstatement in the treatise, there is no doubt that the African trade, because of slaving, ranked high in the assessment of Britain's overseas commerce, the bedrock of her national power.

Important in the day-to-day conduct of the trade were the British settlements or forts and factories in West Africa, situated mostly on the Gold Coast. By the mid-century, these

[1] See R. B. Sheridan, 'The Commercial and Financial Organisation of the British Slave Trade, 1750–1807' in *Economic History Review*, second series, vol. XI, no. 2 (Dec. 1958), pp. 249–63, for changes in the organization of the trade, particularly affecting the West Indies, and for the growing importance of London.

[2] British exports to Africa in 1720 were valued at £130,000 and in 1775 at £866,000; R. Hallett, 'The European Approach to the Interior of Africa in the Eighteenth Century' in *Journal of African History*, vol. IV, no. 2 (1963), p. 196.

[3] *A Treatise upon the Trade from Great Britain to Africa*, by an African Merchant (London, 1772), chap. 1. See also C. Gill, *Merchants and Mariners of the Eighteenth Century* (London, 1961), pp. 74–90.

settlements reflected the victory that had been won by individual merchant enterprise over monopoly organization and control. The Royal African Company, a joint-stock body founded in Charles II's reign, came to an end in 1750 after prolonged attack from 'free traders', and the African trade was thrown open to all merchants. Anyone who paid forty shillings a year and joined the regulated Company of Merchants trading to Africa could participate in it, and the Company was forbidden to trade on a corporate basis. A committee of nine, elected annually by the merchants of London, Bristol, and Liverpool, administered the Company's affairs and managed the settlements; for this purpose, it received an annual parliamentary grant of £10,000, later increased to £13,000.

On the west coast, the transfer of settlements to the new Company and the change-over in management took two years, from 1750 to 1752. Cape Coast Castle, which the Royal African Company had built on the Gold Coast in the seventeenth century, continued as the headquarters of fort administration, and a Council consisting of the Governor-in-Chief and a small number of his colleagues dealt with local matters. They received general directives from the London Committee, although there were many occasions when the exigencies of the situation necessitated an immediate decision on the spot. At least once a year, a store-ship came out to Cape Coast bringing supplies of food, clothing and other commodities intended for the upkeep of the forts, for the purchase of provisions and services, and for the payment of salaries.[1]

Underlying reorganization of the African trade after 1750 was the principle that individual merchant interests must predominate and be safeguarded against the growth of a commercial monopoly, either on the part of the Committee in Britain or of its servants on the west coast. Henceforth, the public settlements were to be maintained on behalf of private traders, whether conducting their business from London, Bristol, or Liverpool or resident in West Africa. The settlements were to exist for the benefit of these traders, drawing the slave trade down from the interior and concentrating it in a particular locality.

[1] K. G. Davies, *The Royal African Company* (London, 1957), especially pp. 97–152; E. C. Martin, *The British West African Settlements, 1750–1821* (London, 1927), pp. 7–48.

But however anti-monopolistic in intention the new system might be, a number of practical weaknesses were brought to light in West Africa. Especially anomalous was the position of the Governor of a fort in the matter of private trade. The payment of part of his salary in goods made such activity necessary. Indeed, the Committee intended that within certain limits a Governor should engage in this sort of trade, and his fort become a market for slaves and other goods, to be sold eventually to British shipping. To define and control all this, however, to ensure that a Governor did not take advantage of his public office to engross trade and cut out the private dealers, to prevent him from exporting slaves on his own account or from doing business with foreigners, was a virtual impossibility, given coastal conditions and the remoteness of direction in London.

Periodically, Governors were suspended for overstepping the mark, and difficulties at the settlements, caused in part by personal antagonism, were legion. Conflict between Governors and private traders, who saw monopoly creeping in under a new guise, proved almost inevitable. Nor were relations improved by the fact that although fort officials were expected to assist private traders in every way, they exercised no authority over them during their periods of residence on the coast. In the absence of any restraining power, a clash of personalities and interests, both public and private, arose in and around the eighteenth-century settlements.[1]

Life there, for the Europeans concerned with the turbulent and speculative business of slave trading, called for special qualities. Most important, perhaps, was the 'unusual degree of toughness, both of spirit and body'[2] necessary for physical as well as economic survival. Yet although the risk of sickness or death through tropical disease ran high, it would be wrong to regard the eighteenth-century communities as completely transient in nature. Their residents often spent remarkably long periods in West Africa, a fact in striking contrast with the record of Europeans during the nineteenth century.

Richard Brew, for example, the central figure in this study, lived for thirty years as a coastal settler. Thomas Westgate, at one stage his business partner, first went out in 1751, and died twenty-eight years later when on his way home, after spending

[1] Martin, op. cit. pp. 10–56. [2] Ibid. p. 38.

the greater part of that time on the coast. Richard Miles, Brew's executor and eventually a Governor-in-Chief, had been in West Africa for fifteen years by 1780 and thought this 'quite sufficient'; the same length of service was achieved by Gilbert Petrie, another Governor-in-Chief. Jerome Bernard Weuves, also executor to Brew, exceeded ten years, and a number of similar cases can be found.[1] Nor was residence punctuated by frequent leaves in Europe; there are instances of as much as fifteen years at a time on the coast.[2]

Among the British, entry into the tough world of West African settlement often came through a family connection or through the patronage of a merchant, following the practice of eighteenth-century society. A nephew of Governor-in-Chief Charles Bell was appointed into fort administration in 1761, and two brothers of Governor Richard Miles, Charles and Thomas, also appeared on the coast. David Mill, in command at Cape Coast during the seventeen-seventies, had a strong link through his family with the African trade, while Horatio Smith, who went out to Anomabu to be associated with the Brew establishment, was a cousin of Brew's London partner, Samuel Smith, a member of the African Committee. Horatio later became a writer at one of the forts; he too had a nephew on the west coast.[3] Local knowledge was accordingly built up over the years, and passed on within a circuit of the Committee's servants, private traders, and ships' captains.

Admirable in the description they gave of the local scene were the Governor-in-Chief's despatches sent to London at regular intervals from the main British settlement, Cape Coast Castle. They portrayed the niceties of the Afro-European

[1] Entry in T. 70/1454, f. 1; entries in T. 70/1455, ff. 1, 2, 5; Richard Miles to Gilbert Petrie, 28 Sept. 1778, T. 70/1483, ff. 156–7; the same to the Committee, 21 Oct. 1779, T. 70/32, f. 92; the same to William Miles, 1 April 1780, T. 70/1483. Richard Miles returned to the coast again, despite his comment in 1780. By 1760 the Dutch President of the Council at Elmina, Mr. Huydecooper, had been on the coast for more than twenty years; William Mutter to the Committee, 15 Oct. 1760, T. 70/30, f. 383.

[2] Richard Brew is a case in point. His first spell on the coast was from 1745 to 1760.

[3] T. 70/69, f. 129; Committee to Governor and Council, Cape Coast Castle, 23 Aug. 1769, T. 70/69, f. 157; entries in T. 70/1455, ff. 22, 27; Horatio Smith to Richard Miles, 7 Aug. 1777, T. 70/1534; Richard Miles to Samuel Smith, 29 Sept. 1778, T. 70/1483, f. 160; E. Donnan, *Documents Illustrative of the History of the Slave Trade to America*, vol. II (Washington, D.C., 1931), p. 538 n. 5.

relationship, whose balance could be disturbed by the death of a chief, a stool dispute or the pressure of an expanding empire like Ashanti. Influential figures in African society were mentioned repeatedly; there were chiefs who were well known to the London Committee over a number of years through these despatches, and whose sons or relatives might be brought over for education in England.[1]

Local news, too, often of a more personal nature, was contained in private correspondence to and from the coast, and revealed the social fact of mixed unions that were a common feature of life there. In one letter, Governor Richard Miles referred to the African 'wife' by whom he had had seven children, although only two were still alive;[2] for a family of this kind it was customary to make some provision, perhaps by giving the 'wife' a house, and educating the sons for possible entry into the Committee's service.[3]

No aspect indeed of eighteenth-century settlement for the purpose of slave trading is more important than the relationship between African and European, with its wide social repercussions. Based on a mutual assessment of advantages, this relationship was characterized by the degree of European dependence on the indigenous population. The term 'fort' may perhaps convey the impression of much greater self-sufficiency and dissociation from the African environment than in practice was the case.[4] Although it had its own small European staff and garrison for administration and defence, the fort relied on the immediate locality for a wide range of services such as those of canoemen, labourers, and domestics, and also for certain foodstuffs, water, and wood. Even the land on which it was built generally remained in African hands and a rent was paid for it. Trade could be offered or withheld at the will of the local people. They were the middlemen and controlled the

---

[1] See below, pp. 19–22, 36–7.
[2] Richard Miles to Gilbert Petrie, 16 July and 28 Sept. 1778, 10 Aug. 1779, T. 70/1483, ff. 130, 156, 225.
[3] Richard Miles to John Cockburn, 5 Feb. 1773, T. 70/1482; H. Debrunner, 'Notable Danish Chaplains on the Gold Coast' in *Transactions of the Gold Coast and Togoland Historical Society*, vol. II, pt. I (1956), pp. 22–3. See also pp. 106–8 below.
[4] See A. W. Lawrence, *Trade Castles and Forts of West Africa* (London, 1963), pp. 46–69 for an account of the organization of a fort and the life there. See also V. R. Dorjahn and C. Fyfe, 'Landlord and Stranger: Change in Tenancy Relations in Sierra Leone' in *Journal of African History*, vol. III, no. 3 (1962), pp. 394–5.

economic web linking the maritime states with the inland supply of slaves along well-established routes. The fact of European
competition—in the eighteenth century mainly Anglo-French
and Anglo-Dutch—also strengthened considerably the bargaining position of Africans and enabled them to play off one
rival against the other.

Settlement, whether represented by the public establishments along the Gold Coast or by the scattered private trading
concerns of Europeans that grew up around them, gave rise to a
unique community that was not divided by the colonial barrier
until the later nineteenth century. From these points of settlement, European culture radiated outwards and affected African
society; it has been well said of the forts that 'nowhere else have
small and transitory communities of traders so changed the life
of the alien peoples who surrounded them, and indirectly of a
vast region beyond'.[1]

The cultural influence, felt most strongly on the coast, also
began to affect the interior long before there was actual physical
penetration. Merchants from Ashanti, pushing southwards towards the fountain-head of European trade, came into contact
with the white man at the forts over a hundred years before the
first British embassy reached Kumasi in 1817.[2] Along the seaboard, the fulfilment of settlers' economic needs led to the
intrusion of new forms of wealth and property into society.
African diplomacy was extended from intertribal affairs to
negotiation with competing groups of Europeans and contrac-
tual relations were established in employment. A degree of
western education brought a small number of Africans into fort
administration as messengers, linguists, and writers; in some
cases these men were the mulatto offspring of mixed unions.

The fact that this early diffusion of European culture took
place in a commercial setting must be stressed. Settlement and
trade involved African consent, and force had only limited
utility.[3] It was therefore incumbent on the European business
communities to make an adaptation to the *mores* of local society.
Failure to do so might well result in the dislocation of the life

[1] Lawrence, op. cit. p. 29.

[2] M. Priestley and I. Wilks, 'The Ashanti Kings in the Eighteenth Century: a
revised chronology' in *Journal of African History*, vol. I, no. I (1960), pp. 85–6.

[3] In only one case—at Keta, on the Gold Coast—was a fort established against
the wishes of the local population; Lawrence, op. cit. p. 66.

of a fort by the refusal of necessary supplies and services, by the withdrawal of trade, or even by attack. Acculturation acted in two ways and the European settlements, for their part, came under African social influence.

The marked difference, from this point of view, between conditions in the eighteenth century and in the later colonial period needs emphasis. During the eighteenth century, physical isolation from Europe, the absence of steam shipping and telegraphic communication, was a matter of no small importance. Letters took up to six months to reach England; the Committee's store-ship was normally an annual event. Visiting shipping certainly traded along the coast and brought news from home, but the daily round of settler existence took place in an environment controlled by Africans in which the British, Dutch, and Danish were small 'stranger' communities. A statement about strangers in West Africa, made in a different context, can be applied with equal validity to the eighteenth-century communities: 'because their very livelihood depended upon the will and patronage of the local Africans, they were compelled to understand the social systems of their hosts and to develop techniques for dealing with them'.[1]

There grew up, in consequence, a geographically restricted trading society which developed its own conventions and modes of behaviour and was shaped by African as well as European interests. Culturally, the situation on the Gold Coast was not that of a dichotomy, with the European community pursuing an independent course of existence and dominating the pattern of events. However repugnant slave trading might be, it acted as a cohesive force and brought two societies together with mutual, long-term effects. The career of Richard Brew demonstrates this. An Irishman of turbulent personality, his life on the Gold Coast from 1745 to 1776 provides a detailed commentary on many facets of slaving and settlement in the highly competitive age of the private trader.

[1] E. P. Skinner, 'Strangers in West African Societies' in *Africa*, vol. XXXIII, no. 4 (Oct. 1963), p. 311.

CHAPTER II

Fanti in the Eighteenth Century

The greater part of Brew's thirty years on the Gold Coast were spent in Fanti, a region long subject to European influence, and it was here that his mulatto descendants became prominent. The history of Fanti is still shrouded in considerable obscurity.[1] Some account nevertheless must be given, focused on the maritime towns of Anomabu and Cape Coast during the second half of the eighteenth century, as a background to the present family study.

Like their eventual Ashanti antagonists, the Fanti were an Akan people;[2] they had migrated from the interior in the past and had formed settlements along the coast and in the hinterland. The eighteenth century deserves special attention as an important period in Fanti development. It was a time of general although not continuous growth and consolidation, with the first indications of the long struggle against Ashanti. It was also a time when seeds of change were sown in Fanti as a result of westernization.

According to the contemporary Dutch writer, Willem Bosman, Fanti territory, at the beginning of the century, consisted of a narrow, maritime strip only nine or ten miles in length,

---

[1] For a good, brief account see A. A. Boahen, 'Asante and Fante A.D. 1000–1800' in *A Thousand Years of West African History*, ed. J. F. Ade Ajayi and I. Espie (Ibadan, 1965), pp. 160–85. See also W. Bosman, *A New and Accurate Description of the Coast of Guinea* (London, 1705); J. Barbot, *A Description of the Coasts of North and South Guinea* (London, 1732); J. W. de Graft Johnson, *Historical Geography of the Gold Coast* (London, 1929); E. J. P. Brown, *Gold Coast and Asianti Reader*, 2 vols. (London, 1929); J. M. Sarbah, *Fanti Customary Laws* (London, 1904); J. M. Sarbah, *Fanti National Constitution* (London, 1906); J. B. Christensen, *Double Descent among the Fanti* (New Haven, 1954). Recent seminar papers on the Akan of Ghana have been printed in *Ghana Notes and Queries*, no. 9 (Nov. 1966), and the publication of other papers is intended.

[2] In modern Ghana the Akan constitute over 40 per cent of the population, and dominate about two-thirds of the country, geographically; A. A. Boahen, 'The Origins of the Akan' in *Ghana Notes and Queries*, no. 9 (Nov. 1966), p. 3.

extending eastwards from the Iron Mount, near Mouri. Cape Coast in the separate kingdom of Efutu was not included.[1] By the close of the eighteenth century, and after displaying military prowess, Fanti consisted of a loose federation of states some sixty miles in extent, between the Sweet river, near Elmina, west of Cape Coast, and Beraku, west of Accra.[2] Ultimately, it was to comprise all the Gold Coast belt except Accra and the district to the east.

Politically, Fanti differed from the Ashanti Empire in its fragmentation and lack of an overriding central authority.[3] It took the form of a flexible association of small and virtually self-governing states. They were devoted to their independence, often antagonistic to each other, and recognized no well-defined paramountcy such as the Golden Stool of Ashanti. Loose ties, in origin of a religious nature, linked the states together. These ties centred on Mankessim ('the big city'), a place significant as the shrine of the three patriarchs who were said to have led the initial migration from the north-west and who became national deities. At Mankessim, through the medium of priests, the Fanti customarily sought guidance from their national deities on major issues of law and politics. A strong rival, however, for the position of *primus inter pares* in the federation was Abura, also, like Mankessim, the scene of an early settlement.[4]

Along with territorial growth in the eighteenth century went a trend towards closer federation. The impelling force here was Ashanti expansion, as the inland kingdom, a supplier of slaves, sought to open up direct trade with the European forts and to eliminate profit-taking middlemen in the exchange of slaves and gold for guns and ammunition. This objective constituted an economic and political threat to the Fanti and recurrent tension with Ashanti ensued.

[1] Bosman, op. cit. p. 55.
[2] H. Meredith, *An Account of the Gold Coast of Africa* (London, 1812), pp. 95–6, 111–12; W. E. F. Ward, *History of Ghana* (London, 1966), p. 143.
[3] See K. Arhin, 'Diffuse Authority among the Coastal Fanti' in *Ghana Notes and Queries*, no. 9 (Nov. 1966), pp. 66–70.
[4] Brown, op. cit. vol. I, pp. 56–61; Christensen, op. cit. pp. 7, 12–13. The rivalry of Mankessim and Abura can be observed during the Fanti Confederation movement, 1871; see p. 163 below. An elderly informant today, summing up the relationship of the two states, said that Mankessim held the head, and Abura held the feet of the Confederacy.

Relations were particularly strained during the years 1765–73 when Richard Brew was living at Anomabu. An Ashanti army, pursuing the Akim and the Wassaw, entered Fanti territory in 1765 and encamped as near the coast as Abura. Initially, the Ashanti had undertaken this action in alliance with Fanti, but discord between the two powers soon developed. It culminated in a brief outbreak of hostilities, the first occasion of direct Ashanti-Fanti conflict. Although there was a withdrawal inland, it was regarded on the coast as the preliminary to a subsequent and better-planned invasion, and for some years rumours and alarms circulated in the European settlements.[1]

Under these pressures, the Fanti states began to develop a greater degree of cohesion and consultation among themselves. They held frequent conferences in the seventeen-sixties, for example, to discuss the terms of a peace settlement with Ashanti, and to determine lines of policy on questions of vital concern to all in the maritime region. The conferences took place at Mankessim, Abura, and Efutu.[2] The first two were Fanti's traditional centres. Efutu, however, lay outside its original confines and was the capital of the kingdom of Efutu to which Cape Coast had owed allegiance.[3] The fact that congresses were held and alliances negotiated there is evidence of Fanti's widening orbit of power during the course of the eighteenth century.

Significant, too, in their effects upon Fanti were the European forts and factories on the coastline. With the British in particular, a long-standing business connection had been established, and the Fanti acted as middlemen in the trade between seaboard and interior. A consequence of European settlement was that it helped to increase Fanti's range of economic influence, and to mould political contours.[4] Maritime towns rose to

[1] M. Priestley, 'The Ashanti Question and the British: eighteenth century origins' in *Journal of African History*, vol. II, no. 1 (1961), pp. 35–59.

[2] Ibid. p. 52.

[3] Brown, op. cit. vol. I, pp. 118–24. In Efutu, sometimes written as Afutu or Fetu, the succession to the stool was not matrilineal, as with the Akan, but patrilineal; Brown, op. cit. vol. I, p. 196. See also D. Birmingham, 'A Note on the Kingdom of Fetu' in *Ghana Notes and Queries*, no. 9 (Nov. 1966), pp. 30–3, and Otutu Bagyire VI, *Abiriwhene*, 'The Guans: a preliminary note' in *Ghana Notes and Queries*, no. 7 (Jan. 1965), pp. 21–3.

[4] The effects of European settlement upon Fanti were complex; both integrating and disintegrating trends were fostered. See Arhin, art. cit. in *Ghana Notes and Queries*, no. 9 (Nov. 1966), pp. 66–70 for a discussion of Fanti as a segmentary society.

prominence around the forts and became the focal points of a
wide, commercial network extending along the seaboard and
into the hinterland. European settlement also aided the establishment of strong dynasties in the coastal region. New centres
of power emerged; the most important of them were Anomabu
and Cape Coast.

The town of Anomabu has special relevance as the home of
Richard Brew for the greater part of his life in West Africa.
One of the earliest Fanti communities to be established on the
coast, it lay at the seaboard end of an accessible inland slaving
route. During the eighteenth century, Anomabu became a
major British commercial centre and one of Fanti's leading
states. At the beginning of the century, its military strength and
independent trading attitude were already evoking European
comment.[1] Towards the end of the century, the chief of Anomabu, who was now designated 'King' by the British, wielded
influence over the rulers of an area stretching as far west as the
river Pra, and ranked high in the British assessment of power
distribution on the Gold Coast.[2]

The advancement of Anomabu owed much to the effective
use, in the middle decades of the century, of opportunities
created by European trade and settlement. A central figure in
Anomabu's advancement was the chief caboceer, Eno Baisie
Kurentsi, or John Currantee in European styling, who was the
founder of a dynasty of powerful chiefs,[3] and, as will be seen,
closely connected with Richard Brew. He is variously described
in the British records as *ohene*, principal caboceer, captain of
Anomabu, and chief magistrate and general on that part of the
coast;[4] he was clearly a dominant personality in local affairs.
At one time he had been formidable on the military scene, and

[1] Bosman, op. cit. p. 56.
[2] B. Cruickshank, *Eighteen Years on the Gold Coast of Africa*, vol. I (London, 1853),
pp. 54–5.
[3] Brown, op. cit. vol. II, pp. 106–7; Ward, op. cit. p. 98 n. 29; J. N. Matson,
'The French at Amoku' in *Transactions of the Gold Coast and Togoland Historical
Society*, vol. I, pt. 2 (1953), p. 47.
[4] Thomas Melvil to Committee, 11 July 1751, T. 70/1517; the same to the same,
11 June 1752, C.O. 388/45, Dd 115; entry dd. 30 April 1763, T. 70/987; *Gentleman's
Magazine*, vol. XX (1750), p. 272; J. J. Crooks, *Records relating to the Gold Coast
Settlements, 1750–1874* (Dublin, 1923), p. 32; Brown, op. cit. vol. II, pp. 106–7.
In the *Gentleman's Magazine*, John Currantee is referred to in one entry as the
'Chinnee of Anamaboe', obviously a misspelling of *ohene*.

had married Ekua, the daughter of King Ansa Sasraku of Akwamu after the defeat of the Akwamu Empire by a coalition in 1730. His marriage led to the adoption of Ekua's son, William Ansah, who was later a protégé of the British, and a daughter, Effua Ansah, who became the 'country wife' of Richard Brew.[1]

As a result of European commercial rivalry, John Currantee found himself a centre of intrigue in the seventeen-fifties, and he was courted assiduously by the British and the French. Each nation wished to build a fort at Anomabu, and for this the permission of the chief caboceer was essential.[2] With considerable bargaining skill, John Currantee extracted from both parties all that he could in the way of material benefits and support; even after the British had secured the advantage and had begun building operations in 1753, he continued to behave in the same way.

There is no doubt that the prospect of a fort had economic attractions for the local population. It would be a stimulus to trade and employment, and no maritime town during the eighteenth century was more actively engaged in the middle-man network that revolved around settlement and slaving than Anomabu. But there was another side to the matter. By the mid-century, John Currantee was advanced in years, and the question of succession to his elective office of 'Captain' loomed large.[3] The chance to strengthen the position of his family through association with a trading settlement could hardly have been unwelcome. Indeed, according to the British, he had 'raised himself to his present greatness' by methods likely to bring eventual retribution, and their suggestion that the caboceer's desire for a fort was not unconnected with protection for his relatives after his death may well have contained an element of truth.[4]

[1] Charles Bell to Committee, 4 Aug. 1762, T. 70/31, f. 10; Richard Miles and Jerome Bernard Weuves to Committee, 10 Sept. 1776, T. 70/32, f. 38; copy of Richard Brew's will, 3 Aug. 1776 (Somerset House, London); *Gentleman's Magazine*, vol. XX (1750), p. 272; T. Thompson, *An account of Two Missionary Voyages* (facsimile reprint, London, 1937), pp. 47–8; Crooks, op. cit. p. 32; Ward, op. cit. p. 111; I. Wilks, 'The Rise of the Akwamu Empire, 1650–1710' in *Transactions of the Historical Society of Ghana*, vol. III, pt. 2 (1957), p. 132 and see pp. 20–1 and 106–8 below.   [2] See p. 38 ff. below.   [3] See p. 15 n. 2 below.

[4] Thomas Melvil to Committee, 11 July 1751, T. 70/1517; Matthew Buckle, H.M.S. *Assistance*, to Secretary to the Admiralty, 19 Feb. 1752, Adm. 1/1485.

In the event, John Currantee lived until 28 June 1764, by which time Anomabu fort had been occupied for seven years. He was succeeded as principal caboceer by a relation, Amonu Kuma, who was likewise committed to the British interest.[1] Under Amonu an important change took place. In 1774, a Fanti congress appointed him to the new position of 'King of the Town of Annamaboe'; the appointment can be interpreted to mean consolidation of the dynasty and higher political status.[2] It reflects the increasing significance of Anomabu, due in no small measure to economic factors.

At Cape Coast in Efutu, the site of Britain's West African headquarters and home of many of the nineteenth-century Brews, similar developments can be observed. Here Fanti was extending beyond its original frontiers. It had defeated the Kingdom of Efutu in 1711,[3] after which closer ties were gradually formed between Cape Coast and the neighbouring Fanti states. In time, Cape Coast was ruled by its own dynasty, independent of Efutu, and became an integral part of Fanti and ultimately its effective capital.[4]

Politico-economic processes during the eighteenth century are illustrated by one of the town's most influential figures, Birempon Cudjo or Cudjo Caboceer, to give him the name used by Europeans.[5] By birth a native of Fanti, Cudjo was

[1] William Mutter to Committee, 20 July 1764, T. 70/31, f. 102; entries dd. 7 Sept. 1764 and 1 Nov. 1765, T. 70/988; entry dd. 10 Nov. 1770, T. 70/1029; Richard Miles and Jerome Bernard Weuves to Committee, 10 Sept. 1776, T. 70/32, f. 38.

[2] Entry dd. 19 July 1774, T. 70/1035. In the British African Companies' records, John Currantee is not referred to as 'King'. According to a contemporary report, his office of 'Captain'—an elective one—generally passed to the eldest son; this would suggest that it fell within the organization of the patrilineal military companies or *asafu*. By the later eighteenth century, it seems likely that a different type of office, predominantly political rather than military, had evolved at Anomabu and was being held by Amonu Kuma. It is interesting to note the tradition that the first Omanhene of Anomabu was elevated to that position because he helped the people financially. The stool today is known as the 'Amonu' stool; Thomas Melvil to Committee, 11 July 1751, T. 70/1517; the same to the same, 11 June 1752, C.O. 388/45, Dd 115; Christensen, op. cit. p. 117.

[3] Boahen, 'Asante and Fante A.D. 1000–1800' in *A Thousand Years of West African History*, pp. 178–9 and see p. 12 n. 3 above.

[4] Brown, op. cit. vol. I, pp. 130–5; de Graft Johnson, op. cit. pp. 148–9.

[5] 'Birempon' (*brempon*) is a Fanti word for a person wealthy through trade or inheritance; 'caboceer' is a corruption of the Portuguese *caboceiro* (captain), and a European designation for one of the chief men of a community; Sarbah, *Fanti Customary Laws*, pp. 11–12.

stepson to the King of Efutu and Cape Coast through his mother's remarriage.[1] He carved a significant position for himself in local society as linguist at Cape Coast Castle, and served the British for almost fifty years, until his death in 1776, guiding their trade through the intricate maze of local politics.[2]

The office of linguist at a fort involved semi-diplomatic duties on behalf of the Governor. It also opened up wide, personal opportunities for trading, and there is every sign that Cudjo achieved a high degree of success on both accounts. He was indispensable, for example, in the Anglo-Fanti discussions held at Cape Coast Castle during 1752 about excluding the French from settlement on the coast, while the next decade saw him prominent in conferences at Efutu on the subject of Ashanti-Fanti hostility.[3] The corollary to Cudjo's involvement in trade and its political ramifications was the building up of his own position. A man of 'immense wealth' through commerce, he was elevated in Cape Coast to the rank of caboceer. But his power extended over a much wider area, and he was also 'made King and Captain of Fantee'; the whole Fanti country, it was reported in 1757, had sworn to support him in any dispute in which he might be engaged.[4] The enhanced importance of Cape Coast and its dynasty under the impetus of European trade, and the multiplication of its contacts with Fanti are brought to light by these events.

Fanti's territorial expansion and political development in the eighteenth century was accompanied by the interaction of cultures, African and European. Along the coast, Akan culture had displayed considerable vitality. It became dominant among the different tribes who had been absorbed into Fanti since the

[1] Brown, op. cit. vol. II, pp. 122–3. Cudjo Caboceer's parents came from Ekumfi-Adansi.

[2] Cudjo's name appears on the establishment list of Cape Coast Castle in 1729 among 'Linguists and Messengers'. He was then receiving £24 a year, in a junior capacity. By 1750, his pay had risen to £72 a year; T. 70/1450, f. 3; entry in T. 70/1516; David Mill to Committee, 7 May 1776, T. 70/32, f. 33. The British regarded his death as a major loss.

[3] Thomas Melvil to Committee, 23 Sept. 1752, C.O. 388/45; entries dd. 8 July and 27 Nov. 1765, T. 70/1022; Priestley, art. cit. pp. 44–5, 52.

[4] Nassau Senior to Committee, 7 Dec. 1757, C.O. 267/6; Brown, op. cit. vol. II, p. 123. According to a contemporary account, it was Cudjo Caboceer who exercised the real power in Cape Coast in the seventeen-fifties, when his half-brother was king; Thompson, op. cit. p. 34.

earliest days of migration and conquest.[1] Cape Coast in Efutu furnishes a good example; by the first decade of the nineteenth century its people were submitting, in general, to Fanti law and custom.[2] Akan culture also made an impact on the European trading settlements, a process that was reciprocal.

The social structure of the coastal Akan, in fundamentals, differed little from that of the Ashanti. Three particular elements must be noted: the matrilineal clan or *abusua*, the patrilineal military company or *asafu* and the all-pervasive force of traditional religion. Among the Akan, it was the eight exogamous matrilineal and patrilineal clans that formed the major units of society and the matrilineal clan within which the lineage was structured.[3] J. M. Sarbah, in his classic work on Fanti customary law, describes the 'family' as consisting of all persons lineally descended through a female from a common ancestress. A child belonged, not to its father's clan, but to that of its mother, and inheritance passed similarly along the female line, not from father to son, but from father to nephew, the son of his uterine sister.[4]

Thus defined, the family possessed certain clearly distinguishable characteristics. It was first and foremost a corporation, whose actions and responsibilities were collective, and the individual had no place in society save as a member of such a group through which alone he acquired rights and duties. Nowhere was this more apparent than in the case of property. Ownership of it, by customary law, was collective and 'the absolute, unrestricted, exclusive' right of the individual to possession an exception.[5] At the head of the corporate family stood a *penin* or elder, chosen from among the senior members and exercising the highest authority. As the family's representative he arranged its internal affairs, settled disputes, had custody of property and acted on its behalf in matters concerning other groups.[6] Following the lines of the social pattern, political authority among the Akan was built up by the association of lineages into villages and of villages into towns and states. At each level, a council of elders assisted headman or chief, and succession to a stool, like

---

[1] Christensen, op. cit. p. 9.
[2] Meredith, op. cit. pp. 95–6, 111–12.
[3] Boahen, art. cit. in *Ghana Notes and Queries*, no. 9 (Nov. 1966), p. 4.
[4] Sarbah, *Fanti Customary Laws*, especially pp. 33, 42–3, 100–2.
[5] Ibid. pp. 61–2.   [6] Ibid. pp. 37–8.

inheritance of property, was reckoned matrilineally, with age and lineage the main determinants of status.

Patrilineal groupings, too, had their place in society. Based on a spiritual bond and on the belief that a child received the intangible quality of soul or personality from its father, the tie between father and son assumed stronger and more pronounced forms on the coast than with the Ashanti inland.[1] The military companies or *asafu* to be found within each Fanti town were one practical manifestation of this, and a son joined the company of his father. The *asafu* played a major part in the life of the maritime towns. They were endowed with civil and religious as well as with military functions, and were officered by captains or *asafuhin*; sons, if considered suitable, were generally elected to succeed to their father's captaincy on death. A general or *tufuhin* commanded all the companies in a state and ranked so high in the politico-military structure that when a paramount stool was vacant, the *tufuhin* might perform the duties of regent.[2]

The binding power of every Akan law and of each institution lay in a deeply rooted traditional religion. There was belief in a Supreme Being, in lesser deities inhabiting natural objects such as the sea, rocks, and rivers, and in ancestral spirits. But it was ancestor worship that predominated as an ever-present feature of daily life. The spirit world was looked upon as constantly close to the living, a powerful influence on events whose course it could affect benevolently or otherwise. This was a view of the universe that found expression in a variety of ways and through many rituals. At the time of death and entry into the spirit world, the lineage performed funeral ceremonies appropriate to the rank of the deceased; the *penin* of a family, like a chief after enstoolment, was regarded as an intermediary with the departed, while among the *asafu*, the mustering post, also a shrine, might be built on the spot where an important member of the company had been buried. Great national festivals, like the annual thanksgiving for the yam harvest, were occasions for commemorating the ancestral spirits of former chiefs, and with

[1] Christensen, op. cit. especially pp. 1, 2–5, 97. For a discussion of patrilineal groups in Ashanti, see I. Wilks, 'Aspects of Bureaucratisation in Ashanti in the nineteenth century' in *Journal of African History*, vol. VII, no. 2 (1966), pp. 215–232.

[2] Christensen, op. cit. p. 107 ff.; J. C. de Graft Johnson, 'The Fanti Asafu' in *Africa*, vol. V (1932), pp. 307–22; Brown, op. cit. vol. I, p. 197 ff.

the Fanti states, veneration of the patriarchs of the migration
constituted the main spiritual bond of their association.[1]

European settlements, dependent on the Fanti middleman,
adapted the pattern of their behaviour to Akan social institutions and beliefs. Hence they acknowledged the importance
of chiefs, elders, and the *asafu* through a system of allowances,
and of gifts on special occasions. At Anomabu, John Currantee
and Amonu Kuma had regular 'Company's pay', Cudjo
Caboceer of Cape Coast was given presents at the annual
celebration of the yam harvest, while in the seventeen-eighties
his son Aggrey, the influential Captain General of Cape Coast,
received £100 per annum as Castle linguist.[2] Europeans also
conformed to Akan practice in the matter of funeral rites. When
Aggrey died on 23 February 1793, the Castle authorities provided goods to the value of over £100 for the celebration of his
funeral custom, and a similar payment was made to the chief
of Anomabu in 1776, after the death of a European, Richard
Brew.[3]

But the coastal Akan were themselves in contact with the
alien culture of the settlements and they could not remain
unaffected. Among western practices, none proved more innovatory and more crucial as a long-term solvent of the traditional order than education.[4] Allied in the eighteenth century
with trade and to a limited degree with Christianity, education
emphasized individual action and rights, and the validity of
personal decision as against the collectivism of extended family
and clan. It led to status based on opportunity and achievement
instead of solely on birth and lineage. At first narrowly restricted in extent, western education embraced a small and
select group in the maritime towns. This included the relatives
of influential Africans as a form of coastal insurance policy
for the safeguarding of trade, and the mulatto offspring of

[1] S. G. Williamson, *Akan Religion and the Christian Faith* (Accra, 1965), pt. 2,
pp. 85–111; Christensen, op. cit. pp. 112–13 and see p. 11 above.
[2] Entries, especially 1 Nov. 1765, T. 70/988; entry dd. 15 July 1771, T. 70/1031;
entry dd. 28 July 1774, T. 70/1035; entry dd. 17 May 1780, T. 70/152; James
Mourgue to Committee, 14 May 1786, T. 70/33, f. 129; William Feilde to Committee, 20 Aug. 1789, ibid. ff. 217-18; M. Priestley, 'Philip Quaque of Cape Coast'
printed in *Africa Remembered*, ed. P. D. Curtin (Madison, 1967), pp. 129–30.
[3] Entry dd. 26 Feb. 1793, T. 70/1063; Archibald Dalzel to Committee, 28 Feb.
1793, T. 70/33, f. 374 and see pp. 85–6 below.
[4] See P. Foster, *Education and Social Change in Ghana* (London, 1965).

merchants like Richard Brew. Between the worlds of European exporter and Fanti middleman, a valuable communicating link was thereby created.

Both Anomabu and Cape Coast, key trading areas in the mid-eighteenth century, provide examples of African education overseas under European sponsorship. The sons and relatives of politically influential figures such as John Currantee and Cudjo Caboceer were among the beneficiaries. Two in particular must be mentioned, William Ansah of Anomabu and Philip Quaque of Cape Coast. Each of them came to London, and on their return to the coast played an important part in the mercantile community.

The circumstances of William Ansah's visit are not completely clear, but it may possibly have been undertaken with the backing of the Royal African Company. After an unfortunate start—he was sold into slavery by the ship's captain but redeemed by the British government—William came under the personal charge of Lord Halifax, a Commissioner of Trade and Plantations. The Earl arranged for his education and instruction in Christianity, and supervised his material welfare. While in England, 'Prince William' moved in fashionable social circles. He tasted the pleasures of a London season and was accorded the deference due to a person of rank. Together with an African companion, he was introduced to George II, and the young men were greeted with applause when they appeared at Covent Garden for a performance of the opera.[1]

In 1750, William Ansah embarked on a British warship, H.M.S. *Surprise*, for the return voyage to West Africa. It anchored briefly off the Sierra Leone coast where he was entertained by the captain of a slaving ship and described by his host in very favourable terms.[2] At Anomabu, the chief caboceer, John Currantee, was awaiting his son and with due form and ceremony Prince William was handed over—'magnificently equipped in a full-dress scarlet suit, with gold lace à la Bourgoyne, point d'Espagne hat, handsome white feather, diamond

[1] Thomas Melvil to Committee, 11 July 1751, T. 70/1517; John Roberts to Earl of Halifax, c. 1751, T. 70/1477; *Gentleman's Magazine*, vol. XIX (1749), pp. 89–90, 522; ibid. vol. XX (1750), p. 272; Brown, op. cit. vol. II, pp. 105–8 and see plate 3.
[2] J. Newton, *The Journal of a Slave Trader, 1750–1754*, ed. B. Martin and M. Spurrell (London, 1962), p. 19.

solitaire buttons, etc.' But his father divested him of all this
finery and replaced it with traditional dress like his own, 'a
piece of broad-cloth thrown over his shoulder', as a symbol of
the return to African society.[1]

Back now in Fanti, William Ansah received the approval
of the British and put his education to good use from their
point of view; in the Governor-in-Chief's opinion, he was a
very honest, modest, and sensible lad of whom John Currantee took considerable notice, and who deserved encouragement.[2]
At a time of intensive Anglo-French rivalry over fort-building at
Anomabu, he became a useful intermediary, passing on information to the British about the activities of the French and
their approaches to his father. When Anomabu fort had been
built and occupied, William was taken on to the establishment
as a writer. He is to be found there during the seventeen-
sixties, one of the handful of literate African clerks, messengers,
and linguists employed in the service of the trading administration.[3]

At Cape Coast, early educational development had the
support of Cudjo Caboceer, the Castle linguist and a man of
progressive outlook; it also had a missionary connection. The
Reverend Thomas Thompson, Britain's first missionary to
West Africa, arrived at Cape Coast in 1752[4] and a school was
started at Cudjo's request, although it was of short duration,
owing to the lack of local support. Thompson, however, set in
motion a scheme to train young Africans overseas as mission-
aries at the expense of the Society for the Propagation of the
Gospel. The choice of candidates fell to Cudjo. He selected

---

[1] Brown, op. cit. vol. II, pp. 112–15.

[2] Thomas Melvil to Committee, 11 July 1751, T. 70/1517.

[3] William Ansah to Earl of Halifax, 20 Feb. 1752, C.O. 388/45, Dd 83; John
Roberts to William Ansah, 27 Oct. 1752, T. 70/1478; William Ansah to Thomas
Melvil, 17 Feb. 1753 (in Captain Cockburne's letters), Adm. 1/1604; entries in
T. 70/988.

[4] During his time on the coast, Thomas Thompson went to see William Ansah
at Anomabu, and subsequently held church services in John Currantee's house;
the construction of Anomabu fort had then started, and the English were living
temporarily with the chief caboceer. Governor-in-Chief Melvil expressed the
opinion that if Thompson could put John Currantee's morals to rights, he would
be performing a miracle. Thompson also stayed with Richard Brew, who at that
time was in charge of Tantumkweri fort; Thomas Melvil to Committee, 11 June
1752, T. 70/1518; John Apperley to Committee, 10 March 1753, T. 70/1520;
Thompson, op. cit. pp. 41–3, 47, 57–8, 62.

three; one of them, Philip Quaque,[1] was a relation of his own.

Quaque came to England, 'that blessed Christian Country',[2] in 1754 at the age of thirteen, and spent eleven years receiving education under missionary supervision. In 1765, he was ordained deacon and then priest, and given a dual appointment— as 'Missionary, Catechist and Schoolmaster to the Negroes on the Gold Coast in Africa' by the Society for the Propagation of the Gospel, and as the first African chaplain at Cape Coast Castle by the Committee of the Company of Merchants. Together with an English wife, he landed at Cape Coast early in 1766, and remained on the Castle establishment for half a century, until his death on 17 October 1816.

Soon after returning, Quaque revived the attempts of his predecessor, Thomas Thompson, to establish a school. With the Governor-in-Chief's approval, he taught a small group of boys and girls in his room at the Castle; religious instruction, reading, writing, and arithmetic made up the content of study. Even on this modest scale, there were obstacles to contend with, including wavering European support and apathy among the local population, not all of whom shared Cudjo Caboceer's views. The number of pupils in attendance fluctuated between sixteen and one, and Quaque never succeeded in his aim of a special school building where he would have the assistance of two Africans educated in London, one of them Cudjo Caboceer's son, Frederick Adoy.[3]

In the late seventeen-eighties, educational effort at Cape Coast assumed a more organized form for a time when a Charity School experiment was sponsored by the gentlemen of the trading settlement. Twelve needy mulatto children were to be educated in the Castle, boarded there and provided with school uniforms. Quaque was placed in charge, assisted by his son Samuel, who had recently arrived back from an English

[1] For the following account of Quaque, see F. L. Bartels, 'Philip Quaque, 1741–1816' in *Transactions of the Gold Coast and Togoland Historical Society*, vol. I, pt. 5 (1955), pp. 153–77 and Priestley, 'Philip Quaque of Cape Coast' printed in *Africa Remembered*, pp. 99–139.

[2] Philip Quaque to the Society for the Propagation of the Gospel, 11 April 1777 ('C' Manuscripts, West Africa, in the Society's Archives, London).

[3] Thompson, op. cit. pp. 34–5. Frederick Adoy was the brother of Aggrey, later Captain General of Cape Coast and Castle linguist; William Feilde to Committee, 20 Aug. 1789, T. 70/33, ff. 217–18.

education, and both the African Committee and the Society for the Propagation of the Gospel gave the scheme their blessing. Unfortunately, this philanthropic venture was short-lived, and within a few years of its foundation the Charity School ran into difficulties, in part financial. Yet the struggling educational plant, however feeble, never died completely. From the ranks of Quaque's school came teachers to carry on his work during the first decades of the nineteenth century, and the arrival of the Methodist Missionary Society on the coast in 1835 owed much to the tradition of Bible study he had instilled in his pupils.

Slight though Quaque's achievements might appear to be, his career is significant in the evolution of a western-educated élite on the Gold Coast. Two aspects of the process are seen— education overseas and the beginnings of a rudimentary system on Fanti soil. Both affected a tiny yet important minority. It included Africans of indigenous stock: Quaque himself, his son Samuel who was the child of a local marriage,[1] Frederick Adoy,[2] and William Ansah. But there was also a strong mulatto element, the offspring of European slave traders and their 'country wives', and most of Quaque's own pupils were of this kind.

In eighteenth-century Fanti, the Anomabu and Cape Coast mercantile communities were intricately enmeshed, and they cut across the facts of literacy and race. John Currantee was linked through his daughter, Effua Ansah, with Richard Brew. Philip Quaque stayed in Brew's house when visiting Anomabu, and Harry, a mulatto son of Richard, subsequently married into Quaque's family.[3] Within this network of trade and influence, the African emerged who had 'acquired his property chiefly by trading with Europeans', and whose house was 'more splendidly furnished than those of any of his neighbours, having many articles of European luxury in it'.[4] Potentially a challenge to the corporate family and its claims, he symbolized individual ownership of property, an inheritance tie between father and son, and social ascent through personal effort. As a result of

---

[1] Quaque married twice after the death of his English wife; see his letters to the S.P.G. dd. 5 Sept. 1769 and 8 March 1772.

[2] See p. 22 n. 3 above.

[3] See pp. 106, 109 and 120–1 below.

[4] J. Adams, *Remarks on the country extending from Cape Palmas to the River Congo* (London, 1823), pp. 18–19.

European trade and settlement, cross-currents in Fanti society now existed and areas where a conflict of attitudes was possible. It was the western-educated group, often—like the Brews—of mixed blood, around whom these cross-currents would revolve throughout the following century.

PART TWO

Richard Brew: European Trader

CHAPTER I

The Irish Background

European settlement in West Africa was fed from many sources. One source was Ireland, and the Irish connection with West Africa over a long period is a subject worthy of fuller investigation.[1] Even a passing glance at the evidence brings to light interesting features. A book of wills, drawn up on the west coast in the late eighteenth and early nineteenth centuries, for example, shows that a number of the merchants residing there were of Irish origin.[2] Commercially, Ireland and Africa were linked through the export of Irish linens, and because of the proximity of Dublin and Waterford to Liverpool and Bristol, Britain's chief slaving ports.[3] Nor was it unknown for a young West African, receiving his education overseas under commercial auspices, to be sent for this purpose to the Irish capital instead of to London or Liverpool. A case of this kind occurred in the seventeen-fifties, when a son of the chief of Dixcove, sponsored by the Company of Merchants, was placed under the educational charge of a gentleman in Dublin.[4]

[1] In the late seventeenth century, numbers of Irish were recruited into the service of the Royal African Company. In the early nineteenth century, Irish residents in Sierra Leone, for example, celebrated St. Patrick's Day with a dinner, speeches and songs. Notable among Irishmen on the west coast during the nineteenth century were Governor Sir Charles Macarthy and Governor John Pope Hennessy, both of whom had dealings with descendants of Richard Brew; entries, 5 June 1819 and 8 April 1820 in *The Royal Gazette and Sierra Leone Advertiser* (Freetown), vol. I, no. 53 and vol. II, no. 96; Davies, *Royal African Company*, p. 254; J. Pope Hennessy, *Verandah* (London, 1964) and see pp. 138–41 and 164–5 below.
[2] Copy of Wills, Committee of Merchants trading to Africa, 1792–1829, ADM. 1/705 (G.N.A.).
[3] Entry dd. 24 Jan. 1759, T. 70/144, f. 103. In the eighteenth century, of course, England exercised a large measure of control over Ireland's trade.
[4] John Roberts to Committee, 25 Feb. and 6 June 1759, T. 70/1530; Thomas Allan to Secretary, African Committee, 10 April 1759, ibid. and see pp. 36–7 below.

Among traders of Irish origin to be found in West Africa during the slaving days of the second half of the eighteenth century, one—Richard Brew—is notable for the length of time, thirty years in all, that he spent on the coast, and for the outstanding mulatto descendants who stemmed from him in Fanti. A reasonably clear picture can be built up today of his public and private activities between 1745 and 1776, and those of his descendants over several generations, even within a context predominantly African. Much more shadowy, however, is Brew's early life in Ireland, and the circumstances that led him to seek a career in the world of West African trade and settlement. Irish family history presents special problems of its own, not the least of them being the destruction of records in a once much-troubled country.[1] But by piecing together the evidence that still exists, it becomes possible to advance reasonable suppositions about Brew's home area, and about the general background of conditions that preceded his arrival in West Africa in 1745.

There are various pointers from the period after 1745 to associate Brew with Ireland, although unfortunately none of them specify the particular part of the country from which he came. Two pieces of evidence are of special importance: a comment made by Britain's trading rivals, the Dutch, whose headquarters were at Elmina Castle, near Cape Coast, and Brew's own will, drawn up in 1776, shortly before he died. To the Dutch, whose reporting of coastal events was detailed and meticulous, Brew was very well known—it might even be said notorious—and the occasions of friction between them numerous. Their reference to him, in 1775, as Irish by birth and hence a subject of the British Crown therefore has considerable significance.[2] Brew himself, in a will dated 3 August 1776, included among its beneficiaries his 'heirs at law now living in that part

---

[1] The Library of the Society of Genealogists in London has an excellent collection of printed material relating to Irish family history. In Dublin, the Genealogical Office, Dublin Castle, the Registry of Deeds, and the National Library of Ireland all contain invaluable manuscript and printed material. Unfortunately, many of the records in the Public Record Office, Dublin, including wills, were destroyed in 1922. See particularly W. Clare, *A Simple Guide to Irish Genealogy* (London, 1938), *passim*, and A. J. Camp, *Wills and their Whereabouts* (Canterbury, 1963), pp. 101–2.

[2] Peter Woortman to David Mill, 16 Oct. 1775, B.T. 6/2, B 52.

of Great Britain called Ireland'; fuller information about persons and place is tantalizingly omitted.[1]

There are other pointers, too, strengthening the fact of a connection with Ireland. It was there that he went for a while in 1760 during the only period he spent away from West Africa, and his accommodation address was care of Dublin merchants, Carleton and Jevers, who had business premises in Eustace Street, Dublin.[2] In Brew's personal life on the west coast, a certain Irish flavour can be detected. The private residence which he ultimately built at Anomabu had the designation 'Castle Brew', doubtless recalling the castles of his home country, and it is interesting to note that his library of books contained three volumes of a *History of Ireland* by an author unstated.

Family history in Ireland is closely bound up with the involved and recurrent processes of conquest and colonization to which that country has been subjected, leading to an admixture of blood and influencing the form and distribution of surnames.[3] The name 'Brew' or 'Broe' has different origins and a long history behind it. It is an anglicized version of the Gaelic 'Ó'Brugha', it appears at the end of the twelfth century in the Norman form of 'de Berewa' and 'de Bruth', and it is also a Manx surname.[4] By the eighteenth century, Brews were to be found in Dublin and in Downpatrick in Northern Ireland.[5] But they were by far the most numerous in the far west, in County Clare.[6] Since earlier references to them in this country are almost

---

[1] Copy of Richard Brew's will, 3 Aug. 1776 (Somerset House, London).

[2] Secretary, African Committee to Richard Brew, 4 Sept. 1760, T. 70/29, f. 209; entry dd. 24 Sept. 1760, T. 70/144, f. 138; Dublin Directory in *The Gentleman and Citizen's Almanack* (Dublin, 1761, 1762).

[3] See E. Curtis, *A History of Ireland* (London, 1961); E. MacLysaght, *Irish Families; Their Names, Arms and Origins* (Dublin, 1957) and *More Irish Families* (Dublin, 1960); P. H. Reaney, *A Dictionary of British Surnames* (London, 1958).

[4] MacLysaght, *More Irish Families*, p. 44; Reaney, op. cit. p. 46.

[5] ed. A. Vicars, *Index to the Prerogative Wills of Ireland, 1536–1810* (Dublin, 1897), p. 53; ed. D. A. Chart, *Marriage Entries from the Registers of the Parishes of St. Andrew, St. Anne, St. Audoen and St. Bride, Dublin, 1632–1800* (Dublin, 1913), p. 23; ed. A. E. Langman, *Marriage Entries from the Registers of the Parishes of St. Marie, St. Luke, St. Catherine and St. Werburgh, Dublin, 1627–1800* (Dublin, 1915), p. 79; *Report of the Deputy Keeper of the Records, 1928* (Belfast, 1929), App. B, p. 35; ibid. *1936* (Belfast, 1937), App. B, p. 37.

[6] See the Molony Collection in the Genealogical Office, Dublin Castle (abbreviated hereafter as Gen. Office). This is an extensive and valuable collection of notes on the genealogy of many families, including the Brews, in the Clare-Limerick area. It results from a private investigation made earlier in the century.

non-existent, it is possible that they moved there under Cromwell's Transplantation Scheme of 1653–5, when a number of Irish landowners were resettled west of the Shannon.[1] On the basis of the information available, Clare can be regarded as the most likely home of Richard Brew.

Historically one of the strongholds of Catholicism in Ireland, it is a remote and lonely county with an Atlantic coastline of rugged beauty. Ennis, capital of County Clare, stands on the river Fergus, a few miles inland from Limerick in the southeast and the Shannon estuary in the south-west; at the beginning of the eighteenth century the capital had a population of about six hundred.[2] Trade in hides, tallow and butter was carried on between Ennis and Limerick by boat. Indeed, water communication proved very much easier than that overland, and the journey across Ireland to Dublin then has been described as an 'arduous' undertaking.[3] County Clare abounded in castles, each the 'Big House' of a member of the Irish gentry, often— like the surrounding peasantry—much impoverished. In this essentially rural county, far removed from the town life of Dublin, many features of traditional Irish society long persisted —a strong feeling for the clan and its ancestors, a detailed knowledge of lineal descent, and a belief in the supernatural world and in the influence of spirits.[4]

Few aspects of life in eighteenth-century County Clare remained unaffected by the severe Penal Laws that sought to

A wide range of records was consulted, including some in the Irish Public Record Office which are no longer available.

[1] Curtis, op. cit. p. 253 and J. Frost, *The History and Topography of the County of Clare* (Dublin, 1893), passim. A 'James Broe' was among those who received Transplanters' Certificates in the City and County of Limerick; see 'Persons Transplanted in Ireland, A.D. 1653–54' in J. O'Hart, *The Irish and Anglo-Irish Landed Gentry when Cromwell came to Ireland* (Dublin, 1884), p. 329. No direct *contemporary* reference has been found to Brews in County Clare during the seventeenth century. In the Molony Collection, Gen. Office MS. 456, p. 12, there is a letter dated 27 Aug. 1923 from a member of the Brew family in which he refers to an Act of Attainder passed by James II against John Brew of Corofin (in Clare). He links this with a story which his father told him of a Brew ancestor who had had to flee the country, and who lived for a while in the north of England. This would suggest a Protestant connection on the part of one branch of the family anyway, by the late seventeenth century.

[2] E. MacLysaght, *Irish Life in the Seventeenth Century* (Cork, 1950), p. 190.

[3] Frost, op. cit. p. 605; MacLysaght, *Irish Life in the Seventeenth Century*, pp. 126, 239–41.

[4] MacLysaght, *Irish Life in the Seventeenth Century*, pp. 6, 18–20, 42, 89–90, 177–8.

reshape society and eliminate Catholicism, a consequence of William III's victories over James II and his Irish supporters in 1690–1. Debarred from the electorate and from most professions and trades, Catholic landowners could only keep their estates intact if the heir accepted Protestantism within a limited period of time; failing this, on a father's death the estate was broken up and divided among all his sons.[1] Socially, the effect of the Penal Laws, aided by a growing indifference to religion, was to bring about conformity, at least of a nominal kind, to the established church, as the necessary price to be paid for continuance of property and status. Also tending in the same direction was the intermarriage that took place between Catholic families and newly arrived Protestant landowners after the upheavals of the mid-seventeenth century. In County Clare the net result was to transform long-established Irish families, such as the O'Briens and the Moloneys, into leading supporters of the Protestant ascendancy.[2]

It is against this background that the Brews in County Clare must be considered. Located in different parts of the county, the majority of them seem to have been Protestant, although an occasional Catholic comes to light.[3] But by and large, they, too, appear as conformists, owning land, voting at elections, entering the church, serving as justices of the peace, and receiving the freedom of the borough of Ennis—in short, displaying all the hallmarks of country gentry.[4] Between the various Brew families, interrelationship is now almost impossible to trace; the crucial links probably lie in the turbulent and confused history of the seventeenth century. One fact in particular, however, deserves comment: the frequency with which the same Christian names are used, making disentanglement of the Clare Brews almost as difficult a problem as that of the Fanti Brews later.[5] At least five 'Richards' are to be found in County Clare during the eighteenth century.[6] Among them was Richard Brew of Ennis,

[1] Curtis, op. cit. pp. 284–6.
[2] Curtis, op. cit. pp. 285, 291–2; MacLysaght, *Irish Life in the Seventeenth Century,* p. 117.
[3] Frost, op. cit. p. 630. Thomas Brew was converted to Protestantism in 1783, however.
[4] Molony Collection, especially 'Extracts from the Poll Book of the Clare Election of 1745' in Gen. Office MS. 450; Frost, op. cit. pp. 606, 619.
[5] See pp. 123–4 below. [6] Molony Collection.

to whom some of the earliest of the eighteenth-century references are made. Described as a brewer, vintner, and gentleman, Richard voted in the 1745 Parliamentary election along with several other Brews.[1] It is he who most probably was the father of Richard, the trader in West Africa.

In the first place, the time sequence is completely appropriate. Exactly what age the trader was when he first went out to West Africa in 1745 is not known, but the assumption that he was in his early twenties, and in his fifties when he died thirty years later seems reasonable.[2] This would make the date of his birth c. 1725. References to Richard Brew, the vintner, begin in 1726, a year in which he leased land and buildings in Ennis,[3] doubtless an indication that he was at an early stage of his working life and establishing a business there. By 1735, he was said to have a 'large helpless family', the eldest son of which bore the same Christian name as his father.[4] Richard, the future West African trader, would then be about ten years old—perhaps a little older—and from this point of view, identifiable with Richard Brew, Junior, of Ennis.

In the second place, adding further weight to the time element, there is the important fact that the vintner ran into considerable financial difficulties, a circumstance that might well send an eldest son overseas in search of better fortune. During the seventeen-thirties, Richard, Senior, had entered into a brewery partnership with the High Sheriff of County Clare, Nicholas Bindon. Land was leased in Ennis and a brewery built. It was completed by 1737 and Richard was appointed manager of it with a salary of £10 per annum above his share of the profits. The partnership was a short-lived one, and following its dissolution in 1743 there were legal proceedings in which Brew attempted to prove that he had been defrauded.

An interesting light is thrown on his financial position by Bindon's claim that Brew did *not* have a share in the business on

[1] Molony Collection, Gen. Office MS. 456, pp. 19, 35, 36; 'Extracts from the Poll Book of the Clare Election of 1745' in Molony Collection, Gen. Office MS. 450. Five other Brew names—Arthur, Francis, George (twice), and Thomas—are given, apart from Richard.

[2] See pp. 36 n. 1 and 81 below.

[3] Gore to Brew, registered 26 May 1731, no. 66–228–45953, Registry of Deeds, Dublin; Molony Collection, Gen. Office MS. 456, p. 35.

[4] Molony Collection, Gen. Office MS. 456, pp. 24, 35.

Pat Carter

1. The town of Anomabu from the air

the terms which he asserted, since he had been unable to contribute enough capital to enter on that basis. According to Bindon, the vintner's whole fortune in the seventeen-thirties had been no more than £350, due to him from a gentleman in County Clare and payable in instalments over three years; a part of it was owed to creditors, and he had not invested £100 in the brewery.[1] Whatever the rights and wrongs of the case may have been, it is clear that Brew, Senior, did not possess an overabundance of the world's goods at that time; in 1744 he was still in debt, and in 1747 he mortgaged some property for £120, giving up his right of redemption in 1750 for a further sum.[2] The arrival of Richard, Junior, on the west coast of Africa, two years after the partnership ended, could well have been the result of these pecuniary embarrassments—an inauspicious start for an eldest son in a country severely limited in opportunities. Nor would he have been the only Irishman to have adopted this course in the middle of the century, and for similar reasons.[3]

Strongest of all, however, in establishing a family link between Richard Brew of Ennis and the west coast trader, is evidence centring on the former's wife, Eleanor, the same Christian name, it should be noted, as the younger Brew chose for his mulatto daughter.[4] Eleanor was the daughter of Turlough O'Brien and Mary Blake, said to be Papists—a fact which caused complications for Richard Brew, Senior, at the time of the 1745 election, and perhaps for his elder children too.[5] Turlough O'Brien died intestate in 1736, followed by his wife Mary, also intestate, in 1741, whereupon Eleanor became the administrator of both her father's and her mother's estates. A series of court cases ensued, in which the name 'Reddan' is recurrent. Unfortunately, complete details of these cases are no longer available, but from what *is* known, it can be deduced that the Reddans and Eleanor Brew were related. In 1742, she

[1] Molony Collection, Gen. Office MS. 456, p. 24 ff.; Frost, op. cit. p. 627.
[2] Molony Collection, Gen. Office MS. 456, pp. 22-3, 35-6.
[3] N. Owen, *Journal of a Slave Dealer* (London, 1930), introduction by E. C. Martin, pp. 1-18.
[4] See p. 107 below.
[5] Molony Collection, Gen. Office MS. 456, pp. 17-18, 31 and 'Extracts from the Poll Book of the Clare Election of 1745' in Gen. Office MS. 450. Richard Brew's vote was objected to on the grounds that his wife was a Papist, but the objection was not proved.

and Richard brought a case against her maternal uncle Andrew Blake, and John Reddan, arising out of Eleanor's role as her mother's administrator. In 1747, John and James Reddan and Richard Brew were all parties to a lawsuit bearing on the affairs of Turlough O'Brien, while in 1750 James Reddan with Mr. and Mrs. Brew appeared as the defendants in further litigation. This time the case concerned a will, of which Turlough O'Brien had been one of the executors. Challenged under the Penal Laws, it affected Eleanor Brew as her late father's representative; another executor was her maternal uncle, Andrew Blake.[1]

It seems obvious, then, that the Reddans, like Andrew Blake, were closely implicated in the property and family affairs of Mrs. Brew after her parents' death, although the precise nature of the relationship remains unknown. The significance of this connection, for present purposes, becomes marked when it is realized that Richard Brew, the trader, had a relation 'Reddan' residing with him at Anomabu. He was mentioned in coastal correspondence by a business friend of Brew's, Thomas Westgate, between 1768 and 1770.[2] 'Reddan' is an old County Clare name that occurs frequently in the seventeenth century.[3] It thus links Brew with this part of western Ireland, and more particularly, when all the foregoing evidence is taken into account, suggests a family tie with Richard Brew of Ennis—brewer, vintner, and gentleman.

The younger Brew's path to West Africa may have taken him through Limerick along the coastal route to Dublin, where contacts with those engaged in world trade would be easier to establish. Once in West Africa, he would find the same method of communication for Europeans—by sea, rather than overland —between the various forts and factories. With his native Ireland, there would be other similarities, too, not least that of a peasant society steeped in ancestor worship and having a tenacious clan structure.[4] Within this society Brew sought to

---

[1] Molony Collection, Gen. Office MS. 456, pp. 9–10, 19, 29–34.

[2] Thomas Westgate to Richard Brew, 28 Oct. 1768, 18 July 1770 and 24 Sept. 1770, T. 70/1536, pt. 2. The vital reference is that of 24 Sept. 1770.

[3] Frost, op. cit. pp. 385, 402 n., 403 n., 405.

[4] A comparison has recently been drawn between the more isolated islands of Scotland and contemporary West Africa from the point of view of social features; see K. L. Little, 'The Study of "Social Change" in British West Africa' in *Africa*,

create the material conditions appropriate to an eighteenth-century gentleman—house, furnishings, pictures and books—transplanting features that were essentially alien to the west coast.[1] But it is his integration with the local community, not the reverse, that stands out prominently. Volatile and quarrelsome in temperament, and endowed with a strong political sense, Brew's Irish background may well have been an important factor in enabling him to adapt as successfully as he did to the kinship pattern and customs of African society.

vol. XXIII (1953), p. 283. On the subject of actual living conditions, it is interesting to note that in the eighteen-forties, African dwellings at Cape Coast and inland were regarded as far superior to those of the Irish peasantry; *Report from Select Committee on the West Coast of Africa*, pt. II, Appendix and Index (1842), App. no. 3, p. 13.
[1] See p. 100 ff. below.

CHAPTER II

Governor of Anomabu Fort

Brew first arrived on the west coast in 1745, during the twilight phase of the Royal African Company. His early activities there remain obscure, and it is not possible to say exactly where he was or in what capacity, although it can reasonably be assumed that he was serving the now almost moribund organization. At the beginning of 1750 Brew held the clerical post of registrar at British headquarters, Cape Coast Castle, receiving a salary of £63 per annum. Two months later, in March 1750, he was appointed to his first command in Fanti—as chief factor of Tantumkweri, a fort on its eastern borders.[1] The rest of his public career, ten years in all, was spent entirely in Fanti except for a brief spell in 1750–1, when he shared the command of Dixcove in Ahanta country, to the west of Cape Coast.

Local disputes there, entangled with Anglo-Dutch rivalry, had led to hostilities, and early in 1751 a gathering of British and Dutch Governors and native rulers was held at nearby Sekondi in an attempt to resolve the problem. Brew remained at Dixcove in sole charge, while his colleague attended the congress at Sekondi.[2] The Ahanta troubles gave rise to one interesting by-product which may well reflect Brew's influence and Irish background. Quamina, the young son of Acca, a Dixcove caboceer and participant in the Sekondi congress, became an educational protégé of the British Company, and was placed

---

[1] Entry dd. 24 Jan. 1750, T. 70/1516; entry dd. 30 March 1750, T. 70/151; Richard Brew to Committee, 31 Aug. 1758, T. 70/30, f. 253; Charles Bell to Committee, 4 Aug. 1762, T. 70/31, f. 10. See Brew's reference, in 1758, to his thirteen years on the coast, p. 48 below.

[2] Entries dd. 26 Oct. and 18 Dec. 1750, T. 70/1467, ff. 95, 109; Nassau Senior and Richard Brew to Governor and Council, 2 Dec. 1750, ibid. f. 256; John Roberts to Nassau Senior and Richard Brew, 8 Jan. 1751, T. 70/1476; the same to Richard Brew, 9 Jan. 1751, ibid.; entry dd. 11 Jan. 1751, T. 70/1130.

under the care of a Mr. Thomas Allan of Dublin, who had him baptized, and educated with his own son for seven years.[1]

After leaving his temporary command at Dixcove, Brew was appointed once again to Tantumkweri, and continued there for two and a half years, from August 1751 until February 1754.[2] The main feature of this period seems to have been the development of his own trade connections in Fanti, with resultant differences between himself and the newly created African Committee. He soon became involved, therefore, in the question of private trading by servants of the Committee, its nature and extent, a recurrent theme throughout his life on the coast, whether from the defending or attacking end.[3]

In 1753, soon after the Company of Merchants had come into existence, he and his senior officer, Thomas Melvil, the first Governor of Cape Coast Castle appointed by the Committee, were under fire for attempting to create a local monopoly in slaves, contrary to the spirit of the Act establishing the new regime. The charges against them, based on the evidence of Liverpool and Bristol merchants and ships' captains, included the formation of a private slave-trading partnership with the aim of obstructing the dealings of ships' officers on the coast. This misuse of their public position was the cause, it was said, of an increase in prices. Brew, according to reports, had gone into the market-place at Legu, a small place near Tantumkweri, and announced that whatever the private dealers offered for slaves, he would pay forty shillings more. Since such behaviour nullified Parliament's intention that the forts should assist shipping and private traders, the Committee, after considering the various complaints made, directed Melvil in November 1753 to suspend Brew for 'very blameable' conduct. His career in the service was to come to an end unless he could prove his innocence. Much to the Committee's relief, the issue was resolved by the fact that Brew sought his own discharge

---

[1] Entry dd. 11 Jan. 1751, T. 70/1130; John Roberts to Committee, 25 Feb. and 6 June 1759, T. 70/1530; Thomas Allan to Secretary, African Committee, 10 April 1759, ibid.; James Laroche to the same, 13 Oct. 1759, ibid.

[2] T. 70/1454, f. 1. In the Register of Servants and Officers of the African Company Brew is recorded as a factor at Cape Coast Castle in June 1751; presumably this was in the brief interval between leaving Dixcove and being reappointed to Tantumkweri on 10 Aug. 1751.

[3] See pp. 51–2, 94–7 below.

early in 1754 in order to set up in a private capacity at Mumford, like Legu, a small trading town near Tantumkweri.[1]

Two years after this, in 1756, officialdom had occasion to revise its previous view that Brew's actions had 'render'd him unfit for the service of this Committee'. He was now reinstated and confirmed in another Fanti command, this time of a new fort at Anomabu, a place henceforth to be his home as a public or private settler for a period of almost twenty years.[2] Significant as this stage was in Brew's career, the coastal circumstances that gave rise to it and brought him to the main theatre of his West African activities need to be explained. In the eighteenth century, Anomabu ranked as one of the chief slave-trading centres on the Gold Coast because of its connection with an accessible route to the interior, and its roadstead was much frequented by shipping.[3] Earlier, the Royal African Company had built a fort there, Fort Charles, but by the seventeen-thirties it was in ruins and no longer used.[4] Some twenty years later, French activity in the neighbourhood opened up the question of whether or not a British settlement should be re-established in order to counter the possibility of a rival foundation. In May 1752, the government eventually decided to do this, soon after the Company of Merchants trading to Africa had taken over control of the forts.[5] Consequently, in the middle of the century, Anomabu became a scene of Anglo-French rivalry, an intrusion into West Africa of a major issue dominating international politics.

Fort-building was linked inevitably from its initial stages with African willingness to co-operate; without this, the decision

[1] Charges against Governor Melvil, 27 April 1753, T. 70/1521; entry dd. 10 May 1753 and copy of an affidavit of David Hamilton, 16 June 1753, C.O. 388/45, Dd 153, Dd 155; Donnan, Documents Illustrative of the Slave Trade to America, vol. II, p. 506; Thomas Melvil to Committee, 4 April 1754, T. 70/1522; Committee to Governor and Council, Cape Coast Castle, 7 Sept. 1754, T. 70/29, f. 25.

[2] Committee to Governor and Council, Cape Coast Castle, 7 Sept. 1754, T. 70/29, f. 25 and see pt. 2, chap. III below.

[3] Bosman, A New and Accurate Description of the Coast of Guinea, p. 56; Lawrence, Trade Castles and Forts of West Africa, p. 349.

[4] Matson, 'The French at Amoku' in Transactions of the Gold Coast and Togoland Historical Society, vol. I, pt. 2 (1953), p. 47.

[5] Entry dd. 28 May 1752, P.C. 2/103, ff. 97–8; Martin, The British West African Settlements, p. 13. The eighteenth-century fort is called 'Fort William' today, but at that time it was simply known as 'Anomabu Fort'; M. Priestley, 'A Note on Fort William, Anomabu' in Transactions of the Gold Coast and Togoland Historical Society, vol. II, pt. I (1956), pp. 46–8.

would scarcely have been a practical proposition. Of much importance, therefore, was the attitude of John Currantee, the chief caboceer of Anomabu, an extremely skilled exponent of the art of bargaining.[1] No better example of the contemporary working realities on the Gold Coast can be found than in the behaviour of John Currantee towards the British and the French. A nice calculation of benefits led him to recognize fully the many uses of a fort, to accept the inducements of the rival claimants, and, even when the balance seemed to have swung in favour of the British, to continue manipulating the situation to Fanti advantage. As a Governor of Anomabu fort said in the early days of its construction, John Currantee was as much French as English and would hold out a hand to each nation. Yet being under his protection, the English had to be very cautious in speech and behaviour.[2] Nothing demonstrates more clearly than John Currantee's actions the limits of European power, its involvement with local affairs, and the '*Common Factor* of interests'[3] binding Africans and Europeans together. The matter was summed up in a letter written by one of his sons in the phrase, 'the English live by us and we by them'.[4]

Hence the chief caboceer of Anomabu found himself the centre of a vigorous dual attempt to win and retain his support; the British reported that the activity of the French was the most determined effort they had yet made to monopolize trade on that part of the coast.[5] Two main avenues of approach were employed over these years—diplomatic missions reinforced by suitable presents, and the offer of education abroad. Between 1749 and 1752, British and French warships visited the coast carrying a variety of gifts, for example, brandy, a large silver cup, a sword, a gun, cloaks, and feathered hats. The officers who took them ashore discussed with the recipient his views about establishing a fort, and sounded opinion as to the strength of their opponents' position.[6]

[1] See pp. 13–15 above.
[2] Christopher Whytell to Committee, 22 April 1753, T. 70/1520.
[3] B. Malinowski, *The Dynamics of Culture Change*, ed. P. M. Kaberry (New Haven, 1945), p. 66.
[4] William Ansah to Earl of Halifax, 20 Feb. 1752, C.O. 388/45, Dd 83.
[5] John Roberts to Lord Duplin, 23 March 1749, T. 70/1476, f. 72.
[6] John Roberts to Lord Duplin, 23 March 1749, T. 70/1476; Patrick Baird, H.M.S. *Surprise* to Secretary to the Admiralty, 25 July 1751, Adm. 1/1485; Matthew

The second method, education abroad, had as its object the personal commitment of leading Fanti to the British or French cause through an eighteenth-century equivalent of the overseas scholarship. Indeed, in the mid-century, there was a reference to the 'Exhibition' received by John Currantee's son, William Ansah, from the Royal African Company, after which he was appointed on the coast as a writer.[1] Measures such as these, it was hoped, would induce in his father a favourable disposition towards the donors, and at the same time provide them with the benefits of an influential local intermediary. One practical aspect of this was William Ansah's reports of any moves made by the French. Letters from him, along these lines, to Lord Halifax at the Board of Trade were taken to London in 1752; the bearer, who wrote back to the coast after arrival, urged Prince William to do all that he could to frustrate French designs and to assist British traders.[2] John Currantee nevertheless found it useful to have a foot in both camps; if two of his sons went to England, a third, like the sons of other Fanti caboceers, went to France. The consequences of having a French party also at Anomabu were revealed in a number of ways. One was in John Currantee's reluctance to sign the 'law' which the British were negotiating with Fanti states to exclude the French from settling between Queen Anne's Point, near Cape Coast, and James Fort, Accra. Another was in the possibility that his successor might favour the rival interest, a prospect that caused the British no little concern.[3]

Behind Fanti manœuvrings there lay a very real awareness of the potentialities of a fort. Apart from its tactical value in local politics, and as a place of defence, it had undoubted commercial significance.[4] Nor was this connected only with the slave trade and the long-standing middleman role of the Fanti.

Buckle, H.M.S. *Assistance* to the same, 19 Feb. 1752, ibid.; William Ansah to Earl of Halifax, 20 Feb. 1752, C.O. 388/45, Dd 83.

[1] John Roberts to Viscount Barrington, n.d., T. 70/1476 and see pp. 20-1 above.

[2] William Ansah to Earl of Halifax, 20 Feb. 1752, C.O. 388/45, Dd 83; John Roberts to William Ansah, 27 Oct. 1752, T. 70/1478.

[3] Thomas Melvil to Committee, 11 June 1752, C.O. 388/45, Dd 115; Committee to Governor and Council, Cape Coast Castle, November 1752, ibid. Dd 107; Thomas Melvil to Committee, 13 Dec. 1752, T. 70/1518; George Cockburne, H.M.S. *Glory* to Secretary to the Admiralty, 14 Dec. 1752, Adm. 1/1604; Matson, art. cit. p. 49.

[4] See pp. 14-15 above.

A fort also stimulated the local economy: for example, labour and food supplies were needed. In 1751 and 1752, before a decision to build had finally been taken in London, John Currantee was offering to supply people to carry stones and lime, and his men were pointing out to the captain of a visiting man-of-war that their women lacked a market for fowls, eggs, and corn because of British tardiness in repairing the old structure or building a new one.[1] Despatches sent to London from the coast stressed that there was a local demand for a fort, which if the British did not meet, the French certainly would. In 1751 it was reported that John Currantee had refused the French permission to establish a settlement. The next year they reappeared to make a second attempt, which was prevented by a British naval squadron. Largesse had strengthened the French party, and the Fanti were saying in 1752 that there was room for both nations to build at Anomabu.[2]

When it was politic to do so, John Currantee made much of his own personal preference for the British, basing this on their historic link with his forefathers. The Anglo-Fanti trading relationship was indeed an old one, originating in the mid-sixteenth century.[3] But even after George II's government, assured of the caboceer's co-operation, had decided to build a new settlement, it was realized on the coast that the position was far from secure. There were no illusions about the Fanti intention to get as much as possible from both sides.[4] A chain of difficulties lay ahead, and indeed heavy expense. Not the least aspect of a fort's local attraction was the building process, the longer the better, during which all kinds of pressure could be exerted with materially beneficial results.[5] In June 1752

[1] Thomas Melvil to Committee, 11 July 1751, T. 70/1517; Matthew Buckle, H.M.S. *Assistance* to Secretary to the Admiralty, 19 Feb. 1752, Adm. 1/1485.

[2] Thomas Melvil to Committee, 11 July 1751, T. 70/1517; Patrick Baird, H.M.S. *Surprise* to Secretary to the Admiralty, 25 July 1751, Adm. 1/1485; Matthew Buckle, H.M.S. *Assistance* to the same, 19 Feb. 1752, ibid.; George Cockburne, H.M.S. *Glory* to the same, 14 Dec. 1752, Adm. 1/1604; entry dd. 28 May 1752, P.C. 2/103, f. 97.

[3] William Ansah to Earl of Halifax, 20 Feb. 1752, C.O. 388/45, Dd 83; J. W. Blake, *Europeans in West Africa, 1450–1560* (Hakluyt Society, 2nd Series, London, 1942), vol. II, p. 293.

[4] Entry dd. 28 May 1752, P.C. 2/103, ff. 97–8; Christopher Whytell to Committee, 22 April 1753, T. 70/1520; Thomas Melvil to Committee, 24 Feb. and 24 April 1753, ibid.

[5] Thomas Melvil to Committee, 22 Sept. 1753, T. 70/1520.

Thomas Melvil expressed the view that the cost would be impossible to determine and would rise or fall as the French pursued or dropped their design of settling.[1] Expenditure on construction, badly planned in London and far exceeding the original estimate, was consequently increased by the special conditions of coast diplomacy and Fanti business tactics.[2] French ships continued to visit Anomabu and to bring presents; three attempts had to be made, owing to difficulties with the Fanti, before the foundations of a new fort were finally laid in August 1753, and during the early stages of unloading materials at Anomabu there was a strike of canoemen for higher wages.[3] In the same year, the cost of food for the British rose to a level described as 'exorbitant'. While the fort was under construction, the Governor, engineer, and their small staff lived in the house of John Currantee who provided accommodation in return for rent. The residents then discovered that they could not buy provisions such as fowls direct from the 'bush people'; John Currantee's household set up a middleman trade and sold at double the price.[4]

The handling of such a complex and unpredictable situation was clearly no easy matter; five and a half years after the foundations of the fort had been laid, work was still in progress.[5] Throughout, much depended upon the person who was

[1] Thomas Melvil to Committee, 11 June 1752, T. 70/1518.

[2] In reply to the Committee's inquiries about increased cost, John Apperley, the engineer (who had never been in West Africa before), pointed out that his estimate had not included freight, landing expenses at Anomabu, or any other contingencies, but only the actual buildings. It should be noted that the account of expenses produced by the Committee in 1755 included £1,000 distributed to the Fanti to obtain a treaty securing the rights of the English to ground at Anomabu. Parliament had made a grant of £6,000 in 1753 for the building of the fort. In 1755, it made a second grant; John Apperley to Committee, 28 March 1755, C.O. 388/46, Ee 60; Account of Expenses incurred in building a fort at Anomabu, 1755, ibid. Ee 47; Martin, op. cit. p. 17. For the technical difficulties involved in fort-building, see Lawrence, op. cit. pp. 90–1 and for Anomabu fort, pp. 349–55.

[3] Thomas Melvil to Committee, 25 Jan. 1753, T. 70/29, f. 54; William Ansah to Governor, Cape Coast Castle, 17 Feb. 1753 (in Captain Cockburne's letters), Adm. 1/1604; John Apperley to Committee, 8 Sept. 1753, T. 70/1520; John Apperley to Thomas Melvil, 21 Sept. 1755, C.O. 388/47, Ff 12; Thomas Melvil to Committee, 22 Sept. 1753, T. 70/1520.

[4] Thomas Melvil to Committee, 30 Oct. 1752, T. 70/1518; John Apperley to Committee, 10 March 1753, T. 70/1520; Christopher Whytell to Committee, 23 June 1753, ibid.; entry dd. 31 Oct. 1756, T. 70/986.

[5] Thomas Westgate and Richard Brew to Committee, 12 Jan. 1759, T. 70/30, f. 276.

Governor of Anomabu and his ability to maintain a *modus vivendi* with John Currantee and the Fanti, and ensure continued building. The possibility that the aged caboceer's[1] successor might favour French designs also had to be taken into account, and with international relations deteriorating into the Seven Years War in 1756[2] the French menace in all its forms became more real. In that year, too, the Governor, John Apperley, became critically ill, causing a vacancy in the command at a critical juncture.

Apperley had first been appointed by the Committee in 1752 as engineer. Two years later, on the death of Governor Christopher Whytell, he had applied to succeed him in office, pointing out that this would be of practical value during the period of construction. The Committee had approved the appointment, although it was contrary to their normal rule of promotion according to experience, on the understanding that Apperley did not intend to remain after the building was finished. By the spring of 1756, he was described as far advanced in consumption and unlikely to live for more than a few months. Doubts were expressed on the coast as to what would happen when he died, since the Anomabu people were so difficult to handle; in their despatch of November 1756, the Committee told the Governor-in-Chief, Charles Bell, to appoint a dependable successor should circumstances necessitate it. But before the Committee's despatch had even been written, Apperley's death had occurred, on 18 August, and his place had already been taken by Richard Brew, who now returned to official life after two years as a private trader at Mumford.[3]

Brew's appointment as Governor of Anomabu fort in July

---

[1] There are many contemporary references in the middle of the century to John Currantee's advanced age. The Rev. Thomas Thompson, for example, who arrived on the coast in 1752, described him as about eighty; Thompson, *An Account of Two Missionary Voyages*, p. 47.

[2] England declared war against France on 18 May 1756; Committee to John Apperley, 28 May 1756, C.O. 388/47, Ff 28.

[3] Entry for 5 Aug. 1752 in 'A Narrative of the Proceedings of the Committee of the Company of Merchants ... relative to the building the fort at Anomabu', C.O. 388/46, Ee 48; John Apperley to Committee, 30 Oct. 1754, ibid. Ee 46; Committee to Governor and Council, Cape Coast Castle, 28 June 1755, ibid. Ee 59; abstract of letter from Andrew Farquhar, 12 March 1756, C.O. 388/47, Ff 35; Charles Bell to Committee, 28 April and 1 Sept. 1756, ibid. Ff 33 and Ff 41; Committee to Governor and Council, Cape Coast Castle, 4 Nov. 1756, T. 70/29, f. 100.

1756[1] was occasioned, then, by the need to fill a post of importance beset with special difficulties. In the words of Charles Bell, it called for 'a thorough Acquaintance with the Temper and manners of the natives and no small Interest with the ruling men'. Brew had already spent some years in Fanti, first at Tantumkweri and then at Mumford, and it was the unanimous opinion of the Council that no white man possessed the needed qualities to a greater degree than he did. In addition, he was said to have 'a remarkable ascendant' over the mind of old John Currantee, an asset not to be underestimated in view of past experience. For these reasons, the Council decided to readmit him into the service on receipt of a petition explaining why he had resigned from Tantumkweri in 1754.[2] Their action was ultimately confirmed by the Committee who expressed the hope, at the same time, that Brew would conduct himself satisfactorily in his new position.[3] For his part, he wrote in April 1758 thanking the Committee for confirming him in the post and admitting him to the Council, and giving an assurance of his constant endeavour to maintain their honour and interest and merit future favour.[4]

The Governorship which Brew held at Anomabu for two periods, 1756–60 and 1761–4, carried a salary of £200 a year in the first instance and a table allowance of £150;[5] as was customary on assuming a command he had to provide bond for £5,000 through two sureties of £2,500 each. There appears to have been some delay in completing the formalities. By July 1758, nobody had offered to stand surety and the Committee sent a reminder that he must write to his friends. It was late in the next year before the bond, duly witnessed, was received at the African Office in London.[6] Brew had been on the coast for fourteen years, and this may have been one of the factors weakening his home connections; the matter was dealt with

[1] Entry dd. 21 July 1756, T. 70/986; T. 70/1454, f. 1. Brew assumed command before Apperley died.

[2] Charles Bell to Committee, 1 Sept. 1756, C.O. 388/47, Ff 41.

[3] Committee to Governor and Council, Cape Coast Castle, 9 Dec. 1757, T. 70/29, f. 119.

[4] Richard Brew to Committee, 16 April 1758, T. 70/30, f. 233.

[5] Entry dd. 21 July 1756, T. 70/986. This was increased to a total of £400 during his second Governorship; entries in March and April 1764, T. 70/988.

[6] Committee to Governor and Council, Cape Coast Castle, 9 Dec. 1757 and 22 July 1758, T. 70/29, ff. 122, 140; entry dd. 28 Nov. 1759, T. 70/144, f. 120.

more expeditiously when he was reappointed while in England and after making influential contacts.[1]

Like his two predecessors, Brew began his Anomabu command of 1756–60 by living in the house of John Currantee. Early in 1757, however, the Committee was informed that the move into the fort had now taken place; hence Brew became the first Governor actually to occupy it.[2] Building was still in progress and it was not until 1759, towards the end of his first spell of office, that it was described as 'near being finished'.[3] Among Brew's colleagues at Anomabu was one Thomas Trinder, another long resident on the coast and eventually Governor of a fort. Trinder, a practical man whose services were much in demand, held the post of Overseer of Works, and until an engineer arrived to replace John Apperley, he was able to continue operations.[4] The new engineer, Captain John Baugh, sent out by the Board of Ordnance, reached Anomabu in 1758 and under him the first stage of the fort was completed, although not without subsequent criticism of his work.[5]

Despite the clashes that were the normal accompaniment of exercising coastal authority, Brew certainly proved useful during the first period at Anomabu, counteracting in so far as it was possible John Currantee's skilful manipulation of events. The advantage veered first to one side, then to the other. Shortly after assuming command, Brew was in trouble with the Anomabu townspeople on the grounds that he had not paid proper respect to the leading men and, more specifically, was displaying less public generosity than Apperley had done.[6] But in 1757 there was a different story to tell. The arrival of French warships to reduce Cape Coast Castle provided the wily John Currantee with a good opportunity for another display of pro-French sentiment. Brew resorted to 'extraordinary expenses' in order to gain the interest of the Fanti, but when the

[1] See p. 49 below.
[2] Charles Bell to Committee, 13 Feb. 1757, C.O. 388/47, Ff 65.
[3] Thomas Westgate and Richard Brew to Committee, 12 Jan. 1759, T. 70/30, f. 276.
[4] Charles Bell to Committee, 10 Oct. 1756 and 23 April 1757, C.O. 388/47, Ff 46, Ff 65.
[5] Nassau Senior to Committee, 15 June 1758, T. 70/30, ff. 239–40; Charles Bell to the same, 16 Dec. 1761, ibid. f. 443. There was subsequent work on the fort in 1761 and 1770; see Lawrence, op. cit. pp. 349–52.
[6] Entry dd. 17 Sept. 1756, T. 70/986.

Anomabu caboceer prepared a present to be sent by sea to the French commander, he did not hesitate to shoot the canoe to pieces with the guns of the fort before it could be launched, and threatened similar action to the town. Not to be thwarted, John Currantee then organized an overland embassy of congratulation to the French on their expected victory at Cape Coast. Hearing that the outcome had been otherwise, he proceeded to send the same message to the British Governor-in-Chief, and assured him that armed men had been waiting at Anomabu ready to march to his assistance the moment they were summoned. [1]

This swift adaptation to the course of events well illustrates how easily local support could fluctuate between one European nation and another, and the need for Governors at all times to be aware of and to assess indigenous pressures. Only occasionally and in exceptional circumstances did they apply force, a method normally incompatible with the aims of a trading community. Dependent in the last analysis upon African goodwill, the customary way for a fort to secure it was by adherence to an established pattern of behaviour. In concrete terms, this was expressed through a network of payments, geared to the social structure of the coastal states and with due regard to rank and traditional practice.

During the time that Brew was in charge at Anomabu a considerable number of payments were made, as the account books reveal. There were allowances of £48 and £24 a year to John Currantee and his heir, and frequent gifts of rum, tobacco, fine chintz, and other commodities to the caboceer, his wives and household, and to William Ansah and the Fanti elders and headmen. [2] Since the increase of these payments, not surprisingly, was an objective of coastal rulers and the palaver a useful means to this end, a Governor needed to have some facility for diplomatic bargaining in order to deal effectively with African demands. Brew's knowledge of Fanti society and of the vernacular undoubtedly assisted him here; in the words of his senior officer at Cape Coast Castle, the Fanti were 'sometimes foiled . . .

---

[1] Entry dd. 24 Jan. 1757, T. 70/986; Crooks, *Records relating to the Gold Coast Settlements*, pp. 31–3, quoting from Smollett's *History of England*, chap. VII, bk. III. See also p. 102 below.

[2] See the variety of entries in the Anomabu Day Books, e.g. T. 70/986, T. 70/987, T. 70/988.

at their own weapons'.[1] It was certainly not the case that there were no palavers while he was Governor; under another man there might well have been more, prolonging even further the completion of the fort.

Apart from the benefits to be derived from his Fanti influence, the new Governor of Anomabu had another significance, recognized even in the quarters where his official behaviour was criticized. This was the capacity to keep the fort supplied at times when the public stock was depleted. Such a situation must have arisen periodically on the coast, given the circumstance of a store-ship usually sent out once a year, and especially during the Seven Years War, when normal shipping delays would have been accentuated. A Governor like Brew, whose resources were increased by considerable private trade, could thus be extremely useful in advancing necessities without which the life of a fort would come to a standstill. During 1758, 1759, and 1760, he was furnishing the fort with goods, on one occasion totalling £161 in value, and shortly after he had left for England in 1760, the Council at Cape Coast Castle placed it on record that the next person appointed ought to be someone in a position to do likewise.[2]

In the last three years of this Governorship, awareness of Brew's practical services was counterbalanced, however, by complaints of a high-handed and disrespectful attitude. These complaints emanated particularly from Nassau Senior, Governor-in-Chief at Cape Coast Castle, and successor to Charles Bell who had been responsible for Brew's appointment in 1756 and who had thought highly of his capabilities in dealing with the Fanti.[3] It is clear that Brew and Nassau Senior did not get on at all well, and under the latter coastal friction reached such a point that in 1760 the Committee contemplated sending Bell back to restore harmony.[4] Charges and counter-charges were advanced to London by both men. After he had received a strongly worded letter of criticism from Anomabu about his policy,

[1] Charles Bell to Committee, 23 April 1757, C.O. 388/47, Ff 65.
[2] Entry dd. 30 Oct. 1758, T. 70/986; entry dd. 1 Jan. 1760, T. 70/987; Act of Council, Cape Coast Castle, 13 March 1760, T. 70/30, f. 345.
[3] See pp. 43-4 above. Nassau Senior had shared the command of Dixcove with Brew in 1751; see p. 36 above.
[4] Committee to Governor and Council, Cape Coast Castle, 1 March 1760, T. 70/29, f. 188.

Senior sent a copy of it to the Committee, regretting that the Governor there had ever been appointed a member of Council. This was soon followed by an accusation against Brew of trading with the enemy French in wartime. Brew explained this incident to the Committee in very different terms, and at the same time reported the arbitrary actions of the Governor of Cape Coast Castle in dismissing and demoting officers without reference to the Council. In August 1758 Nassau Senior gave it as his opinion that his Anomabu colleague was 'determined to be under no authority' and should be discharged from the service, but added in his despatch that this could not be done until stores arrived on the coast, however bad his behaviour, since no one else could supply the fort, a fact of which Brew was said to be well aware.[1]

It was in the second half of 1758 that Brew announced to the Committee his probable intention of leaving the coast; he had been in that part of the world for thirteen years, he said, and wished to revisit his 'native country'.[2] There may have been family reasons why this was so, although no details are available; on his return he went to Ireland for a time, and correspondence was forwarded to him at a mercantile address in Dublin.[3] It is also possible that health may have had some bearing on his decision.[4] Not until 31 January 1760, however, did he take his discharge from the service.[5] On the day that Brew gave up his command, Nassau Senior came over from Cape Coast Castle to pay a formal visit, and was escorted from the Anomabu waterside to the fort by soldiers, drums, and flutes—an occasion important enough to call for 'dashes' to John Currantee and other caboceers.[6] On 1 February William Goodson, the factor at Anomabu, assumed temporary charge of the fort, and a few

[1] Richard Brew to Nassau Senior, 5 July 1758, T. 70/30, f. 245; Nassau Senior to Committee, 7 July and 6 Aug. 1758, ibid. ff. 245, 256–7; Richard Brew to Committee, 6 Aug. 1758, ibid. ff. 251–3; Committee to Governor and Council. Cape Coast Castle, 1 Jan. 1759, T. 70/29, f. 156.

[2] Richard Brew to Committee, 31 Aug. 1758, T. 70/30, f. 253. On 23 July 1759, Brew expressed his intention of leaving Africa in six or at most eight months' time; Richard Brew to Committee, 23 July 1759, T. 70/30, f. 306.

[3] Secretary, African Committee to Richard Brew, 4 Sept. 1760, T. 70/29, f. 209, and see p. 29 above.

[4] On 25 Feb. 1761, Brew attended a meeting of the Committee and renewed his offer of serving them again, 'he having recovered his Health'; T. 70/144, f. 151.

[5] T. 70/1454, f. 1.

[6] Entry dd. 31 Jan. 1760, T. 70/987. 'Dash' was the coastal word for 'gift'.

3. William Ansah, from the portrait in the *Gentleman's Magazine*,
vol. xx (1750)

4. James Hutton Brew, 1844–1915

days later Brew sailed for home in the *Chesterfield*, completing his first spell of almost fifteen years in West Africa.[1]

The period now spent in Europe can be considered a decisive one, although whether or not he had always planned a return to West Africa must remain an open question. During his time in London, Brew forged a strong business association with Samuel Smith, one of the members of the African Committee. This event was to be of demonstrable significance in giving him powerful backing for the next phase of public office as well as for the establishment of a substantial private trading concern, the Smith and Brew Company.[2] In August 1760, while in Dublin, Brew was in correspondence with Smith, who sent him an inquiry from the Committee about recent happenings at Anomabu.[3] A few months later, by the early spring of 1761, negotiations were under way for Brew's re-entry into the service, and his personal appearance at a meeting of the Committee on 25 February was followed on 18 March by their consideration of a written petition. It was then resolved that the applicant should be appointed again to Anomabu and to membership of the Council.[4] A bond was required of him and of two sureties for £10,000; it was arranged on this occasion without delay. Brew guaranteed £5,000, and Samuel Smith and William Dacres, a one-time coastal resident, £2,500 each.[5]

Between May and June 1761, the month of embarkation in the *Duke of Marlborough*,[6] arrangements were made at the African Office which reflect the influence wielded by Samuel Smith on his partner's behalf. Nor should the latter's own capacity to secure for himself conditions regarded as appropriate to his rank be overlooked. It was agreed, for example, that Anomabu should have a garden to supply the fort with green vegetables and other foodstuffs, and a gardener was appointed who also sailed in the *Duke of Marlborough*. Charles Bell,

---

[1] Entries dd. 1 Feb. to 15 March 1760, T. 70/987; Nassau Senior to Committee, 3 Feb. 1760, T. 70/30, f. 338.
[2] See p. 59 ff. below.
[3] Secretary, African Committee to Richard Brew, 20 Aug. 1760, T. 70/29, f. 208.
[4] Entries dd. 25 Feb. and 18 March 1761, T. 70/144, ff. 151, 153.
[5] Entries dd. 29 April and 6 May 1761, T. 70/144, f. 154; T. 70/1454, f. 5.
[6] Entry dd. 10 June 1761, T. 70/144, f. 157.

once again Governor-in-Chief after the upheavals under Nassau Senior, received instructions from London to obtain a suitable piece of ground near the fort and to enclose it with a wall. Fifty pounds was authorized for building, and it was to be effected without delay. Another prestige symbol was to be the firing of a morning and evening gun at Anomabu as well as Cape Coast, one of its purposes being to assist ships in Anomabu road in setting their watch. Brew's rank in Council was made clear; there had previously been a dispute about precedence. The Committee informed Bell that Brew was to rank third after himself and William Mutter, who eventually became Bell's successor.[1]

The returning Governor, well established in favour, arrived back on the coast at the end of September, some twenty months after leaving it.[2] On 1 October, Patrick Greenhill, who had been in charge at Anomabu, handed over to him the castle stores of which an inventory was taken, and on 5 October, John Currantee officially visited the new arrival, being greeted with a salute of eleven guns.[3] This second command of the fort, which Brew now assumed and held between 1761 and 1764, should be considered in the light of an adjunct to the establishment of a large, private business, supported by Samuel Smith in London and continuing until Brew's death on the coast fifteen years later. As far as his public role was concerned, the general pattern of events resembled that of 1756–60, except for the fact that the main structure of the fort was now finished. Internationally, the scene up to 1763 was still one of Anglo-French war, the local scene one of continued efforts to retain the friendship of John Currantee and his family. Before his return to the coast, Brew had been asked by the Committee to approve the choice of a blue velvet umbrella with a gold fringe for the caboceer, and to bring it out with him, which he duly did.[4] But John Currantee, it soon transpired, had not lost the art of making the most of his advantages, and an attempt to create a

[1] Entries dd. 3 June and 1 July 1761, T. 70/144, ff. 157, 158; Committee to Governor and Council, Cape Coast Castle, 1 March 1760 and 24 Jan. 1761, T. 70/29, ff. 188, 231–2; Charles Bell to Committee, 16 Dec. 1761, T. 70/30, f. 443.

[2] Entry dd. 1 July 1761, T. 70/144, f. 158; Act of Council, Cape Coast Castle, 21 Oct. 1761, T. 70/30, f. 454.

[3] Entries dd. 1 and 5 Oct. 1761, T. 70/987.

[4] Entries dd. 29 April and 17 June 1761, T. 70/144, ff. 154, 157.

palaver, which would mean compensation, led Charles Bell in
1762 to charge him with ingratitude to the Governor who had
been 'too much his Friend'.[1] As before, Brew kept the fort
supplied with goods when its stores were at a low ebb, and the
mark of the Committee's approbation was seen in the progress
of the garden, for which a ground rent of thirty shillings a
month was paid in Anomabu, and in the firing, until 1763, of a
morning and evening gun.[2]

The public career of a Governor was always liable to reversal
through changing circumstances and the shifting balance of
interests; this was to be Brew's experience in 1763–4, when
private trading operations once again resulted in his suspension
as at Tantumkweri ten years earlier.[3] He had been reprimanded
during his first Anomabu command for selling slaves to the
Dutch,[4] and two years after reappointment, in 1763, the Committee's suspicions about the scale of his commercial activities
and personal shipment of slaves to the West Indies and North
America caused them to seek 'authentick Information' on the
subject from Bristol merchants. A warning was sent to the
coast that he must obey trading instructions and watch his
future conduct.[5] At the end of the year, on the receipt of further
complaints from Liverpool, the Committee decided that such
transactions while in public office must be stopped, and in a
despatch dated 15 December 1763 they ordered suspension until
Brew could prove himself innocent of the accusations advanced
against him.[6] The precise charge in this second major clash was
retrospective, dating back to 1761, at which time he was said to
have shipped 512 slaves on his own account in the *Duke of
Marlborough*. Attacking the Committee some years later as a
private merchant, Brew made the point, in his own defence, that

[1] Charles Bell to Committee, 16 June 1762, T. 70/31, ff. 7–8.
[2] Entries dd. 31 Oct. 1761, 3 Nov. 1761 and 31 Oct. 1762, T. 70/987; Charles
Bell to Committee, 16 Dec. 1761, T. 70/30, f. 443; Committee to Governor and
Council, Cape Coast Castle, 28 Feb. 1763, T. 70/29, f. 279.
[3] See pp. 37–8 above.
[4] Committee to Governor and Council, Cape Coast Castle, 9 May 1759,
T. 70/29, f. 173; Richard Brew to Committee, 23 July 1759, T. 70/30, ff. 304–6;
Journal of the Commissioners for Trade and Plantations from January 1759 to December 1763
(London, 1935), pp. 73–4.
[5] Committee to Governor and Council, Cape Coast Castle, 28 Feb. 1763, T.
70/29, f. 279; Donnan, op. cit. vol. II, p. 524.
[6] Committee to Governor and Council, Cape Coast Castle, 15 Dec. 1763, T.
70/29, f. 302.

the Act forbidding their servants to trade in this way had not been passed when the disciplinary measures were taken.[1]

His suspension followed close on the successful ending of the Seven Years War in 1763 and the publication, in the same year, of a treatise, *Considerations on the Present Peace*. Its unknown author dealt at some length with the African trade, of whose organization and the misdemeanours of the Committee and its servants he was extremely critical; the existing form of management never lacked opponents. Brew and Samuel Smith, for instance, were singled out to illustrate the evils of public encroachment on the sphere of the private trader, with the implication that a new form of African monopoly had been developing since the reorganization of 1750. In 1761, said the author of the treatise, the Committee had appointed Brew to the command of Anomabu, although they must have known that he was fitting out ships for the pursuit of his own trade on the coast with Smith as a London agent. An additional complaint made against him, calculated to appeal to contemporary economic nationalism, was that he shipped Dutch merchandise to West Africa to the detriment of British manufactures and the re-export of East India goods.[2] Such attacks indicate that Brew was becoming a source of embarrassment to the Committee, a disadvantage that outweighed his earlier value in an area of Anglo-French rivalry. The matter was summed up in 1764 by a coastal contemporary, who wrote that the Governor of Anomabu had been suspended because of the Committee's determination that the fort and public money should no longer contribute to the furtherance of his schemes of private trade.[3]

The events leading to Brew's rift with authority at Tantum-kweri and Anomabu demonstrate clearly a major practical problem of fort management in the second half of the eighteenth century—that of deciding upon and enforcing reasonable limits

[1] Donnan, op. cit. vol. II, pp. 536–7 n. 1; Richard Brew to Liverpool merchants, 25 Aug. 1771, T. 70/1531. In the Committee's letter of 15 Dec. 1763, the charge against Brew was that of shipping 312 slaves to Jamaica in the *Duke of Marlborough* in 1762. Brew, however, in his letter of 25 Aug. 1771 gave the figure as 512 slaves and the year as 1761. The *Duke of Marlborough* was the ship in which he had returned to the coast in 1761. An Act was passed in 1765 forbidding the African Committee's officers to sell slaves off the coast; Martin, op. cit. p. 40.

[2] Donnan, op. cit. vol. II, pp. 515 n. 1, 520–1.

[3] John Hippisley, 'On the Necessity of erecting a Fort at Cape Appolonia' in *Essays* (London, 1764), pp. 58–9.

of trade for a Governor. To quote the words of the Committee, 'all persons in our service should thrive, but they ought to keep within the bounds prescribed'.[1] The difficulty was to distinguish between keeping 'within the bounds prescribed', and pursuing 'too much trade',[2] at a time of economic individualism and weak administrative machinery. Furthermore, the Governors were invariably linked with one or another mercantile concern at home, and it is not surprising that a web of discord and intrigue resulted from the different cross-currents at work.[3] Although Brew may have been an extreme example, his was not the only case where service in a public capacity became the avenue to setting up as a private trader. In 1762 the Governor of Cape Coast Castle told the Committee that whenever any of their servants saw a proper opening in this direction, they behaved in such a way as to necessitate dismissal.[4]

It is unlikely that on this occasion suspension caused its victim many qualms. Brew took his own discharge from the end of April 1764, preferring this to the uncertain process of an attempted re-establishment.[5] But his departure from the service may have been nothing more than an action always intended at some point after his return to the coast. During the second Governorship at Anomabu, he had begun to build a house there, a significant preparation for the future, although it was not completed by the summer of 1764.[6] The influence of Samuel Smith at the African Office also continued to work to his advantage during the period of transition from public to private settlement. At the end of the Committee's despatch of 15 December 1763 ordering disciplinary measures, there was an interesting postscript. It directed that Brew should be given an apartment in the fort for securing his effects over a reasonable length of time and assuming good behaviour. This was because of representations made to the Committee, obviously by Smith, regarding the possible hardship to Brew of immediate

---

[1] Martin, op. cit. p. 40.

[2] Hippisley, op. cit. p. 58.

[3] See pp. 94–7 below for Brew's subsequent attack on the Committee and its officers.

[4] Charles Bell to Committee, 4 Aug. 1762, T. 70/31, f. 10.

[5] Richard Brew to Liverpool merchants, 25 Aug. 1771, T. 70/1531; T. 70/1454, f. 14.

[6] See pp. 57–9 below.

suspension.[1] Six days later, at the request of Smith, the Secretary made these instructions more explicit in a second letter to the Governor and Council. Personal accommodation and storage space in the fort was authorized for six months, under the conditions already laid down, should Brew's affairs necessitate this.[2] Brew received a copy of this letter from Smith; the Governor-in-Chief, William Mutter, for some reason did not get one, a fact which led him to give vent to certain feelings of irritation.[3] The arrangements concerning Brew brought him further difficulties. In July 1764 the period of six months was extended to twelve by the Committee, and Mutter later received an official rebuke because he had not been sufficiently responsive, at the coastal end, to the needs of private traders.[4] There was no small touch of irony in a situation whereby the ex-Governor of Anomabu, at the close of his public career in the service of the forts, now found himself the recipient of generous consideration from London as a private trader who was in partnership with a Committee member.

[1] Committee to Governor and Council, Cape Coast Castle, 15 Dec. 1763, T. 70/29, ff. 302, 306.

[2] Committee to Governor and Council, Cape Coast Castle, 21 Dec. 1763, T. 70/29, f. 306.

[3] Committee to Governor and Council, Cape Coast Castle, 21 Dec. 1763, T. 70/29, f. 306; William Mutter to Committee, 10 May 1764, T. 70/31, ff. 81–2.

[4] Committee to Governor and Council, Cape Coast Castle, 25 July 1764, T. 70/69, f. 23; William Mutter to Richard Brew and William Webster, 15 July 1764, ibid. f. 40; Committee to Governor and Council, Cape Coast Castle, 8 Feb. 1765, ibid. f. 39; William Mutter to Committee, 20 July 1765, T. 70/31, f. 136.

CHAPTER III

Private Trader

The events of 1764 meant a change of residence for Brew and the discarding of administrative function; the pattern of his commercial activity continued unaltered, shaped by the mechanics of the African trade. Once organized monopoly had broken down—and this happened effectively long before the statutory dissolution in 1750 of the Royal African Company—economic control lay in the hands of individual merchants.[1] Acting usually in small partnerships, they fitted out the vessels whose captains then spent up to several months at a time on the coast, acquiring slaves for export across the Atlantic.[2] In some cases shipping traded direct with African or mulatto dealers—this was particularly so in Sierra Leone—in other cases with the Governors of forts or with resident Europeans who maintained their own factories in West Africa.[3] It is the latter category to which Richard Brew belongs; he operated a private company based on Anomabu from the early seventeen-sixties[4] until 1776, the year of his death. From surviving records, it is possible to attempt some reconstruction of its workings, although the absence of account books and ledgers limits the statistical side. But the standing of the company, its partnership aspect, coastal organization, and methods of trade can be described, and a

---

[1] Davies, *The Royal African Company*, pp. 135–52.

[2] Gill, *Merchants and Mariners of the Eighteenth Century*, pp. 75, 91; Newton, *Journal of a Slave Trader*, passim. The two-masted sailing ship known as a 'snow' was frequently used in slave trading; see *Journal of a Slave Trader*, p. 117 for a sketch of a snow.

[3] Between 1737 and 1743, a ship known as a 'floating factory' was permanently stationed off Anomabu, to receive European goods from visiting ships, and transfer slaves and other commodities; Gill, op. cit. pp. 91–7.

[4] Brew was clearly in partnership with Smith before he left the Company's service in 1764, but conducting business from Anomabu fort. See p. 65 n. 5 below.

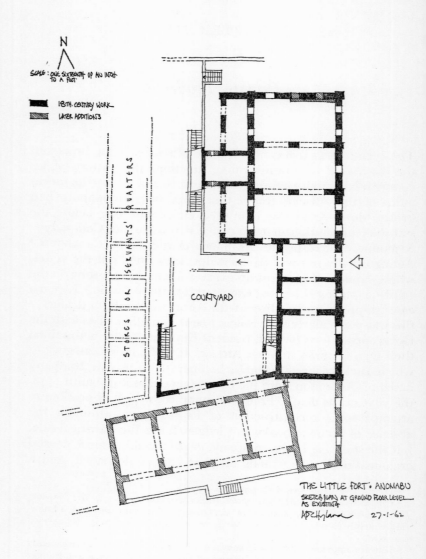

N

SCALE : ONE SIXTEENTH OF AN INCH TO A FOOT

18TH. CENTURY WORK
LATER ADDITIONS

SERVANTS' QUARTERS
OR
STORES

COURTYARD

THE LITTLE FORT · ANOMABU
SKETCH PLAN AT GROUND FLOOR LEVEL
AS EXISTING
AD Hyland   27·1·62

general economic assessment made. The relations between private trader and public fort, officially there to defend his interests, are also thrown into sharp relief.

The centre of the company was Richard Brew's Anomabu residence, called in Irish fashion Castle Brew, a title suggestive of his intention that it should rival the fort in the eyes of the Fanti population. Eighteenth-century references make it quite clear that Castle Brew was a large and impressive building enclosed by high walls, and with its own warehouses, and guns for defence. Writing to Amsterdam from Elmina, the Dutch Director-General reported that Brew's house was equal in size to Anomabu fort, while according to the British Governor-in-Chief, it occupied 'more Ground in length', could shelter two or three hundred men under its walls, and in cost had exceeded all that he himself was worth.[1] The present-day ruins, known as the 'Little Fort', reveal a brick structure built in 'obvious imitation' of the public establishment, with later extensions and renovations carried out probably in the nineteenth century after a period of disuse and decay.[2] Of particular interest is the siting of Castle Brew. It stands at the north-west corner of Anomabu fort and so near to it—the distance was described by Brew as '50 yards'—that it could interfere with the line of fire and area of observation in matters of defence.[3]

[1] Gilbert Petrie to Committee, 7 June 1767, T. 70/31, ff. 254–5; Richard Miles to Horatio Smith, 28 Sept. 1776, T. 70/1534; 'Inventory of the Effects of Richard Brew ... taken this 5th day of August, 1776', ibid.; J. P. T. Huydecooper to Assembly of the X, 8 Nov. 1765, W.I.C. 116.

[2] Lawrence, *Trade Castles and Forts of West Africa*, p. 355 and see diagram on facing page. I am indebted to Mr. Anthony Hyland for an architectural report on the ruins and a sketch plan, and to the Director of the Ghana Museum and Monuments Board for access to the file relating to the 'Little Fort'. From the stylistic evidence, it would appear that the latter was built in the mid-eighteenth century or soon afterwards, and was enlarged more than once. It has been partly restored by the Ghana Museum and Monuments Board, and bears the name 'Blankson House', since it was occupied in the nineteenth century by a prominent Anomabu merchant, George Blankson—a contemporary of Samuel Collins Brew, one of Richard Brew's descendants in Anomabu; see pp. 147–8 below. Local knowledge of the house today does not go back, in detail, as far as the eighteenth century, although it is recognized that it may have been built then.

[3] Richard Brew to Richard Miles, 22 Feb. 1776, T. 70/1534. There are contemporary references to Castle Brew being damaged by the sea, in one instance encroaching within twelve feet of the walls. This would suggest that the beach was closer to the house then than it is today, owing to subsequent building-up of the ground level. I am grateful to Mr. Paul Ozanne for advice on this matter. See Richard Brew to Samuel Smith's assignees, 20 Feb. 1776, T. 70/1534.

Governor Gilbert Petrie, describing Castle Brew in 1767, made mention of its proximity to the fort. The Committee, in reply to his letter, said that whoever had been in command there at the time the house was under construction had been very much at fault in allowing a part of it to be built so very close.[1]

It was, of course, Brew himself who had been in command, serving his second Governorship.[2] Exactly when work started on the house cannot be ascertained with certainty, but it was probably in 1763, the year before his suspension came into effect. The fact that Castle Brew was not finished by the summer of the next year, shortly after Brew had quitted the service, gave rise to exchanges between him and Governor William Mutter of Cape Coast Castle. Brew's request, in these circumstances, for continued use of the fort's storage space brought the reply that he and his associate, Webster, should not have indented for cargoes so soon. Permission was grudgingly granted, with the comment that Mutter expected the house to be ready within the six weeks that had been specified. A copy of this letter, sent by its recipients to Samuel Smith in London, was duly laid before the Committee, who conveyed to the Governor-in-Chief their disapproval of his unhelpful attitude towards private traders on the coast. Mutter made the rejoinder to the Committee that had he been as anxious as Mr. Brew to bring up complaints, 'Materials' were not lacking. He quoted from an earlier letter, received during Brew's Governorship of Anomabu, in which Mr. Johnson, the second-in-command there, had referred to the building of the Governor's house and the manner of its construction. Anomabu fort was being neglected, Johnson had told Mutter. Brew was concentrating on his own affairs and an inventory could not be taken. The garden, that had cost so much, was going to waste, and the gardener and the rest of the castle slaves were fully employed on the house: for the past fortnight they had been cutting timber in the bush.[3] It is worthy of note that these coastal allusions to the

---

[1] Gilbert Petrie to Committee, 7 June 1767, T. 70/31, ff. 254–5; Committee to Governor and Council, Cape Coast Castle, 17 Nov. 1767, T. 70/69, f. 111.

[2] See p. 50 ff. above.

[3] William Mutter to Committee, 10 Jan. 1764, T. 70/31, f. 50; the same to Richard Brew and William Webster, 15 July 1764, T. 70/69, f. 40; Committee to Governor and Council, Cape Coast Castle, 8 Feb. 1765, ibid. f. 39; William Mutter

use of the fort's labour for Brew's private purposes, in about 1763, do not seem to have been conveyed to the Committee until 1765, and then as a form of self-defence by the Governor-in-Chief against criticism of his dealings with Brew made at that time in London.

The explanation for this silence, as for so much else that worked to Brew's advantage in his relationship with the forts, lay in the fact of his partnership with Samuel Smith, a merchant engaged in the African trade and a member of the Committee.[1] The Dutch at Elmina described Smith in 1765 as the biggest participant in the Anomabu company. His credit emboldened the other partners, they said, and caused the Committee's servants on the coast to be cautious and apprehensive.[2] Any consideration of Brew's company, its functioning and importance, must therefore pay special attention to the activities of his London partner.

About Smith's background and emergence into mercantile society very little is known, although it should be observed that he had a connection with Ireland. He was at Waterford in December 1777 and proposing to return to London in the spring. Furthermore, the commodities which he exported to the coast included Irish linens.[3] In the City, his address was the Old Jewry, but there were also business connections with Bristol and probably with Liverpool, and it is clear that he had a considerable interest in African affairs.[4] The firm of Barton and Smith, in which he was a partner, was among the Committee's contractors, shipping goods to the Gambia and to Cape Coast Castle for the supply of the forts, and it was Smith's cousin, Horatio, who eventually went out to assist the

to Committee, 20 July 1765, T. 70/31, f. 136; Gilbert Petrie to Committee, 31 March 1768, ibid. f. 294. See also p. 49 above. Johnson was appointed second-in-command in 1763; he and Brew quarrelled shortly afterwards. See Mutter's letter to the Committee, dd. 10 Jan. 1764.

[1] See p. 49 above.

[2] J. P. T. Huydecooper to Assembly of the X, 8 Nov. 1765, W.I.C. 116.

[3] Samuel Smith to Richard Miles, 23 Dec. 1777, T. 70/1536, pt. 2; entry dd. 24 Jan. 1759, T. 70/144, f. 103 and see p. 27 above.

[4] Thomas Westgate to Samuel Smith, 7 Nov. 1766, T. 70/1531; Samuel Smith's letter dd. 30 June 1771 in *A Treatise upon the Trade from Great Britain to Africa*, App. G. A 'List of the Company of Merchants trading to Africa' for 1754 includes the name 'Samuel Smith' under Liverpool, Bristol and London, although the address in London was Cateaton Street; T. 70/1522.

partnership at Anomabu, bought the house after Brew's death and settled there.[1]

Introduction to his future business associate may have come to Brew through a fellow Governor, Thomas Westgate, for whom Smith had stood security in the seventeen-fifties.[2] By 1759, the two Governors were acting together as a local faction,[3] and it was shortly after this, when Brew returned to London, that he and Smith made contact, possibly for the first time. The latter now became one of Brew's securities on his reappointment to Anomabu, and during the sojourn in England, they were in close touch as a preliminary to the setting up of a company on the coast.[4]

The new partnership benefited in a number of ways from Smith's membership of the Committee, a circumstance that illuminates the administration of the West African trade in the eighteenth century and the extent to which a small group could secure a dominating hold. Although the Act establishing the Company of Merchants stipulated annual election to its executive body as a way of avoiding monopoly,[5] it is clear that this objective was by no means always achieved. In Smith's own words, he represented London and Bristol on the Committee for 'several years'. A member of it in the seventeen-fifties, he remained so until 1767, although he declined to stand for election in the next year as he was 'under a cloud'—in fact of a financial nature culminating in bankruptcy—which he hoped would soon dispel.[6] He was back in official favour by 1777, and had by then obtained 'a pretty little appointment' under the government; the letter conveying this news to the coast

[1] Entry dd. 24 Jan. 1759, T. 70/144, f. 103; 'In the matter of Samuel Smith ... a bancrupt', entry dd. 4 Nov. 1775, B. 1/66, f. 67; Donnan, *Documents Illustrative of the Slave Trade to America*, vol. III (Washington, D.C., 1932), p. 194 and see p. 69 below. The firm of 'Burton and Smith' on whom Richard Brew drew a bill in 1763 (Donnan, vol. III, p. 194) can be equated with 'Barton and Smith', one of the Committee's contractors.

[2] T. 70/1454, f. 1. The other security was William Dacres, who later stood security for Brew, along with Samuel Smith; see p. 49 above.

[3] Committee to Governor and Council, Cape Coast Castle, 7 Aug. 1759 and 1 March 1760, T. 70/29, ff. 179, 189.

[4] See p. 49 above.

[5] Martin, *The British West African Settlements*, pp. 29–30.

[6] Samuel Smith to Richard Brew, 4 Aug. 1768, T. 70/1531; Samuel Smith's letter dd. 30 June 1771 in *A Treatise upon the Trade from Great Britain to Africa*, App. G; entries in London Minute Book, 1755–62, T. 70/144 and see p. 63 below.

unfortunately did not specify its nature.[1] Smith's business dealings certainly gave rise to plenty of criticism, and he was attacked in 1763 for turning his public position on the African Committee to private commercial advantage.[2] But in West Africa, as the Dutch indicated, the Committee's servants were decidedly circumspect in matters concerning him, and recognized an influence here that could be wielded in London with men of power.[3]

Until he fell 'under a cloud', this influence worked strongly on behalf of the Smith and Brew Company. There was firstly the building of Castle Brew, so close to the fort, with the assistance of its labour supply, a fact apparently unreported officially for the best part of two years.[4] Next, Brew's transition from Governor to private trader, resident in Castle Brew, was helped by prolonged use of the fort's accommodation, which the Committee approved at Smith's instigation. Even after the house had been finished, Governor William Mutter pointed out that Brew was monopolizing the public storage space for slaves to the disadvantage of other traders, who had an equal right to it.[5] Mutter's rather cool response to Brew in 1764 over warehouse facilities earned him a rebuke from the Committee; this had been occasioned by Smith who had drawn their attention to the matter. Smith also took it upon himself personally to reprimand the Governor-in-Chief in two letters described by the latter as 'of extraordinary kind'.[6] It was Smith who kept Brew informed of the public side of coast affairs by sending him copies of official despatches. In 1765, there had been a complaint about this. Three years later, Governor Gilbert Petrie wrote that it was still happening and would continue to do so as long as Mr. Smith was a member of the Committee and had connections at Anomabu; on the coast, too, certain of the Committee's servants in the forts were charged with transmitting

[1] Horatio Smith to Richard Miles, 10 Feb. 1777, T. 70/1534.
[2] Donnan, op. cit. vol. II, p. 521. See also Westgate's attacks on Smith, pp. 68–9 below.
[3] J. P. T. Huydecooper to Assembly of the X, 8 Nov. 1765, W.I.C. 116; Samuel Smith to Richard Brew, 4 Aug. 1768, T. 70/1531.
[4] See pp. 57–9 above.
[5] William Mutter to Committee, 25 Oct. 1765, T. 70/31, ff. 148–9 and see pp. 53–4 above.
[6] William Mutter to Committee, 20 July 1765, T. 70/31, f. 136 and see p. 58 above.

official information to Brew.[1] Significant, also, was Governor
Petrie's wariness in dealing with a palaver between fort and
townspeople that developed at Anomabu. It was not only
a case of the version of affairs that would reach London through
the Brew–Smith line of communication. Petrie feared damage
to Castle Brew if the Fanti took reprisals on private traders. In
that event, he envisaged the possibility of legal action in
England against himself and the Governor of Anomabu for
perhaps as much as £5,000 or £6,000.[2]

His assessment of the value of Castle Brew raises the question
of the Smith–Brew partnership agreement. While it is known
that Smith had management of the business at its English end,[3]
full details of the agreement are not available; nevertheless the
general lines of the relationship can be established. There is
every reason to suppose that Smith's participation in the
company was crucial. Without him Brew, even though a trader
of no mean order, could never have set up such a large establishment on the coast. It seems very probable that it was Smith
who took the main financial responsibility for the building of
Castle Brew, and who owned the house or the greater part of it.
As a Committee member and contractor,[4] he would be in a
position to ship out materials on favourable terms, and the
London side of a partnership operating at such long range
would find it useful to retain a fairly concrete hold on the
coastal organization, which ownership of the house would give.
In the company's normal working, Smith's most important
function was to provide the credit so necessary in this branch of
commerce, where the interval between export of cargoes to the
west coast and returns from the sale of slaves in the New World
was a lengthy one. From the point of view of continued bartering on the coast, the exporting merchant in Britain had a
vital part to play. This was Smith's role as merchant and ship-
owner, sending out cargoes on credit, in which textiles would
be a leading commodity, to supply his partner at Anomabu and
its subsidiary factories. The firm of Barton and Smith also

---

[1] William Mutter to Committee, 25 Oct. 1765, T. 70/31, f. 151; Gilbert Petrie
to Committee, 15 May 1768, ibid. ff. 300–1; entry dd. 25 July 1768, ibid. ff. 327–9.

[2] Gilbert Petrie to Committee, 7 June 1767, T. 70/31, ff. 251–5.

[3] 'In the matter of Samuel Smith . . . a bancrupt', entry dd. 3 Nov. 1775, B. 1/66,
f. 188.

[4] See pp. 59–61 above.

acted as Brew's London agents on whom he could draw bills of exchange for coastal transactions with visiting ships.[1]

After the year 1768, the partnership was adversely affected by Samuel Smith's financial difficulties and ultimate bankruptcy, implicating Richard Brew at a time when the company law of limited liability was non-existent. The intricacies of Smith's position came to light in the course of bankruptcy proceedings during 1774–5. His troubles had first become obvious six years earlier, at which stage he had stopped payment, since he was in debt as a result of his partnership trading in the Smith and Brew Company, and also on account of his own separate dealings. In 1768 an agreement was made with the separate and partnership creditors for Smith's estate to be collected in and disposed of under Inspectors, the proceeds to be used for meeting proportionately the various debts incurred. As most of these debts were not paid within the time allotted, a commission of bankruptcy was awarded against Smith on 25 May 1774, under the designation of merchant of the Old Jewry in the City of London, partner with Richard Brew, merchant of Anomabu on the Gold Coast of Africa. His creditors included two London linen drapers and a Mrs. Elizabeth Cock, who in 1756 had lent the sum of £500 to John Barton and Samuel Smith, partners in trade. Smith's estate and effects now passed under the control of three assignees. They were to keep distinct accounts of his separate estate and that of the Smith and Brew partnership, and apply them appropriately to the settlement of the debts. But it was found that the two estates were in fact 'very much intermixed', and the accounts 'very much involved', so that it was difficult, if not impossible, to distinguish between them with any accuracy. By arrangement, the joint and separate estates were instead merged into one for equal division among the respective creditors according to their debts.[2]

---

[1] Thomas Westgate to Richard Brew, 24 Aug. 1767, T. 70/1536, pt. 2; Richard Brew to William Devaynes, 2 May 1770, T. 70/1531; Donnan, op. cit. vol. II, p. 520; ibid. vol. III, p. 194 and see p. 60 n. 1 above.

[2] Application for Commission of Bankruptcy against Samuel Smith, 25 May 1774, B. 4/21 (Ind. 22654); 'In the matter of Samuel Smith . . .', entries dd. 3 and 4 Nov. 1775, B. 1/66, ff. 188–92, 67–9. In Smith's own account of his difficulties, he said that he could have paid a respectable dividend in 1768 had not the Inspectors decided to send a large quantity of goods to Africa, purchased with money belonging to the estate, instead of at once dividing it among the creditors, a course of action to which the creditors had agreed. In April 1771, at Smith's request, the

The repercussion of these events at Anomabu first took the form of a period of credit uncertainty for Brew in the early seventeen-seventies, as Smith failed to extricate himself from the morass of indebtedness. Next, bankruptcy was followed by the absorption of Castle Brew, its contents, and all Smith and Brew's property in Africa into Smith's total estate, irrespective of individual or company ownership of the property. In December 1774, as a consequence of the commission of 25 May, the assignees appointed Governor Richard Miles of Anomabu to be their attorney on the coast, to take possession of Castle Brew, effect the necessary sales, and remit the proceeds to London.[1] An agreement was then reached between the assignees and creditors to release Brew from any claims that there might be upon him arising either out of his partnership trading with Smith, or out of his separate dealings with Smith, on payment of the sum of £6,000 sterling. This was the same amount which in 1768, it had been rumoured Brew might offer Smith to buy up the latter's share of the partnership, at the beginning of their troubles.

In the case of Castle Brew, a separate arrangement was made between Brew and the assignees. They agreed to sell him the house and premises for £1,000, provided that the £6,000 consideration was received on or before 11 April 1777. Brew, for his part, expressed the hope of an 'Abatement' since it would cost 'Every Shilling of Four Hundred Pounds Sterling' to repair the house.[2] He died in 1776 without paying either sum and thereby freeing himself from the partnership, and the proceeds of his estate accordingly went to the assignees.[3] After his death, Brew's own financial affairs were found to be in an extremely parlous and confused condition. A number of

Inspectors gave a certificate confirming this; failure to pay a respectable dividend to creditors had been one of the obstacles to renewal of his candidacy for the African Committee; see Samuel Smith's letter dd. 30 June 1771 in *A Treatise upon the Trade from Great Britain to Africa*, App. G. In 1768, Smith wrote to Brew saying that the insolvency of another company—Sedgley and Company—would affect him, since he had been heavily involved with them to support his own credit; Samuel Smith to Richard Brew, 4 Aug. 1768, T. 70/1531.

[1] Peregrine Cust and others to Richard Miles, 19 Dec. 1774, T. 70/1534.

[2] Samuel Smith to Richard Brew, 4 Aug. 1768, T. 70/1531; 'In the matter of Samuel Smith . . .', entry dd. 3 Nov. 1775, B. 1/66, f. 190; Richard Brew to Samuel Smith's assignees, 1 April 1776 in Peregrine Cust and others to Richard Miles and Jerome Bernard Weuves, 19 Feb. 1778, T. 70/1536, pt. 2.

[3] See pp. 82–3 below.

reasons can be advanced for this. One is the entangled state of his partnerships with Smith and others.

To the Smith–Brew concern, other partners were added from time to time on the basis of separate agreements. Three in particular should be noted: William Webster, John Fleming, and Thomas Westgate, all at some point in the service of the African Committee. When Webster, then Governor of Komenda, took his discharge in 1763 in order to join Brew, the comment was made at Cape Coast Castle that he had received a much more advantageous offer, and could now expect to better himself considerably by having a share in Brew's trade and capital.[1] Webster thus associated himself with the private company at an early stage, while Brew was still in fact Governor of Anomabu, and it was their names that were coupled frequently in 1764–5, during the transition to Castle Brew and the early episodes there.[2] His connection with the Smith–Brew partnership was not a very long one owing to illness and death; in 1767 the Webster family was experiencing difficulty in obtaining satisfaction from Samuel Smith about his share of the profits.[3] Fleming and Westgate's involvement in the concern was likewise for a limited time, but in the case of the latter, correspondence has survived which is very revealing on the subject of the partnership and its pecuniary difficulties.

Thomas Westgate, whose entry into the Committee's service in 1751 had been backed by Samuel Smith, was very probably the initial source of the Smith–Brew alliance.[4] In 1760, taking umbrage over a matter of promotion, Westgate resigned his Governorship of Komenda and after a spell in London, came back to the coast in 1761 as a private trader. For eighteen months he was a partner with Richard Brew, until ill health caused him to return to England, when his place was taken by William Webster.[5] Once in London there ensued some years of

[1] Charles Bell to Committee, 14 April 1763, T. 70/31, f. 29; T. 70/1454, ff. 1, 7; Donnan, op. cit. vol. II, p. 521.
[2] M. Priestley, 'Richard Brew: an eighteenth century trader at Anomabu' in *Transactions of the Historical Society of Ghana*, vol. IV, pt. I (1959), pp. 39–40. See also p. 58 above.
[3] Thomas Westgate to Richard Brew, 24 Aug. 1767, T. 70/1536, pt. 2.
[4] T. 70/1454, f. 1 and see p. 60 above.
[5] William Mutter to Committee, 10 Aug. 1760, T. 70/30, f. 372; Secretary, African Committee to Governor and Council, Cape Coast Castle and to all Chiefs of outforts, 4 June 1761, T. 70/29, f. 229; Thomas Westgate to Samuel Smith's

hard endeavour by Westgate to persuade Smith to meet his claims, a process accompanied by strong denunciation of Smith in a series of letters to Brew, in which Westgate bemoaned his unfortunate plight. Failing to secure adequate settlement, Westgate was ultimately driven to re-enter the service, although he was appointed in the first instance only to the junior position of writer.[1]

A number of features emerge from a study of his connection with the Smith–Brew Company. In the first place, its financial embarrassments are further illustrated. Westgate's 'articles of co-partnership' were drawn up with Richard Brew; when he had to leave the coast, Brew made an offer of £3,000 for his share of the profits, since their eighteen months of trading together had been very successful, and a copy of the agreement was sent to Smith.[2] Westgate's subsequent problem was to persuade Smith to meet his partner's draft for this amount. The profits arising from joint dealings were held in London, and it is obvious that by the later seventeen-sixties, Smith did not have enough funds available to meet demands. In 1766 Westgate complained to Brew that Smith was only allowing him very small amounts of money and sometimes refusing him any, with the excuse that expenses abroad were enormous and that Brew had already drawn far more than he had put into the partnership. Westgate then made fruitless efforts with the Inspectors appointed to investigate Smith's affairs. Their reply was that they were waiting to hear from Brew who would have to send a special remittance for the purpose of settling this debt.[3] On Brew's advice, his late partner returned to service on the coast in 1770, and almost twelve months afterwards there was a quarrel on the grounds that during that time payment had never once been mentioned.[4]

trustees, 29 June 1769, T. 70/1536, pt. 2; T. 70/1455, f. 2. Smith and Brew were probably in partnership from 1761.

[1] Thomas Westgate to Richard Brew, 18 Feb. 1770, T. 70/1536, pt. 2; T. 70/1455, f. 2.

[2] Thomas Westgate to Samuel Smith's trustees, 29 June 1769, T. 70/1536, pt. 2.

[3] Thomas Westgate to Richard Brew, 12 Sept. 1766, 24 Aug. 1767, 28 Oct. 1768, and 17 Aug. 1769, T. 70/1536, pt. 2; the same to Samuel Smith, 20 Nov. 1767, ibid.; the same to Samuel Smith's trustees, 29 June 1769, ibid. Westgate always referred in his letters to Smith's 'trustees'. The latter pointed out to him, however, that they were not *absolutely* trustees, but only people deputed to inspect the affairs of the concern; see Westgate's letter to Brew dated 17 Aug. 1769, T. 70/1536, pt. 2.

[4] Thomas Westgate to Richard Brew, 18 Feb., 17 Dec., and 19 Dec. 1770, T. 70/1536, pt. 2 and see p. 90 below.

Good relations were restored by 1773 when Brew asked for an opinion about the concern, and gave an account of Smith's debts described by Westgate as 'very astonishing'.[1] At the time of Brew's death, the claim was still outstanding, although according to Governor David Mill at Cape Coast Castle, nearly £1,700 of it had already been paid. There is no means of knowing whether or not this was actually so.[2]

Apart from revealing the fact that within a few years of the company's establishment Smith was short of ready cash, the episode gives further indication of the uncertainty of eighteenth-century partnership agreements. There was some doubt as to whether Westgate's articles of co-partnership with Brew gave him a claim upon the concern as a whole, or only upon Brew as one of its principals. Originally an agreement between the two of them, Brew then 'brought it to the general account', informed Smith and secured his own personal draft to Westgate by a bond on himself and the company. In Westgate's opinion, this entitled him to be considered a claimant on Smith's estate when matters were eventually placed in the hands of assignees. The latter, from their side, did not regard it as a partnership debt, but as one that was the responsibility of Brew and affected them in so far as Brew's affairs were bound up with Smith's. It was said by Governor Mill in 1776 that the assignees had constantly denied responsibility for the debt, on the grounds that Westgate's connection lay entirely with Brew whose 'simple bond' he had had for the £3,000. As Brew was not worth this amount when he died, continued Mill, Westgate's debt consequently died with him.[3] Here can be seen the complications to which an eighteenth-century business arrangement could give rise. Westgate was a partner through an agreement with Brew; how far did this involve a company commitment?[4] In the case of Smith and of Brew, partnership trading coexisted with individual transactions, and also with other joint dealings, for

---

[1] Thomas Westgate to Richard Brew, 29 Aug., 12 Sept., Nov. [sic], 2 Dec., and 8 Dec. 1773, T. 70/1536, pt. 2.

[2] David Mill to Richard Miles, 11 Aug. 1776, T. 70/1534; see also p. 82 ff. below.

[3] Thomas Westgate to Samuel Smith's trustees, 29 June 1769, T. 70/1536, pt. 2; the same to Richard Brew, 17 Aug. 1769, ibid.; David Mill to Richard Miles, 11 Aug. 1776, T. 70/1534.

[4] It is possible that Brew originally made the separate agreement with Westgate in order to keep Smith out of the situation, and confine the profits to themselves.

example, Barton and Smith, and Brew and Westgate, both linked to some extent with Smith and Brew. In practice, these various currents of activity became interconnected and resulted in a position of some confusion.

Personal factors could also increase the hazards inherent in business partnerships, and there is reason to suppose that this was so in the case of Samuel Smith. While it is extremely unlikely that Brew himself was over-scrupulous in his business life, the impression gained from the Westgate affair, and from his activities in general, is that Smith certainly was not. It is worth noting that some expressions of concern about Westgate's fate did emanate from Brew. Writing to Smith after the former had returned to the coast, Brew said that he was behaving very well in the matter of his demand on them, and would be incapable, he believed, of taking any steps to their prejudice. He also urged Smith to use influence to secure Westgate the command of a fort in place of the present lowly position of writer; a similar letter of appeal was sent to a member of the Committee.[1] It was on Smith, not on Brew, that the main burden of Westgate's disapproval fell as a 'villain' and a 'scoundrel'. Undoubtedly he was biased against the man unable to satisfy his demands, but the warnings to Brew over a number of years about Smith's underhand behaviour very probably contained an element of truth. In 1766, Westgate told Brew that in his opinion Smith's brother, recently arrived back from the coast, had represented the Anomabu situation in an unfavourable light, and in subsequent letters he sounded a cautionary note about Smith's business connections, describing him as plausible, deceitful, and likely to cause his partner at Anomabu 'an infinite amount of trouble'. It would be unwise, Westgate advised, to entrust him with too much money. In 1773, when affairs were mounting to the crisis of bankruptcy, Westgate informed Brew that total freedom from the concern would enable Brew to enjoy more satisfaction in six months than he had done hitherto in so many years.[2]

As a commentary on these remarks, it can be said that while

---

[1] Richard Brew to Samuel Smith, 10 March 1770, T. 70/1531; the same to William Devaynes, 2 May 1770, ibid.

[2] Thomas Westgate to Richard Brew, 12 Sept. 1766, continued on 18 Sept.; 24 Aug. 1767 and Nov. [sic] 1773, T. 70/1536, pt. 2.

Smith's credit and support had enabled the company to be built up on the coast, the complexity in his affairs and the indistinguishable separate and partnership accounts have implications that cannot be ignored. They suggest, at the very least, mismanagement on Smith's part, and perhaps a good deal more—some deliberate obscuring of the records as a result of his own speculation and financial juggling.[1]

Analysis of the Smith and Brew Company must include not only its partnership angle and London ramifications, but the workings of the company in West Africa, directed from Castle Brew. The organization of the house as well as its material structure resembled that of a fort, and Castle Brew had its European residents participating in trade, and an African complement of house slaves, labourers, and canoemen.[2] In the case of the former, there might be a family relationship with one or other of the partners. This was true of Horatio Smith, Samuel Smith's cousin and his clerk for a number of years. Horatio went out to Anomabu in 1769 as assistant to Brew at the time when Smith's estate, both separate and joint, was under investigation by Inspectors; he was intended as an intermediary between them and the coastal side of the partnership. Receiving a salary of £200 a year for services which Brew considered inadequate and of little benefit to the concern, Horatio quarrelled with Brew in 1775 over a debt the latter owed him, and returned to England to lay the matter before the assignees. Eventually he bought Castle Brew from them, renamed it Smith House, and settled there for a brief period as a private trader before entering public service under the Committee.[3]

[1] According to his letter of 30 June 1771 in the *Public Advertiser*, Smith managed to put across a favourable view of his assets to the Inspectors in 1768. This may have been only a partial representation of the position, however; see Samuel Smith's letter, dd. 30 June 1771 in *A Treatise upon the Trade from Great Britain to Africa*, App. G.

[2] For an account of the organization and personnel of forts, see Lawrence, *Trade Castles and Forts of West Africa*, pp. 46–56.

[3] Thomas Westgate to Richard Brew, 17 Aug. 1769, T. 70/1536, pt. 2; Committee to Governor and Council, Cape Coast Castle, 23 Aug. 1769, T. 70/69, f. 157; Richard Miles's Statement, Dec. [*sic*] 1775, T. 70/1533; Richard Brew to Samuel Smith's assignees, 30 March 1776, T. 70/1534; Richard Brew to Peregrine Cust, 5 April 1776, ibid.; Richard Miles's letter dd. 9 May 1776, T. 70/1482; Peregrine Cust and others to Richard Miles and Jerome Bernard Weuves, 19 Feb. 1778, T. 70/1536, pt. 2; Richard Miles to Samuel Smith, 16 July 1778, T. 70/1483, f. 124; T. 70/1455, f. 22. When Horatio Smith took over Castle Brew, renaming it 'Smith House', it was already in a bad state of repair, and a considerable

A family connection with the concern, although of a short-lived nature, was also developed on Brew's part through his mulatto son, Richard Brew, Junior. Richard, Junior, was taken into the business as a clerk after a 'liberal education' in England, but was eventually disowned and discarded by his father because of his wild behaviour. The Council at Cape Coast Castle, who later employed him, nevertheless held a favourable opinion of his qualities as an accountant, a function he had probably undertaken in his father's business.[1] Towards the end of Brew's life, clerical responsibilities were entrusted now to a Mr. Williams on a salary of £100 a year. It was Williams who wrote out Brew's will during the last days of his final illness, and informed the ships' captains, assembled at Castle Brew, of the depleted state of the warehouses from which they had hoped to withdraw their barters.[2]

Like the Governor of a fort, a private trader maintaining an establishment on the coast had to arrive at an accommodation with the African peoples through proper observance of accepted practices and conventions.[3] The difference between public office and private position in this respect lay in the degree of local expectation rather than in kind. But with Brew there is every indication that he aimed at outdoing the fort in trade and status; consequently his commitments to the Fanti were heavy as an essential condition for the achievement of this. Governor Richard Miles made an apt comment when Castle Brew was renamed Smith House by its new owner, a prudent move, he wrote, since 'its late Incumbent paid for calling it a Castle'. Miles also said in a letter to Horatio Smith that Brew's 'Interest' among the Fanti had been as great as that of any man ever settling at Anomabu, and he had behaved 'with as high a hand' as anyone; nevertheless, 'amazing Expences' had resulted from small disputes between him and the Fanti.[4]

part of it collapsed at the beginning of November 1778; Richard Miles's letter dd. 5 Nov. 1778, T. 70/1480; Thomas Westgate's letter dd. 6 Nov. 1778, ibid. See also p. 90 below.

[1] Entry dd. 22 Dec. 1780, T. 70/145, ff. 13–14; entry dd. 2 July 1781, T. 70/152, f. 109; see also p. 122 below.

[2] Richard Miles to Horatio Smith, 28 Sept. 1776, T. 70/1534; Executors' Accounts, expenses incurred after Brew's death, entry dd. 15 Sept. 1776, T. 70/1504. See also p. 84 below.   [3] See p. 19 above.

[4] Richard Miles to Samuel Smith, 16 July 1778, T. 70/1483, f. 124; the same to Horatio Smith, 15 Sept. 1778, T. 70/1536, pt. I.

The considerable influence which Brew exercised in Fanti arose particularly out of a long personal association with John Currantee; it was demonstrated by his entering local politics as a rival authority to the fort.[1] Yet strong though Brew's position might appear to be, when it came to a clash of interests it was the Fanti who could exert effective pressure and refuse to supply him with provisions or even attack his house. This happened in 1776 when Brew tried to eliminate his goldtaker as a middleman in the purchase of slaves and to buy direct from a country trader coming down to Anomabu, a move which he hoped would lower the price. About half the population of Anomabu consisted of goldtakers who saw in this action a threat to their middleman profits. They staged a major demonstration and threatened to send off the coast as a slave anyone who sold Brew 'the smallest article of provisions'. On his refusal to meet their demands for compensation, a large crowd stormed his house in the middle of the day, firing continually from every quarter, until Castle Brew's own muskets caused them to disperse. The palaver was then talked over in the fort.[2] The conclusion to be drawn from this is that the Fanti could impose severe limitations on the freedom of action and trading manœuvrability of a private settler as well as on the Governor of a fort, a circumstance which Brew could not fail to take into account.

Ambitious in his planning, Brew intended that from Anomabu a personal trading empire should be built up in West Africa stretching far beyond the confines of the Gold Coast. Its geographical range certainly gives substance to the comment, made by the Dutch at Elmina, that he and Webster had established a company which would gradually swallow up and spoil the whole trade on that coast.[3] In Fanti and the adjacent area, Brew already had a firm hold dating back to the early

[1] See pp. 73–4, 106, and 110–11 below.
[2] Richard Brew to Richard Miles, 22 Feb. 1776, T. 70/1534. Goldtakers were originally responsible for the quality of gold obtained in barter, weighing and examining it, for which they received a commission. They acted as intermediaries between African traders and the captains of ships, or—as in the case of Brew—resident Europeans, their functions ultimately extending to the slave trade. Special payments were made to them. Goldtakers often became wealthy and important in local society. They were described as 'sagacious fellows, and keen observers, who soon find out the weak side of a man, and treat him accordingly'; Adams, *Remarks on the country extending from Cape Palmas to the River Congo*, pp. 9, 11.
[3] J. P. T. Huydecooper to Assembly of the X, 8 Nov. 1765, W.I.C. 116.

seventeen-fifties when he had been at Tantumkweri and Mumford.[1] Factories were set up, sometimes in an African house, and a rival private trader was liable to find himself ousted with the assistance of the local population, and his own factory taken over by one of Brew's people.[2] Beyond the river Volta, the eastern limit of the Gold Coast, there were factories at Ouidah and Popo on the Slave Coast, at Lagos and Benin, and, furthest of all from the Anomabu base, at Cape Lopez. Lagos and Cape Lopez, both in an area of extremely active trade, were the most important of the subsidiaries. Schooners, brigs, and sloops, of which Brew's company was the owner, plied between Anomabu and the out-stations carrying cargoes for their supply and returning to Anomabu with slaves to be shipped off the coast, although sometimes there was direct exporting from a subsidiary factory to the West Indies. Castle Brew, under the shadow of Anomabu fort, must thus be seen as the controlling centre of a line of trading establishments extending south of the equator, linked by the ships of the concern and manned by its factors, drawn from as far afield as New England.[3]

A survey of Brew's transactions at this central point of his 'empire' throws light on the widespread ramifications of the slave trade, which embraced both the seaboard and interior in West Africa, and across the Atlantic, the New World and Europe. On the coast, it was the Fanti with whom he had commercial dealings as 'the influential and wealthy agents between the African producers of the interior and European merchants on the seaboard'.[4] His efforts in 1776 to bypass the Anomabu goldtakers in purchasing slaves, although unsuccessful, touched one aspect of a highly organized and far-reaching middleman structure. This extended along trading paths into the interior

[1] See pp. 36–8 above.
[2] John Grossle to Committee, 26 Oct. 1769, T. 70/31, f. 367; Richard Brew to Thomas Westgate, 29 Sept. 1773, T. 70/1532.
[3] Charles Bell to Committee, 14 April 1763, T. 70/31, ff. 29–30; Richard Brew to Richard Miles, 26 July 1774, T. 70/1532; the same to the same, 14 June 1776, T. 70/1534; Richard Brew to Thomas Eagles, 10 Nov. 1774, T. 70/1532; the same to Samuel Smith's assignees, 20 Feb. 1776, T. 70/1534; Richard Miles to Horatio Smith, 28 Sept. 1776, ibid.; the Council's Answer to the Return of the Lords of Trade, 25 June 1778, T. 70/1535; Donnan, op. cit. vol. III, p. 187 n. 2. The sale of effects from Lagos and Cape Lopez after Brew's death realized £728 6s. 6d.; Executors' Accounts, entry dd. 16 Dec. 1776, T. 70/1504.
[4] K. O. Diké, *Trade and Politics in the Niger Delta* (Oxford, 1956), p. 7.

where the Fanti met Ashanti suppliers at markets bordering on the hinterland country of Assin. As the powerful Ashanti Empire pushed southwards during the eighteenth century in an attempt to eliminate entrepreneurs on the coastal routes and set up a direct trade with the forts, the middleman issue became a crucial one in tribal politics. No state was likely to be more affected than Fanti;[1] a period of complex local diplomacy ensued in which both the British and Dutch participated. One of its facets was the intervention of Brew, who used the opportunity to seek regular communication between Castle Brew and the main producer of Gold Coast slaves, the King of Ashanti.

The appearance of an Ashanti army only a few miles from the coast in 1765, followed by brief hostilities with Fanti, led to tension in the relations of the two states that lasted until the seventeen-seventies and deeply implicated European commercial interests. The possibility of conquest of the seaboard was one that could not be ignored. Europeans had anyway long recognized the desirability of opening up the paths to the forts for inland merchants, which was resisted by Fanti middlemen. In the uncertain and delicate situation prevailing after 1765, it was politic for settlers to aim as far as possible at a favourable standing with each of the contending parties. Brew, no less than the British and Dutch Governors, was ready to act along these lines, and aware of the commercial advantages that might arise if he could at least form a trading connection between Castle Brew and Ashanti.

This explains his incursion into Ashanti-Fanti politics in 1765–72 as a competitive mediator alongside the British and the Dutch, and the efforts to bring himself to the notice of Osei Kojo, the Ashanti King. It was for this reason that Brew sent messengers into the interior in 1765, offering to be a negotiator in the dispute with Fanti. Similarly he aimed at securing the fulfilment on the coast of the most important of Osei Kojo's peace terms. His hope that by achieving this he would win 'a small part of the lustre' that would reflect on those who took part 'in settling the peace of the country and opening the trading paths' was not motivated by the disinterestedness which he claimed. Tortuous in the extreme, and designed to raise the prestige of Castle Brew in Fanti above that of the forts, one

[1] See pp. 11–12 above.

aspect of his policy was to explore the chances of an inland connection with Osei Kojo, through messengers, gifts, and attempted negiotiations. Thus an Ashanti hostage going back into the
interior was entrusted with trading goods to a considerable
amount. When the political turmoil of these years eventually
subsided, leaving the internal conduct of the slave trade funda-
mentally unchanged, Fanti middlemen were still enjoying their
controlling position. But, like his contemporaries in the forts,
Brew had looked ahead to direct trade with Ashanti, of whose
power and commercial importance Europeans were already
well aware.[1]

Operating in conditions of political uncertainty from which
it could not remain immune, the coastal slave trade turned,
economically, on the bartering of goods that were acceptable
to an African taste made sharper by European competition. In
general terms, the most popular items were textiles—particularly East India cottons and linens—weapons, gunpowder, and
spirits, with many variations of kind and of assortment.[2] Brew,
for example, provided his regular correspondents, the Liverpool merchants and ships' captains, with information as to the
commodities most in demand at a particular time. Indicative,
too, of the nature of local requirements was his specification of
the colour blue when buying cloth to be sent to the Gabon
region in 1776.[3]

The ways in which he acquired the stock of trading goods
necessary to deal with an irregular and unpredictable flow of
slaves were numerous, showing the wide range of his commercial
contacts. In some cases, he bought from local Governors, a form
of trading that would be regarded by the Committee as entirely
commendable in its servants: Richard Miles, Governor of
Tantumkweri, was supplying him with textiles in 1773.[4] Other

[1] David Mill to Committee, 7 May 1776, B.T. 6/2; Priestley, 'Richard Brew:
an eighteenth century trader at Anomabu' in *Transactions of the Historical Society of
Ghana*, vol. IV, pt. I (1959), pp. 37–41 and 'The Ashanti Question and the British:
eighteenth century origins' in *Journal of African History*, vol. II, no. 1 (1961), pp.
35–59.

[2] Martin, op. cit. pp. 45–6; Gill, op. cit. pp. 76–7.

[3] Richard Brew to Benjamin and Arthur Heywood, 1 Aug. 1774, T. 70/1532;
the same to Thomas Eagles, 10 Nov. 1774, ibid.; the same to Mr. Gwyther, 21
June 1776, T. 70/1534; Miles Barber to Richard Brew, 16 May 1770, T. 70/1531.

[4] Richard Miles to Richard Brew, 1 Sept., 9 Sept., and 18 Nov. 1773, T. 70/1479.
See also p. 79 below.

sources were the ships frequenting the coast, as many as fourteen at a time anchoring in Anomabu road. Brew might then contract with their captains for the whole of a cargo or part of it, and give in payment a bill drawn on Samuel Smith in London, or else give slaves and other commodities in exchange. The vessels were of different nationalities. From the British he took cloth, from the Americans and Portuguese rum, provisions, and tobac-co.[1] A third method was for Smith or Brew to procure a cargo in Europe, and have it sent out in one of the concern's own ships, the *Antelope*, the *Albany* or the *Brew Packet*. Here Smith's credit would be an important factor. Goods might be taken on board at Dutch as well as British ports. In Holland, East India cottons were cheaper, and mixtures of Dutch and British items were popular on the west coast.[2]

As to the actual process of buying and selling slaves in West Africa, many aspects still remain obscure, particularly details of bartering and of price. On the Gold Coast, the standard of measurement for important transactions was gold dust, with ounces and ackies among the weights most commonly used; an ackie equalled one-sixteenth of a troy ounce whose nominal value was four pounds sterling. Slaves and imports might be valued in relation to gold for the purpose of exchange—hence the references to the cost of men and women in terms of ounces.[3]

[1] Gilbert Petrie to Committee, 13 Sept. 1766, T. 70/31, ff. 217–18; Receipt for a Bill on Samuel Smith, 17 May 1767, T. 70/1534; entry dd. 5 Sept. 1766, Jan Woortman reporting from Kormantin, W.I.C. 967; Certificate dd. 2 Nov. 1770, Anomabu road in *A Treatise upon the Trade from Great Britain to Africa*, App. H; Donnan, op. cit. vol. III, pp. 224–5, 232–3.

[2] Charles Bell to Committee, 14 April 1763, T. 70/31, ff. 29–30; Gilbert Petrie to Committee, 30 Dec. 1768, ibid. f. 331; list of ships at Cape Coast and Anomabu, 11 March 1769, T. 70/31, f. 347; Richard Brew to Liverpool merchants, 25 Aug. 1771, T. 70/1531; *Journal of the Commissioners for Trade and Plantations from January 1776 to May 1782* (London, 1938), pp. 141–2; Donnan, op. cit. vol. II, pp. 520–1; Gill, op. cit. pp. 77–8.

[3] There was, however, an 'ounce trade' as well as a gold ounce, in terms of which slaves and goods might be valued. The 'ounce trade' has been described by Karl Polanyi as a 'fictitious money unit', valued *on the coast* at an average of 40 shillings or half the *European* price of an ounce of gold; K. Polanyi, 'Sortings and "Ounce Trade" in the West African Slave Trade' in *Journal of African History*, vol. V, no. 3 (1964), pp. 381–93. The conclusions he then draws are based on a comparison between the prime cost of goods *in Europe*, the ounce value of gold *in Europe*, and the exchange value of these goods *on the coast*. This ignores the essential facts of freight and other costs, and does not take into consideration that the value of gold *on the coast* fluctuated, and that gold was itself both an item of trade and a measure of exchange. The most illuminating discussion of the 'ounce trade' is given by

When making the initial purchase on the coast, the price which European dealers had to pay to African middlemen was determined by a number of factors including, in particular, the supply of slaves then available. In 1770 Brew reported that slaves were scarce and dear. After three months, he said, one of his ships had still not obtained half her complement.[1] Political conditions could also affect supply; intertribal warfare did not always increase the flow to the coast as is sometimes assumed. Equally well it could lead to a stoppage of the inland paths and a disruption of trade; this was one of the reasons why the forts expended so much time and money mediating in local disputes.[2] Prices were influenced by the strongly competitive nature of European dealings in response to which African middlemen displayed a shrewd business sense,[3] while the amount of shipping on the coast at any time and the number of prospective buyers left their mark on the sellers' market. Complaints were frequently made about the high price of slaves, which Brew attributed to the commercial activities of the Governors of forts.[4] On the British side there was an interesting attempt at Cape Coast Castle in 1766-7 to secure an agreement with traders and ships' captains for a reduction in price. It was recognized that the concurrence of Brew, a large-scale dealer, would be essential to it. But there was always a dissenting party

Marion Johnson, who shows that the *coast* price of gold was a variable, that the 'ounce trade' changed its meaning during the eighteenth century, and that the clue to an understanding of it lies in further knowledge of the gold trade; M. Johnson, 'The Ounce in Eighteenth-Century West African Trade' in *Journal of African History*, vol. VII, no. 2 (1966), pp. 197–214. See also pp. 79–80 below. It must be pointed out that much semantic confusion surrounds the reporting of coastal prices in eighteenth-century records. The term 'ounce', for example, was often used without any specification as to kind. Quite apart from trade or gold ounces, transactions on the Gold Coast might also be recorded in sterling, in gallons of rum, or without value, reflecting the varying patterns of commercial activity. Difficulties arose, during the discussion of West African economic affairs in Britain, when traders and ships' captains attempted to explain the coastal price structure, differentiated from European levels by cost factors and by supply and demand conditions; their terminological equipment for making this explanation was limited.

[1] Richard Brew to William Devaynes, 2 May 1770, T. 70/1531.

[2] There are constant references in the records of the Royal African Company and the Company of Merchants trading to Africa (T. 70 series in the P.R.O.) to the stoppage of the trading paths through war.

[3] Of slaving transactions in general, it has been said that 'the pattern of trade was imposed by the African on the European rather than *vice versa*'; Davies, op. cit. p. 235.

[4] See pp. 94–6 below.

to obstruct the agreement. At the times when Brew was prepared to co-operate, certain ships' captains or the Dutch Director-General held out in opposition, and rendered inoperative, in practice, any plans for European price fixing.[1]

The disposal of slaves by Brew took different forms. There were sales to visiting ships, British, New England, Dutch, and French, with the first two predominant. In such cases, textiles, rum, and tobacco as well as foodstuffs and stores were given in exchange, often on credit. At the time of Brew's death, the captains of ships anchored in Anomabu road contemplated withdrawing from his warehouses the barters for which they had expected eventually to receive payment in slaves.[2] Another method was for him to ship off a cargo on his own account to the West Indies—to Jamaica, Barbados, or the Grenadines. The point of export might be Anomabu. Here Brew collected not only the slaves he had obtained on the Gold Coast, but also those brought by his schooners and sloops from the factories at Ouidah, Lagos, and Benin. Alternatively, he might tell a factory to ship direct across the Atlantic. He was planning this in 1776. The agent at Cape Lopez, Mr. Jonathan Hildebrand, was to send to the West Indies a cargo of 120 slaves, and the master of the schooner, on arrival at the Grenadines, had instructions to sell to the trading house that made him the best offer. Sometimes the exporting ship was owned by Brew and had been bought by him on the west coast, together with its cargo. In this way, he acquired in 1763 a vessel belonging to merchants in New England.[3]

The part played by Brew in the New England trade to West Africa deserves mention. Apart from Samuel Smith, and the Liverpool merchants and ships' captains, his most regular contacts were on the American continent. By the middle of the eighteenth century another three-cornered exchange, of which New England was the starting-point, had developed within the overall framework of the triangular trade. Rum, New England's most important manufacture, was exported to West Africa, and slaves

---

[1] Gilbert Petrie to Committee, 13 Sept. and 20 Oct. 1766, T. 70/31, ff. 217–18, 223; John Hippisley to Committee, 25 April 1766, ibid. ff. 185–6.

[2] Donnan, op. cit. vol. III, pp. 224–5, 232–3 and see p. 84 below.

[3] Richard Brew to Thomas Eagles, 10 Nov. 1774, T. 70/1532; the same to Samuel Smith's assignees, 20 Feb. 1776, T. 70/1534; the Council's Answer to the Return of the Lords of Trade, 25 June 1778, T. 70/1535; Donnan, op. cit. vol. III, p. 194 and see p. 72 above.

then shipped to the West Indies in return for the molasses used in rum distilling.[1] One of the ports actively engaged in this trade was Newport, Rhode Island, with whose merchants, particularly the Vernons, Brew formed an early connection dating from the seventeen-fifties. He traded with Rhode Island captains on the coast over a long period, and in 1776 he proposed that one of his schooners should proceed there from the West Indies for repairs, taking on board a cargo of rum before its return to Anomabu.[2] Interesting, too, is the fact that letters from Castle Brew about coast matters—the Ashanti-Fanti troubles of 1765 and the danger of piracy, for example—were published in American newspapers, including the *Newport Mercury*.[3]

With the Vernons, Brew had a number of business dealings. In 1771 they recommended him to a Virginia correspondent as their 'Friend', who shipped 'perhaps . . . more slaves than any one man in the Kingdom'.[4] A transaction which had taken place between them in 1763 illustrates well the financial workings of the slave trade. Buying from the Vernons a vessel and cargo which they had sent to the coast, Brew gave in payment a bill drawn on Barton and Smith in London. He then used the vessel to ship slaves to Barbados, where their purchaser, Mr. Valentine Jones, paid by a bill for £1,590 sterling drawn on *his* London agents, Allen and Marlar. At Brew's request, the two bills were offset against each other, and Valentine Jones made his bill payable to Champion and Hayley, the London agents of the Vernons, cancelling Brew's original bill to the latter on Barton and Smith. In this way, Barton and Smith would ultimately receive any balance due from Brew's sale of slaves after the settlement of his purchase of the Vernons' vessel.[5] Here can be seen in operation a widespread system of payments centred on London, whose financial facilities were used in trade negotiations involving merchants in New England and the West Indies as well as West Africa.

---

[1] D. P. Mannix and M. Cowley, *Black Cargoes* (London, 1963), pp. 159–60.
[2] Richard Brew to Samuel Smith's assignees, 20 Feb. 1776, T. 70/1534; Donnan, op. cit. vol. III, pp. 165–6, 194–5, 232–4 and 248 n. 2.
[3] Donnan, op. cit. vol. II, pp. 528 and 526 n. 1. See pp. 11–12 above.
[4] Donnan, op. cit. vol. III, p. 248 n. 2.
[5] Donnan, op. cit. vol. III, pp. 194–5. 'Barton and Smith' appears in the document printed in Donnan as 'Burton and Smith'. See pp. 59–60 above.

While slaves were unquestionably Brew's chief economic
concern, his participation in other trades—gold, beeswax, the
export of Ijebu cloths from Lagos, and the provisioning of ships
—must not be overlooked.[1] Among these, gold is of particular
interest. West Africa's main source of attraction during the
early days of European contact, it still occupied an important
place in the eighteenth century, although the trade is one less
easy to document than slaving. Nevertheless it is clear that the
cargoes shipped out were often intended for its purchase as well
as for the purchase of slaves. If slaves were reasonably priced,
then apart from a full complement, gold and ivory could also
be bought, in Brew's own words, at a profit on these items of up
to 50 per cent.[2]

Traders living on the coast aimed at accumulating a gold
reserve, not only because it was valuable as a commodity, but as
a medium of exchange. When Brew's death seemed likely,
arrangements were quickly made to safeguard his stock at
Anomabu.[3] Locally, it might be acquired by barter with
Africans (for this purpose Brew sold them tobacco in 1773), or
by dealing with the Governors of forts. Cape Apollonia on the
western Gold Coast was noted as a specially good area of
supply. In 1771 Brew corresponded with Richard Miles,
Governor of the fort there, to obtain a balance due to him of
34 ounces 2 ackies, since he was 'in great want'. It should be
observed that he returned the consignment sent as inferior and

---

[1] The Executors' Accounts, drawn up by Richard Miles and Jerome Bernard
Weuves after Brew's death, show that 4,213 Ijebu cloths, valued at five shillings
each and totalling £1,053 5s. 0d. were shipped from Lagos to Anomabu and then
consigned to Ross and Mill in London, presumably for export to the West Indies.
In February 1776, Brew referred to his intention to ship off, by the end of the year,
as many 'Guinea cloths' and as much wax as would pay Samuel Smith's assignees
the £1,000 he owed them for the house. The province of Ijebu, to the north-east
of Lagos, formed an almost independent part of Yorubaland. According to an
early nineteenth-century account, its people were 'very industrious', and manufactured for sale 'an immense number of common Guinea cloths' which went to
Lagos, whence they were exported to the New World. 'Guinea cloths' were dyed
blue with the indigenous indigo plant; Richard Brew to Samuel Smith's assignees,
20 Feb. 1776, T. 70/1534; Executors' Accounts, entries dd. 17 Dec. 1776 and January 1777, T. 70/1504; Adams, op. cit. pp. 96–7, 108, 173; Donnan, op. cit. vol.
III, pp. 223–4; M. Crowder, The Story of Nigeria (London, 1962), p. 49.

[2] Richard Brew to Liverpool merchants, 1 Oct. 1771, T. 70/1531.

[3] David Mill to Richard Miles, 3 Aug. 1776, T. 70/1534. A ship belonging to
Brew and carrying fifty ounces of gold dust was seized on one occasion by pirates;
Donnan, op. cit. vol. II, p. 528.

unsuitable for the trade at Anomabu and insisted on 'good market gold' rather than fine siftings.[1]

As a medium of exchange, its use was becoming more frequent. Gold formed part of the coastal transactions of visiting ships. Brew bought tobacco and provisions with it from Rhode Island captains; in the same way they purchased stores on the coast before sailing to the West Indies.[2] Nor was exchange of this kind confined to Europeans. At the beginning of the eighteenth century, Bosman had referred to the small bits of gold, impure in quality and of little value, a form of manufactured currency, with which bread and fruit could be obtained from African market women,[3] and gold had a place in Afro-European slaving negotiations. According to Brew, writing in 1771, the 'pernicious practice' had developed of giving it to indigenous traders in return for slaves, to the great advantage, he said, of the Governor of Cape Coast Castle, who was plentifully supplied from Apollonia and the western forts.[4] The extent to which gold was taking the place of goods in the slave trade cannot readily be ascertained, but its increasing circulation on the coast does suggest that by the later eighteenth century African commercial practices were growing in sophistication.[5]

The organization and range of Brew's company leads next to an inquiry into its financial position, bearing in mind that Brew, like Smith, carried on separate as well as partnership trade. To make a complete assessment, more statistical evidence would be required, although fortunately a fair amount of correspondence has survived relating to the winding up of the coastal estate following Brew's death at Anomabu on 5 August 1776, together with a record of transactions in Africa by his executors there. From these sources, general if not specific conclusions can be drawn about the state of Brew's commercial affairs in the later years. Their unfavourable nature can only be

---

[1] Richard Brew to Richard Miles, 4, 14, and 15 Jan. 1771, T. 70/1532; the same to Thomas Westgate, 29 Sept. 1773, ibid.

[2] Donnan, op cit. vol. III, pp. 177, 180, 232–4.

[3] Bosman, *A New and Accurate Description of the Coast of Guinea*, pp. 81–2.

[4] Richard Brew to Liverpool merchants, 1 Oct. 1771, T. 70/1531. By accepting gold, African traders would be able to use it to purchase goods at a time and place suitable to themselves.

[5] For a well-developed trading system on another part of the west coast, see G. I. Jones, *The Trading States of the Oil Rivers* (London, 1963), pp. 90–2.

fully explained by reference to the whole range of his activities, both economic and otherwise. It is in the broader context of life on the coast that a consideration of him as a trader must finally be made, revealing some of the problems that the authorities in the forts had to face as a result of private European settlement within their spheres of influence.

The circumstances of Brew's death and its aftermath are well recounted by Richard Miles, Governor of Anomabu at the time and shortly afterwards of Cape Coast Castle, and appointed executor by Brew together with Jerome Bernard Weuves, who was likewise in the Committee's service.[1] Brew was taken ill towards the end of July 1776, and his condition became serious enough for Miles, who was on a visit to Cape Coast, to be summoned back on 3 August by Captain Eagles, the master of a ship in Anomabu road. On 4 August Brew was unconscious and Miles spent the night at his house. Two doctors and nine or ten ships' captains whom the Governor had sent for were also there. He died at about 1 a.m. on 5 August and was buried later that day; a ship's carpenter made the coffin.

Miles was now confronted with a difficult situation which David Mill, the Governor-in-Chief at Cape Coast, had foreseen and commented on when he received the news of Brew's dangerous illness. Firstly, wrote Mill, there was the question of safeguarding Brew's property against seizure by the Fanti, who had often been told that they were to be his heirs in the event of his dying at Anomabu. This operation should be effected, if possible, without using force and dragging the fort into a dispute likely to be detrimental to trade. Secondly, once the property was secured, the demands of his many creditors would have to be met; the division must be a fair one, and Mill did not think that Miles himself could be authorized to make any payment. The latter's position as Governor of Anomabu fort implicated him, of necessity, in the affairs of a deceased private trader long

---

[1] Richard Miles has been described as 'the most energetic and enterprising of the Governors in the eighteenth century'. He was appointed a writer in the Committee's service in 1765, and became Governor-in-Chief on 1 Jan. 1777, a few months after Brew's death. Suspended in 1779 from this office, he was reinstated in 1781 and resigned, finally, on 1 Jan. 1784. Miles, therefore, had a long career on the west coast. Jerome Bernard Weuves was appointed a writer in 1769; his final resignation, too, was in 1784; T. 70/1455, ff. 1, 5; Martin, op. cit. p. 43 and see p. 6 above.

resident in the town. The fact, discovered on his return to Anomabu, that Brew had named him an executor in the will drawn up by Captain Eagles on 3 August at the sick man's request, did so further, even after his promotion to Cape Coast Castle.[1]

It is clear that Richard Miles had no liking for the role of executor, that it came as a considerable surprise to him, and occasioned 'amazing trouble' over the space of two years, with repercussions as late as 1781.[2] His immediate reaction to the will on learning of its contents on 3 August was one of disapproval. Brew had stipulated that the executors were to fulfil his agreements on the coast and pay all just debts there before remitting anything to creditors in England or to his heirs-at-law in Ireland. In Miles's opinion, such a provision favoured the coast creditors at the expense of those in Europe, reflecting the influence of the former on the making of the will. A suggestion that it should be altered the next day could not be implemented as Brew then lapsed into unconsciousness. Miles's and Weuves's dislike of the tone of the will led Captain Eagles, also an executor, to refuse to act. The task of realizing the estate, 'a very disagreeable business', consequently fell on the two servants of the Committee. 'Never did two persons take charge of an Estate with greater reluctance than we have done this', they wrote to the African Office on 10 September 1776.[3]

For Miles, matters were further complicated by the action of Samuel Smith's assignees, who on hearing a rumour of Brew's death appointed him their agent in December 1776. If necessary, he was to turn Brew's effects, to which they laid claim, into slaves and money for speedy shipment home and

[1] David Mill to Richard Miles, 3 Aug. 1776, T. 70/1534; Richard Miles to Horatio Smith, 28 Sept. 1776, ibid.; Executors' Accounts, entry dd. 18 Dec. 1776, T. 70/1504 and see p. 81 n. 1 above.

[2] Richard Miles to Horatio Smith, 28 Sept. 1776, T. 70/1534. In 1781, while in England, Miles applied to be granted probate of Brew's estate, and swore an affidavit before the Public Notary on 27 April 1781 that the copy of Brew's will which he and Weuves had sent to England in 1776 was authentic; Richard Brew's will, 3 Aug. 1776 and subsequent proceedings (Somerset House); Richard Miles and Jerome Bernard Weuves to Committee, 10 Sept. 1776, T. 70/32, ff. 37–9; Richard Miles to Gilbert Petrie, 10 Nov. 1776, T. 70/1482. See also pp. 86–7 below.

[3] Richard Miles and Jerome Bernard Weuves to Committee, 10 Sept. 1776, T. 70/32, f. 37; Richard Miles to Horatio Smith, 28 Sept. 1776, T. 70/1534; Richard Brew's will, 3 Aug. 1776.

division of the proceeds among the creditors. Subsequently, they took legal steps to prevent any person obtaining administration of the estate, and regarded it as under their control since Brew had not paid the agreed sum of £6,000 to release himself from partnership with Smith. Long before the power of attorney reached Miles on the coast, however, he had acted by virtue of his authority as executor. The assignees expressed satisfaction with the measures he had initiated, but there is no doubt that Miles had a far from easy part to play in his dual capacity as their agent and Brew's executor, and that he was fully aware of it. In West Africa, there were the ever-present realities of Fanti pressure and the demands of coast creditors; in London, the complications of the Smith bankruptcy. To satisfy everybody was impossible, and the prospect that an aggrieved party might sue him could not be overlooked. As to the legal implications, Ross and Mill, the merchant firm in the City to whom Miles sent remittances on behalf of the Brew estate, informed him in February 1777 that they would do all they could to ensure his safety.[1]

In the course of their onerous duties, Miles and Weuves naturally acquired much insight into Brew's business affairs at the close of his life. The features which struck them forcibly were the muddled records and the inadequacy of the estate to meet the many claims made upon it. On the first point, Miles expressed his astonishment, within a few weeks of Brew's death, at finding the books 'in such terrible confusion'. Considerable in quantity, they were so badly kept, he said, that it was impossible to determine any man's account from them, or to ascertain what property lay in the leeward factories. Since Brew's connection with Samuel Smith first began, hardly a single account appeared to have been properly settled or closed. As for the estate, Miles reported that 'amazing demands' had been advanced by the numerous creditors, but that the sum to be divided between them was 'very small'. It was his opinion that Brew's recently

---

[1] Peregrine Cust and others to Richard Miles, 20 Dec. 1776, T. 70/1534; Committee to Richard Miles, 25 Dec. 1776, T. 70/69, f. 247; Ross and Mill to Richard Miles and Jerome Bernard Weuves, 14 Feb. 1777, T. 70/1534 and see p. 82 n. 2 above. Brew's will was ultimately proved in London, and Miles was granted limited probate until the original will and codicil or a more authentic copy should be brought to the Registry of the Prerogative Court of Canterbury; Richard Brew's will, 3 Aug. 1776 and subsequent proceedings.

announced hope of returning to England 'with a genteel fortune' could not have been realized for many years.[1]

Miles subsequently claimed that he had been well aware, during Brew's lifetime, of the latter's financial difficulties, as a result of which many would eventually suffer, and there is no reason to doubt his statement.[2] Their full extent, nevertheless, may well have been greater than he anticipated. An incident the day before Brew died was a precursor of what lay ahead. Disturbed by the will he had been shown, Miles invited those captains in Anomabu road who were Brew's creditors to come on shore for a discussion about methods of payment. It was then decided that they should ask Brew to let them withdraw their respective barters or goods of equivalent value from his warehouses. The Governor agreed, provided that Brew was in a fit state to acquiesce validly. Miles's eventual opposition to the action proposed, on the grounds that the sick man was now unconscious, occasioned an announcement by the clerk at Castle Brew that anyway there were insufficient goods in all the warehouses to pay one man's debts. Miles was 'amazed' and the captains 'thunderstruck' at the news. An investigation of the warehouses before they were sealed up confirmed its truth.[3]

It was on the basis of the will of 3 August, unaltered because of Brew's rapid decline, that the Miles and Weuves executorship proceeded. Their first task was to ensure the safety of the effects at the house and to take an inventory. This inventory was made on 5 August, the day of the funeral. It indicates substantial furnishing and equipment in eighteenth-century style.[4] Miles next had to determine what course to follow, consonant with his obligations under the will, and in the face of Fanti expectations, the known demands of ships' captains, and those of European creditors about which he had less information. On 6 August, a meeting was held at Cape Coast Castle attended

[1] Richard Miles to Horatio Smith, 28 Sept. 1776, T. 70/1534; the same to John Schoolbred, 19 Oct. 1776, T. 70/1482; Richard Miles and Jerome Bernard Weuves to Committee, 10 Sept. and 18 Oct. 1776, T. 70/32, ff. 37–9.
[2] Richard Miles to G. Burton, 6 Jan. 1777, T. 70/1482; the same to the same, 25 June 1778, T. 70/1483, ff. 82–3.
[3] Richard Miles to Horatio Smith, 28 Sept. 1776, T. 70/1534.
[4] Thomas Westgate to Richard Miles, 10 Aug. 1776, T. 70/1536, pt. 2; Inventory of the Effects of Richard Brew deceased, 5 Aug. 1776, T. 70/1534; see also p. 100 ff. below.

by Miles and the ships' captains and resolutions were taken. Regrettably these are not specified in his account of events. What does emerge is that Miles decided not to abide by them and became the object of abuse by many of the coast creditors. Plainly they thought their interests had been neglected. The plan of action he adopted was to gather in all Brew's effects, including those from the outlying factories, sell them by public auction at Anomabu where applicable, and ship the proceeds home—in broad outline, the measures Samuel Smith's assignees later recommended him to carry out as their agent. Miles thus left the question of the division of the estate to be settled in London. The provision of the will for meeting coastal debts before remitting overseas was implemented only in so far as it concerned the Fanti.[1]

Rightly anticipating censure whatever he did,[2] the priority given by Miles to the claims of the Fanti over those of European coast creditors reflects the strength of their position in the trading relationship. To offend them might lead to the worst consequences of all.[3] At an early stage Miles sought the Governor-in-Chief's advice about wages and debts due to Africans. Mill gave it as his private opinion that they should be paid.[4] Accordingly a number of items are listed in the Executors' Accounts—the wages of house slaves, sailors, and the cook, and payments to African creditors, a total in the latter instance of £146 often substantiated on notes.[5] These notes were sometimes for household provisions and necessities—fowls, eggs, and wood —and small in amount. In one instance, however, there was a trading debt of £31. Illustrative, too, of European conformity to the Fanti setting was a charge on the estate of £67, expended

[1] Richard Brew's will, 3 Aug. 1776; Richard Miles and Jerome Bernard Weuves to Messrs. Beard and Deakin, 17 Aug. 1776, ADM. 1/701 (G.N.A.); Richard Miles to Horatio Smith, 28 Sept. 1776, T. 70/1534; Richard Miles to Gilbert Petrie, 10 Nov. 1776, T. 70/1482; James Mourgue to Messrs. Beard, Graves and Deakin, 9 Dec. 1776, ADM. 1/701 (G.N.A.); Peregrine Cust and others to Richard Miles, 20 Dec. 1776, T. 70/1534.
[2] Richard Miles to Archibald Dalzel, 22 Sept. 1776, T. 70/1482.
[3] See the Governor-in-Chief's instructions to Richard Miles when Brew's death seemed imminent. For example, he was to try and secure Brew's property without resorting to force against the Fanti; David Mill to Richard Miles, 3 Aug. 1776, T. 70/1534.
[4] David Mill to Richard Miles, 10 Aug. 1776, T. 70/1534.
[5] Details, in round figures, relating to the settlement of Brew's estate in this and subsequent paragraphs are taken from the Executors' Accounts, T. 70/1504.

in rum, gunpowder, cloth, and a cow, for Brew's funeral
custom. This was received by Amonu Kuma, successor to
John Currantee at Anomabu, and by the inhabitants of the
town. Earlier they had been given rum, valued at £15, 'in
order to induce them to lessen their demand for custom'.[1]

Amonu Kuma was a figure of special prominence to Miles
because of Brew's connection with the ruling dynasty through
the late John Currantee's daughter who had been his 'wench',
and because of the promise of inheritance Brew had made to the
Fanti. Difficulties were anticipated, quite apart from the question of Fanti debts, and in November 1776 Miles reported that
he had experienced 'incredible' trouble. In his will the deceased had formally bequeathed to his 'wench', Effua Ansah,
and her two mulatto daughters, Eleanor and Amba, the Castle
Brew house slaves, together with the proceeds of the sale of
plate, wearing apparel, and household furniture. Miles believed that these provisions or the equivalent would have
to be fulfilled since Effua Ansah, who was of Amonu Kuma's
family, had powerful supporters to press home her claims.[2]
There can be little doubt that Brew's personal connections with
Fanti, which are disclosed in his will, complicated even further
the process of settling his affairs.

After a clearance lasting nearly two years, Miles and Weuves
completed their Executors' Accounts on 30 June 1778.[3] Brew's
coastal estate is there shown to have realized in all £8,739. Of
this, the sum of £4,145, almost half the total estate, was derived
from the sale of Castle Brew's effects and those of the subsidiary
factories, shipped to Anomabu. In the former instance, an
auction of furniture, apparel, and goods held in the hall of
Anomabu fort brought in £3,327, payable in slaves, gold, and
ivory at current coast prices; Miles gives the impression that

[1] Executors' Accounts, entries dd. 9 and 10 Sept. 1776, 31 Oct. 1776, T. 70/1504.
See also pp. 18-19 above.

[2] Richard Brew's will, 3 Aug. 1776; David Mill to Richard Miles, 3 Aug. 1776,
T. 70/1534; Richard Miles and Jerome Bernard Weuves to Committee, 10 Sept.
and 18 Oct. 1776, T. 70/32, ff. 37-9; Richard Miles to Gilbert Petrie, 10 Nov.
1776, T. 70/1482; James Mourgue to Committee, 9 July 1785, T. 70/33, f. 109. The
house slaves absconded and took refuge with the Anomabu people; subsequently
they were delivered up to Horatio Smith, purchaser of Castle Brew, on the understanding that they would not be sold off the coast. See also pp. 13-15 above and
106-8 below.

[3] T. 70/1504.

he had expected this property to yield more.[1] The shipment of slaves, primarily from Lagos and Cape Lopez, and of Ijebu cloths, also from Lagos, made up a further £4,033. Of the remaining small assets, the debts due to Brew are recorded as only £229; Miles himself owed £82, one of the two largest amounts.[2] The charges on the estate, including coastal payments, expenses and 5 per cent executors' commission[3]—£460 each— came to £2,166, leaving a net total of £6,572.[4] The bulk of this, £5,927, was remitted in cloth and slaves, and £530 in bills. The balance of £115 was paid at Anomabu on 30 June 1778 to Horatio Smith, the purchaser of Castle Brew from the assignees, and empowered by them to deal with any matters still outstanding on the coast.[5]

But Miles's troubles were not yet over, and he and Weuves were to be caused the 'deepest concern' by 'the unfortunate end' of Brew's affairs. This took the form of American seizure, during the War of Independence, of the vessels transporting Brew's property and also carrying, separately, the request for insurance. On 25 June 1778, Miles wrote to his father in a state of anxiety saying that the assignees had not yet sent a final release and asking him to ascertain, legally, whether the late Brew's creditors could claim damages from the executors in view of the recent occurrence. It is not surprising that Miles expressed his determination never to act again in such a capacity, and regretted that the good intentions of himself and Weuves in speedily remitting the estate were unlikely to bring them the credit that was their due.[6]

[1] Richard Miles and Jerome Bernard Weuves to Messrs. Beard and Deakin, 17 Aug. 1776, ADM. 1/701 (G.N.A.); Richard Miles to John Schoolbred, 19 Oct. 1776, T. 70/1482. Apart from one reference to the sale of an old boat for £12, there is no specific mention of the sale of ships.

[2] See pp. 88–9 below.

[3] At the time of independence in Ghana, the executor's commission was still 5 per cent in the case of expatriate officers who died while in government service. The general procedure followed by Miles and Weuves in clearing up Brew's estate was very similar to the modern one.

[4] Miles and Weuves took their commission on the basis of an estate valued at £9,219. There was a loss of £478, as a result of slaves dying on board ship before it had left Anomabu; this reduced the total value of the estate to £8,739. See p. 92 below.

[5] Executors' Accounts, T. 70/1504; Peregrine Cust and others to Richard Miles and Jerome Bernard Weuves, 19 Feb. 1778, T. 70/1536, pt. 2.

[6] Richard Miles to Sir William Miles, 25 June 1778, T. 70/1483, ff. 92–9; the same to Samuel Smith, 25 June 1778, ibid. ff. 83–5.

What light does the evidence relating to the settlement of his estate throw on Brew's financial circumstances? In the first place, the view that he died insolvent should be noted. It was expressed, not only by Richard Miles, but also, more colourfully, by the Dutch who described him as having travelled, in this condition, to eternity.[1] The Executors' Accounts, however, are not themselves proof of bankruptcy, in that they refer solely to Brew's African estate and do not provide all the information necessary for a complete financial statement. Two omissions must be mentioned: shipments off the coast prior to death which would result in assets in his favour in London, and a list of European creditors, both in Africa and in England.

As to the former, Brew certainly gave the impression, in the early months of 1776, that he was engaged in current transactions that would clear the £6,000 debt due to Samuel Smith's assignees and pay for Castle Brew. Yet it seems very probable that these transactions were not completed until the beginning of 1777, when Miles and Weuves exported 205 slaves and 4,213 cloths that had been brought round to Anomabu from Lagos and Cape Lopez. The shipments are recorded in the Executors' Accounts; what earlier ones there had been in the months before August 1776 cannot be determined. It must be pointed out that while Brew had mentioned his recent trade, in April 1776, as very prosperous, Miles believed, after making investigations, that this opinion of his prospects had been markedly over-optimistic.[2]

On the second matter of creditors, only those in Fanti are listed in the Executors' Accounts, although the extent of other claims can reasonably be regarded as considerable. Apart from known debts

[1] P. Woortman to Assembly of the X, 26 Sept. 1776, W.I.C. 119; Richard Miles to James Campbell, 10 Nov. 1776, T. 70/1482; the same to John Coghlan, 25 June 1778, T. 70/1483, f. 85; Ledger Account, Richard Brew, entry dd. 10 Dec. 1777, T. 70/1504.

[2] Richard Brew to Samuel Smith's assignees, 20 Feb. 1776, T. 70/1534; the same to the same, 1 April 1776, T. 70/1536, pt. 2; Richard Brew to Peregrine Cust, 5 April 1776, T. 70/1534; Richard Miles and Jerome Bernard Weuves to Committee, 10 Sept. 1776, T. 70/32, ff. 37–9; Richard Miles to Horatio Smith, 30 Jan. 1777, T. 70/1482; Executors' Accounts, T. 70/1504. It would appear that Brew's letter to the assignees, written on 20 Feb. 1776, was not in fact sent until 1 April. The assignees refer to this as the last one they received from him; Peregrine Cust and others to Richard Miles and Jerome Bernard Weuves, 19 Feb. 1778, T. 70/1536, pt. 2.

(the £6,000 owed in London, a further £1,000 that would have secured Brew the house, some £900 due to Horatio Smith, and the demands of Westgate), the amounts owed to shipping in the road were large, according to an American report, and this is borne out by the captains' own actions. The value of one cargo which Brew had recently received from England was given as £1,050. Other consignments could well have been on a similar scale.[1] In October 1776 Miles advanced the supposition that Brew's estate would fall short of his liabilities by £20,000.[2] There is no way of checking this figure which may have exaggerated the position, nor can the executors' own handling of the business or any private negotiations on their part be investigated. The confusion reported in Brew's books would certainly make it difficult for them to give full details of creditors and debtors on the coast. It is a curious fact, if true, that as little as £229 appears to have been owed to him locally.[3] Incomplete data must limit the precision of the picture, but it seems fair to conclude, on weighing up the situation, that opinion was right in regarding Brew as insolvent, and that his net estate, totalling £6,572 on the coast, would have been insufficient to meet his debts. By what margin this was so, however, cannot be ascertained.

It is probable that bankruptcy resulted from a gradual rather than a sudden decline in Brew's fortunes, extending over a number of years. The reputation he enjoyed as one of the largest slave traders on the coast secured him a degree of credit even when troubles were in the offing. Contemporary comment would suggest that the seventeen-sixties was his most profitable period. Between 1765 and 1771, the Dutch, the British, and the Americans independently bore testimony to the magnitude of his business, 'the most flourishing trade ever known at Annamaboe', whence he shipped 'perhaps . . . more slaves than

[1] Richard Brew to Samuel Smith's assignees, 30 March 1776, T. 70/1534; Thomas Westgate to Richard Miles, 8 and 9 Aug. 1776, T. 70/1536, pt. 2; George Burton to Richard Miles, 27 Jan. 1778, ibid.; Donnan, op. cit. vol. III, p. 320 n. 2 and see pp. 64, 66–7, 69, 84 above. Westgate, now Governor of Winneba, does not seem to have entertained much hope of being paid. On 8 Aug. he wrote to Miles saying that when he knew who would act as executors, he would put in some claims, 'if it were no more than for form's sake'.
[2] Richard Miles to John Schoolbred, 19 Oct. 1776, T. 70/1482.
[3] If Brew really had so few debtors, this would suggest that his trading had fallen to a very low level; see pp. 86–7 above.

any one man in the Kingdom'.[1] After his death, too, it was
stated at Cape Coast Castle that he had monopolized the local
trade in slaves between Lagos, Benin, Gabon, and the Gold
Coast, prior to export overseas, although this trade was described as small in quantity.[2] By the seventeen-seventies many
indications can be found that Brew was experiencing a rougher
passage to which the embarrassments of Samuel Smith at the
London end of the concern contributed in material fashion.
Despite Smith's portrayal in 1771 of solid assets and the fact
that the Inspectors had agreed to send out further goods to the
coast to finance the partnership, it was unable to extricate itself
from the difficulties and became increasingly affected by credit
limitations. Westgate's correspondence substantiates this. At
the end of 1773 he described Brew's condition as 'critical', and
bankruptcy as the likely consequence of Smith's indebtedness.[3]

Faced with doubt about continued backing from London,
Brew began to display an uncertain temper where his financial
position was concerned. During a quarrel in 1771, Charles Bell,
Governor of Anomabu, chose to insult him by use of the phrase
'the Bancrupt Brew', and Bell's deprecatory references at the
end of 1774 to the state of Brew's credit with the shipping
seemed likely to result in a duel, until the Governor thought
better of the matter and apologized. In December 1775 Brew
and his assistant, Horatio Smith, came to physical blows; their
altercation began over Smith's request for payment of a debt.
It was in this year, too, that Brew made reference to disappoint-

[1] J. P. T. Huydecooper to Assembly of the X, 8 Nov. 1765, W.I.C. 116; Gilbert
Petrie to Committee, 13 Sept. 1766, T. 70/31, ff. 217–18; Donnan, op. cit. vol. III,
p. 248 n. 2. It is impossible to say how many slaves Brew exported in a year. In
1765, the Governor of Cape Coast Castle told the Committee that of the 440 or
450 slaves sometimes lodged in Anomabu fort, all but 50 or 60 might belong to
Brew and Webster. On 5 April 1776, Brew wrote that he had bought and sold
780 slaves since 12 July last. At this time, however, he was anxious to portray his
trade in as favourable a light as possible; William Mutter to Committee, 25 Oct.
1765, T. 70/31, ff. 148–9; Richard Brew to Peregrine Cust, 5 April 1776, T.
70/1534.
[2] The Council's Answer to the Return of the Lords of Trade, 25 June 1778,
T. 70/1535.
[3] Richard Brew to William Devaynes, 2 May 1770, T. 70/1531; Thomas Westgate to Richard Brew, 10 Aug. 1770, T. 70/1536, pt. 2; the same to the same,
Nov. [sic], 2 Dec., and 8 Dec. 1773, ibid. and see pp. 63–5 and 63 n. 2
above.

ments and misfortunes which for some time would prevent his departure from the coast.[1]

That he should have depicted a very different state of affairs in the following year is somewhat surprising, since trade is unlikely to have improved within a few months to an extent that would justify the optimism expressed in a letter of 5 April 1776. It can be assumed that he was anxious now to impress Smith's assignees with his capacity to pay off the £6,000 due to them by 11 April 1777, and that all his trading efforts were directed towards this end. A belief that his prospects were brighter may well have grown up in mercantile circles after the agreement to buy himself out of the Smith partnership. When Brew died, credit had been received from ships' captains to the extent of some 300 slaves. Although there is no certain proof, it is possible that most of the goods advanced were sent to supply Lagos and Cape Lopez in accordance with his plan to consign slaves and cloth from there to the assignees in 1776; this would account for the depleted state of the warehouses at the beginning of August.[2]

If the above was the case, then Brew's trading capital had really reached a low ebb and he had few reserves available upon which to draw for current transactions. Miles later drew attention to the warnings he had given against over-much trade with Brew, being aware of the latter's real circumstances. There seems little reason to doubt that by 1776 these circumstances had deteriorated markedly since the early days at Castle Brew, and that in the words of a New England captain 'times wass much alterd with him for the worse'.[3] The condition of the house, damaged by the encroachment of the sea, symbolizes this. At the close of Brew's life it was in need of repairs which he had

[1] Charles Bell to Richard Brew, 24 Jan. 1771, T. 70/1531; correspondence between Charles Bell and Richard Brew, 19 and 20 Dec. 1774, T. 70/1532; correspondence between the same, 5 and 6 Jan. 1775, T. 70/1533; Richard Miles's statement, Dec. [sic] 1775, ibid.; Richard Brew to Mr. Coghlan, 28 Aug. 1775, ibid.; the same to Samuel Smith's assignees, 30 March 1776, T. 70/1534. Charles Bell was the nephew of the Governor-in-Chief of that name; see pp. 6, 43–4 above.

[2] Richard Brew to Samuel Smith's assignees, 20 Feb. and 1 April 1776, T. 70/1534; the same to Peregrine Cust, 5 April 1776, ibid.; Richard Miles to Mr. Burton, 25 June 1778, T. 70/1483, f. 81 and see p. 84 above. It should be noted, too, that in 1776, Horatio Smith returned to England to lay the question of his quarrel with Brew before the assignees. Obviously Brew would wish to counteract any unfavourable impression that Smith might give about his financial situation.

[3] Richard Miles to G. Burton, 6 Jan. 1777, T. 70/1482; Donnan, op. cit. vol. III, p. 307 n. 3.

92 WEST AFRICAN TRADE AND COAST SOCIETY

reckoned would cost £400. Part of the structure collapsed in 1778 when its new owner, Horatio Smith, was in residence.[1]

A number of causes, in part economic, had combined to bring about deterioration in the Brew concern. Slave trading, for example, the main prop of his business, was by no means always highly lucrative. Recent research has 'modified the African trade's reputation for huge profits and shown that some voyages were attended with losses. . . . The truth is that the trade was a gamble: profits might be made, but the risk of loss was always present.'[2] This view echoes one expressed in the eighteenth century by John Newton, contemporary with Brew, and a participant in the trade for a while: 'there were some gainful voyages, but the losing voyages were thought more numerous; it was generally considered as a sort of lottery in which every adventurer hoped to gain a prize'.[3]

Among the factors that determined gain or loss was the availability of slaves on the coast at any period, and the length of time it might take a ship to secure a full cargo.[4] Mortality presented another problem, and it has been reckoned that about 10 per cent of slaves died between purchase in Africa and arrival at their destination in the New World. According to the accounts of Brew's executors, this was the fate of twenty-six on board ship at Anomabu at the end of 1776, before it had even set sail for the West Indies. Their value totalled £478, some 11 per cent of the whole slave cargo.[5] Piracy and privateering were further hazards. In 1766 Brew lost a vessel with 50 ounces of gold on board and goods worth £1,200 sterling, and the ulti- mate fate of his property, captured at sea during the War of American Independence together with its insurance coverage, has already been noted.[6] Price fluctuations both in Africa and the New World affected profits, and there were the expenses

---

[1] Richard Brew to Samuel Smith's assignees, 20 Feb. 1776, T. 70/1534; the same to Richard Miles, 14 June 1776, ibid.; Richard Miles to Thomas Westgate, 5 Nov. 1778, T. 70/1480; the same to Charles Bell, 10 Jan. 1779, T. 70/1483 and see p. 57 n. 2 above.
[2] Davies, op. cit. p. 348.
[3] Newton, *Journal of a Slave Trader*, p. 81 n. 2.
[4] Richard Brew to William Devaynes, 2 May 1770, T. 70/1531 and see p. 76 above.
[5] Executors' Accounts, entry dd. 31 Dec. 1776, T. 70/1504; Gill, op. cit. pp. 81-2.
[6] Donnan, op. cit. vol. II, p. 528 and see p. 87 above.

of freight and insurance, and, for Brew, of maintaining and supplying Anomabu as well as its subsidiary factories.[1] If to all this is added the need for a constant stock of trading goods, and the slowness of returns, it is not difficult to envisage a situation in which capital would be subjected to considerable strain. In the case of Brew, fully committed as he was in the 'lottery' with all its attendant risks, this is what happened, and Smith's financial difficulties must have weakened considerably the resources of a partnership already affected, perhaps, by over-extension of its trading activities on the west coast.

While it was essential for the management of a business of this kind that Brew should give it his full attention, it is only too plain that much of his energy in the period 1765–74 was diverted into a field broadly definable as politics. One major aspect of this, arising out of the close relationship between trade, European rivalry, and African affairs, was his lengthy participation in the disagreements between Fanti and Ashanti consequent upon the Ashanti coastal advance of 1765. Brew's mediating attempts, aimed at 'settling the peace of the country and opening the trading paths' into the interior, brought nothing but trouble and embarrassment to the public forts.[2] An endeavour to outstrip the Dutch in winning favour with the King of Ashanti, for example, led him into one of many disputes with them, during which he and his associate, Webster, seized the Dutch Director-General's messenger on 26 August 1765 and placed him in double chains at Castle Brew. The repercussions of this—protests to Cape Coast Castle by the Dutch, their report to the States-General in Holland, and a discussion of the matter in London by the Board of Trade—illustrate the complications, extending even to the level of two metropolitan governments, that could result from the presence of a private trader on the coast. The Governor-in-Chief at Cape Coast Castle might

[1] Davies, op. cit. p. 349. In 1776 Brew intended insurance to be taken on slaves who were valued at £25 sterling a head; his schooner was valued at £300 for the purpose of the trip from Africa to America and the West Indies. After Brew's death, the bill for the freight of 148 slaves from Lagos and Cape Lopez to Anomabu, together with other charges, came to £341. Davies comments on the difficulties of assessing the profits or losses of the Royal African Company, and the same is true in the case of Brew; Richard Brew to Samuel Smith's assignees, 20 Feb. 1776, T. 70/1534; Executors' Accounts, entry dd. 3 Jan. 1777, T. 70/1504; Davies, op. cit. pp. 237–8.
[2] See pp. 73–4 above and 110–11 below.

express his Council's disapproval of Brew's arrogant behaviour, and attribute it to the great indulgence which he had received from the Committee. Significant was the admission that no legitimate authority could be exercised over him.[1]

To the British no less than to the Dutch, Brew was a thorn in the flesh, through his machinations to secure an overriding advantage in local diplomacy. For this purpose he dispensed presents on a lavish scale in Fanti. His tactics caused successive Governors-in-Chief to denounce him in their reports to the Committee as abusive in language, domineering in behaviour, and imbued with romantic notions of impressing upon the population his superiority in power, wealth, and importance to the servants of the Committee. They also pointed out that the effect of rival European peacemaking in the Ashanti-Fanti dispute had been to increase the cost in terms of cloth, silk, liquor, and other goods distributed to the Fanti. It was said in October 1768 that Brew's expenditure had already exceeded £1,200 sterling, far more than that of the other negotiators.[2] His aim of surpassing the British and Dutch forts in a display of local ascendancy was extremely heavy on the purse, and it is difficult to believe that commensurate economic rewards resulted. Until his death, reported to Amsterdam with relief by the Dutch, they, like the British, regarded him as the source of much coastal friction.[3] The records of both Companies substantiate the view that he must have devoted a considerable amount of time as well as money to activities that were not particularly productive in nature.

Evidence to support this can be found in Brew's association with another political question, the organization of the African Company. When living as a private trader at Anomabu, his dealings with the forts were distinguished by a vigorous attack on their administration, directed principally at the Governors. The main ground of his complaint was that the Governors' widespread trade defeated the purposes for which they had been

[1] William Mutter to the Committee, 25 Oct. 1765, C.O. 388/53; Priestley, 'Richard Brew: an eighteenth century trader at Anomabu' in *Transactions of the Historical Society of Ghana*, vol. IV, pt. I (1959), pp. 39–40. Mutter said in his letter that war between England and Holland was even considered a possibility by some at Anomabu.

[2] Priestley, art. cit. pp. 40–1.

[3] P. Woortman to Assembly of the X, 26 Sept. 1776, W.I.C. 119.

appointed, charges similar, in fact, to those that had earlier led
to his own suspension from Tantumkweri in 1753 and Anomabu
in 1764.[1] For six years, between 1768 and 1774, Castle Brew
served as the coastal headquarters of a pressure group whose
object was to effect radical changes in fort management, while,
in England, the Liverpool merchants and principally Miles
Barber became the recipients of prolific correspondence on the
subject. Bristol and London merchants displayed less enthusiasm
for the suggested reforms.[2]

Brew's case against the Committee's servants was expressed
forcibly and with great detail in letters and documents sent
out from Anomabu, on one occasion extending to some sixty
paragraphs in length.[3] His description of this activity as the
preparation of a few anecdotes to be thrown at an appropriate
time into the 'pallaver house', as he picturesquely termed the
British Parliament, was something of an understatement.[4] Brew
argued along the lines that the forts were a practical necessity
for the conduct of trade on the coast, but were not fulfilling the
objects intended of them. Far from aiding and protecting private
traders, he said, the latter were placed at a considerable disadvantage by the commercial activities of the Governors, who used
their position and the public funds to amass large private fortunes. With warehouses, labourers, and canoes all ready to
hand, and supplies sent out from England for the upkeep of the
public establishments, the Governors had the minimum of
overhead expense, declared Brew, and could trade without the
long-term credit necessary to private dealers in obtaining cargoes from Europe. Assisted in this way and effectively un-
restrained by the Committee in London, they were able to
engross the slave trade, causing an increase in prices to the
detriment of British shipping and of private settlers. In his
opinion, the situation could only be remedied at the level of
fort command, either by appointing military officers whose
profession would be a barrier to trade, or by paying salaries

---

[1] See pp. 37–8, 51–3 above.
[2] Miles Barber to Richard Brew, 28 Nov. 1769, 27 Jan. 1771, 23 March and
4 July 1771, T. 70/1531; Richard Brew to Mr. Coghlan, 28 Aug. 1775, T. 70/1533;
Copy of a letter from Richard Brew to Messrs. Richard Farr and Sons, 17 March
1768 (Balme Library, University of Ghana).
[3] Richard Camplin to Miles Barber, 25 Feb. 1771, T. 70/1531.
[4] Richard Brew to William Devaynes, 2 May 1770, T. 70/1531.

large enough to make private trade unnecessary, or by allowing such trade but under certain restrictions. A set of regulations to achieve the last objective was submitted by Brew in 1770.[1]

During the seventeen-seventies, when there was considerable agitation in England for reform in coastal administration, Brew's party, focused on Liverpool, made full use of the Anomabu catalogue of complaints.[2] *A Treatise upon the Trade from Great Britain to Africa*, published in 1772 to illustrate the need for change, contained in its appendixes a number of the letters which he had written to Liverpool merchants.[3] These merchants formed the spearhead of the attack; they set up their own committee in 1770 to consider the evidence, and sent Brew's 'very voluminous production' to the African Committee in London early in 1771.[4] Arrangements were made there for its detailed study, and an immediate inquiry ordered into the charges, although the Secretary declared that this was solely the result of deference to the Liverpool gentlemen. Brew's assertions were regarded as unauthenticated without the properly attested proof of ships' captains. To accept them, the Secretary said, would be contrary to law and justice and to the principles that had earlier governed the Committee in their lenient treatment of Brew, a point of view which the latter strenuously denied.[5] This cool official reception did not deter the reform party either on the coast or in England. Brew next emphasized that failing redress by the Committee, it would probably be necessary to bring the matter before Parliament, and in 1774 he inquired of Captain Eagles what had become

[1] Richard Brew to Benjamin and Arthur Heywood, 1 Aug. 1774, T. 70/1532; Copy of a letter from Richard Brew to Messrs. Richard Farr and Sons, 17 March 1768; Richard Brew's letters dd. 1 July and 15 Oct. 1770, 10 April, 25 Aug., 1 Oct., and 15 Oct. 1771 in *A Treatise upon the Trade from Great Britain to Africa*, App. H.

[2] David Mill to Richard Miles, 12 Oct. 1771, T. 70/1531.

[3] *A Treatise upon the Trade from Great Britain to Africa*, App. H. Extracts are printed in Donnan, op. cit. vol. II, p. 536 ff.

[4] Miles Barber to Richard Brew, 28 Nov. 1769, T. 70/1531; the same to Ebenezer Price, 7 May 1770, ibid.; the same to Richard Brew, 16 May 1770, ibid.; Arthur Heywood, Miles Barber and others to Committee, 25 January 1771, ibid.; Miles Barber to Richard Camplin, 25 Jan. 1771, ibid.; the same to Richard Brew, 27 Jan. 1771, ibid.; Richard Camplin to Miles Barber, 25 Feb. 1771, ibid.; Richard Brew to Miles Barber, 5 Aug. 1774, T. 70/1532.

[5] Richard Camplin to Miles Barber, 25 Feb. 1771, T. 70/1531; Richard Brew to Liverpool merchants, 25 Aug. 1771, ibid.

of the 'African Bill', and whether the Committee's influence had been sufficient to get it thrown out of the House a second time.[1]

In view of the zeal displayed, Brew's change of attitude one year later, in 1775, seems remarkable. He now declared it his intention, as far as the Governors were concerned, 'never to write a syllable more about them', a striking contrast with the earlier mood of 'very voluminous production'. For this volte-face, a twofold explanation was given. Firstly, said Brew, he had come to believe that no alteration would be made in the administration of the forts; only the Liverpool merchants had supported his efforts over the past few years. Secondly, he was motivated by the dictates of prudence as well as by inclination, and was at that time 'upon very decent terms' with Governor David Mill of Cape Coast Castle and Governor Richard Miles of Anomabu. This fact is borne out by the correspondence between them in 1775-6, and especially by Brew's choice of Miles as one of his executors.[2] It is possible that discouragement, together with ill health, had damped his enthusiasm. Doubtless more potent, however, was Brew's second reason. It may well have been connected with the need to re-establish confidence in his business and to enjoy good relations with anyone, including the Governors of forts, who might be able to help him in the period of break-away from the Smith partnership.[3]

Hence it can be seen that throughout the years at Castle Brew, there were matters other than trade absorbing a large measure of Brew's time and interest. This was partly the result of his highly individual personality, and of long residence overseas in a confined European society that lacked any effective framework of authority. In consequence, Brew was diverted

[1] Richard Brew to Liverpool merchants, 25 Aug. 1771, T. 70/1531; the same to Thomas Eagles, 10 Nov. 1774, T. 70/1532. In 1777, when the Committee petitioned for an increased grant for the upkeep of the forts, the House of Commons requested the Board of Trade to examine the state of the African trade. The Board of Trade's report, made on 30 April 1777, was then considered by a Committee of the House of Commons; Donnan, op. cit. vol. II, p. 553 n. 3.

[2] Richard Brew to Mr. Coghlan, 28 Aug. 1775, T. 70/1533. In June 1776, for example, Brew wrote to Miles asking for his assistance in securing labour to repair Castle Brew, damaged by the rains, and saying that he was dependent on Miles's friendship at that critical juncture; Richard Brew to Richard Miles, 14 June 1776, T. 70/1534.

[3] See pp. 90-1 above.

from strict concentration on commercial affairs, perhaps at the
very moment when concentration was most necessary; during
the early seventeen-seventies, credit restriction due to Smith's
impending bankruptcy was paralleled by Brew's involvement
in Fanti politics and in plans to change fort management.
There is another fact that must be taken into account—that of
declining health after thirty years on the coast. In 1773, Westgate expressed concern about this. He referred to Brew's
appearance as 'emaciated' and suggested remedial measures.
Brew himself, in a letter to Richard Miles shortly before he
died, enlarged on his ailments and wished Miles continued
good health, 'the first of all earthly blessings'.[1] When all these
circumstances are borne in mind, the confused state of Brew's
account books, revealed after his death, and the unsatisfactory
financial position of a business once 'the most flourishing . . .
ever known at Anomabu' become much more understandable.

[1] Thomas Westgate to Richard Brew, 10 Aug. 1773, T. 70/1536, pt. 2; Richard
Brew to Richard Miles, 28 May 1776, T. 70/1534.

CHAPTER IV

Castle Brew

Repugnant though the slave trade now appears as a traffic in human lives, Europeans who took part in it were not necessarily the uncultivated desperadoes that might be expected. As far as eighteenth-century Britain was concerned, those engaged in the trade display many of the characteristics of that age of contrasts—hard-headed business realism, adventure and crudeness, the 'unusual degree of toughness, both of spirit and body' necessary for survival on the coast.[1] Combined with this was a measure of sophistication and a literary style of considerable merit. While ships' captains might be less endowed with these qualities of refinement,[2] the coastal residents certainly included men of education who sought to introduce into their establishments something of the manner of life of the gentry.

Their social origins are perhaps best summed up in the broad general category of 'middle class'. The prospect of rapid promotion in the Committee's service, and the hope of acquiring substantial wealth ranked high among inducements that led to West Africa.[3] For the first reason, Thomas Westgate abandoned the navy, where he had been a surgeon's mate, in order to take up a similar appointment with the African Company. The second inducement applied in the case of two resident dealers in Sierra Leone, the Irishman Nicholas Owen and Richard Hall, a gentleman 'who has, like a great many others, spent his estate at home, therefore obliged to go abroad in search of a

---

[1] Martin, *The British West African Settlements*, p. 38.
[2] See, however, Newton, *Journal of a Slave Trader*, ed. B. Martin and M. Spurrell, and his 'Thoughts upon the African Slave Trade', contained in the same volume. Newton, the master of a slaving ship, later became ordained and an opponent of the slave trade.
[3] Martin, op. cit. pp. 38–9.

new one'.[1] Both no doubt were applicable to Richard Brew, whose appearance on the coast may well have been due to family financial difficulties and the limited opportunities available to him in his native Ireland.[2]

There was both an Irish flavour and a touch of feudalism about the name 'Castle Brew', an appropriate choice for a house of its kind, with high walls, battlements, a 'most noble Hall' and twenty guns in the parade.[3] Equipped with warehouses and slave accommodation, Castle Brew has been seen as the centre of a widespread trading concern. Now it must be considered as the home of a 'settler on this coast'.[4] On the day that Brew died, 5 August 1776, Richard Miles took an inventory of its contents, the first of many tasks that fell to his lot in winding up the estate, and from this document the material setting of Brew's life can be envisaged.[5]

At Castle Brew he achieved a standard of comfort in keeping with the requirements of an eighteenth-century gentleman. His bedroom and the hall were furnished in mahogany. The former contained a bedstead, a settee, two arm chairs, a table, and a bureau and bookcase used for the storage of valuables such as gold. In the hall, which was clearly of spacious dimensions and the scene of his social and business dealings, there were two settees, twenty-three Windsor chairs, four mahogany tables, two bureaux and bookcases, and a sideboard. Four bedsteads provided extra sleeping accommodation. Lighting was in the form of candles, and the hall was adorned by a glass chandelier. There were also four looking-glasses and '66 pictures of different sizes', a miniature art gallery about which the inventory, alas, is uninformative. An organ, listed in the effects, must have been played in the hall when religious services were conducted there by the Reverend Philip Quaque, the African chaplain at Coast Cape Castle and an occasional visitor to Anomabu.[6]

---

[1] Thomas Westgate to Committee, 2 Feb. 1751, T. 70/1517; Newton, op. cit. p. 17 n. 9; Owen, *Journal of a Slave Dealer*, pp. 1–18.

[2] See pp. 32–3 above.

[3] Inventory of the Effects of Richard Brew, deceased, 5 Aug. 1776, T. 70/1534; Philip Quaque to the S.P.G., 7 March 1767 and see p. 57 above.

[4] Richard Brew to Liverpool merchants, 25 Aug. 1771, T. 70/1531.

[5] Inventory, 5 Aug. 1776, T. 70/1534 and see p. 84 ff. above.

[6] See p. 109 below.

Brew's tastes and mode of existence are further revealed by his household equipment and personal possessions. These included a quantity of silverware (candlesticks, a large salver, cream jug, and teaspoons) and a plentiful stock of china, glassware and linen—over five dozen plates, two dozen cups and saucers, Queen's Ware, decanters for wine, punch, and water, wineglasses and some twenty-six tablecloths.[1] Brew had obviously equipped himself well to play the host when he was visited by the captains of ships anchored in Anomabu road.[2] His wardrobe of clothes, in eighteenth-century style, was a substantial one. There were fifteen waistcoats, nine coats laced and plain, sixteen shirts, nine velvet collars, cravats, patterned black silk breeches, and several pairs of stockings, some of them silk.[3] Old gold lace was kept in a bureau in the bedroom. Cards and a backgammon table give an insight into his leisure pursuits. But from this point of view, particular interest attaches to his books, which are fortunately described more fully in the inventory than the pictures.

Brew's library consisted of nearly one hundred works, some of them in several volumes. Thirty-one are listed by title, and the rest under the general definition of '65 volumes of odd books'.[4] They can be described as the normal reading matter of any well-educated contemporary, with the addition of one or two works of more specialized attraction. To the former category belong the periodicals, novels, poems and essays popular in eighteenth-century Britain, where 'a wider public was being educated to a taste in good literature'.[5] The shelves of Castle Brew contained the *Spectator*, the *Rambler* and the *Connoisseur*, *Tom Jones* and *Sir Charles Grandison*, twenty volumes of Pope, eleven of Swift and some volumes of Addison. Dr. Johnson's *Dictionary* had a place, also the *Annual Register* and Postlethwayt's *Universal Dictionary of Trade and Commerce*, as might be expected in the house of a merchant. For historical literature, Brew seems to have had a special liking. There were sixteen volumes of Rollin's *Roman History*, a *History of Guinea*, a

---

[1] Inventory, 5 Aug. 1776, T. 70/1534. 'Queen's Ware' was Wedgwood china.
[2] See pp. 108–9 below.
[3] Brew had a mulatto tailor, presumably to make him items of clothing such as shirts; Executors' Accounts, entry dd. 22 Oct. 1776, T. 70/1504.
[4] Inventory, 5 Aug. 1776, T. 70/1534.
[5] B. Williams, *The Whig Supremacy, 1714–1760* (Oxford, 1945), p. 395.

History of Ireland in three volumes,[1] a *History of London* in six, and nine volumes of Smollett's *History of England*. The works of Shakespeare were there, and among miscellaneous titles, *Don Quixote*, borrowed from Westgate in 1770 and presumably never returned,[2] a book on geography and the *Art of Cookery*. More unusual were the *Life of Cleveland*, a mid-seventeenth-century metaphysical poet of small popularity in the eighteenth century, and two volumes of the works of William Shenstone, a contemporary poet.

Brew's literary taste was thus a cultured and discriminating one, suggesting a social background appropriate to this. Some of his books may have been acquired from the family home, but a number must have been bought as they were published. It is interesting to find him writing to a ship's captain in 1774 that 'some new publications' would be 'very acceptable', and his library was well up to date.[3] Smollett's *History of England* is a case in point. Brew himself is mentioned in it as the Governor of Anomabu fort, and Smollett recounts the episode of 1757 when John Currantee tried to send a present to the French naval squadron which had come to attack Cape Coast Castle. The presence of this work in Brew's collection indicates that he kept well abreast of current literature.[4]

How much leisure time he devoted to reading, of course, is impossible to determine, although the many letters emanating from Castle Brew show that he was influenced by the excellent prose writing of the age. A mark of their literary quality, as of the Governor-in-Chiefs' despatches to London, is that they can portray with such clarity developments in trade and politics, the tension of personal relationships and minutiae of daily existence. Brew's style was direct and forceful, with the polished

[1] In 1763, vol. I of a *History of Ireland* by Ferdinando Warner was published; this may have been the work purchased by Brew. See the *Gentleman's Magazine*, vol. XXXIII (1763), p. 259.

[2] Thomas Westgate to Richard Brew, 7 Aug. 1770, T. 70/1536, pt. 2; Inventory, 5 Aug. 1776, T. 70/1534.

[3] Richard Brew to Thomas Eagles, 10 Nov. 1774, T. 70/1532.

[4] See pp. 45–6 above. It is interesting to note that according to a modern informant in Cape Coast, James Hutton Brew (1844–1915), one of Richard Brew's descendants, was very interested in Tobias Smollett's *History of England* and suggested to a Fanti contemporary that the latter should purchase a copy of it from Foyle's. Brew, who spent many years in England, said that the work contained information about their ancestors. See p. 169 ff. below.

turn of phrase and the well-placed allusion typical of the century, and was adaptable to a variety of circumstances, from formal exposition of coastal maladministration intended for the benefit of Liverpool merchants to hard-hitting abuse directed at a personal enemy.

Much of his literary effort after 1764 went into attacks on the African Committee and its servants.[1] Criticizing the Governors for misuse of their time, Brew neatly described them as seized with 'the spirit of engineering'. The result of this, he said, was that the forts were badly maintained; 'and yet these gentlemen are all professed engineers and will talk of a bastion, ravelin, horn work, cornered way, etc. with as much facility as either a Vauban, or a Coehorn'.[2] In well-chosen phrases, he announced that he was 'preparing a few anecdotes to be thrown into the pallaver house at a proper time', a reference to the hoped-for parliamentary inquiry into African affairs. Similarly he passed on trading information to Liverpool—'gold is still the greatest *of all articles* in this golden country'.[3] On occasion there was recourse to Shakespeare, and to Swift during quarrels with Charles Bell, Governor of Anomabu fort: 'I have however somewhere read in Swift and I think it very applicable to this man, vizt. of how small estimation is wealth in the sight of God by his bestowing it on the most unworthy of all mortals.'[4] Brew's personal onslaught on Bell produced a stream of invective that expressed the writer's feelings with vigorous effect. 'Farewell thou wretch of wretches', he ended one letter, 'and believe that I neither am nor never will be, Your humble servant.'[5]

Life at Castle Brew, bringing to West Africa the embellishments of the Georgian age in furnishing, silverware, china, pictures, and books, had a decidedly turbulent side. While Brew's own character and his quick temper, perhaps due to Irish blood, contributed to this, it must be emphasized that

[1] See pp. 94–7 above.

[2] Richard Brew to Liverpool merchants, 1 July 1770 in *A Treatise upon the Trade from Great Britain to Africa*, App. H.

[3] Richard Brew to William Devaynes, 2 May 1770, T. 70/1531; the same to Liverpool merchants, 15 Oct. 1771 in *A Treatise upon the Trade from Great Britain to Africa*, App. H.

[4] Richard Brew to William Devaynes, 2 May 1770, T. 70/1531; the same to David Mill, 20 Dec. 1774, T. 70/1532.

[5] Richard Brew to Charles Bell, 23 Jan. 1771, T. 70/1531.

friction was a marked feature of the European trading community of the time. A small and restricted society, driven to hard and competitive bargaining with African middlemen, there is little wonder that its tensions found an outlet in displays of animosity and back-biting. This was true of the officers in the British forts, and concern was expressed in London at the 'want of a good Understanding' among them.[1] It was no less true of private traders both in their dealings with each other and with the British and Dutch administrations. Coastal existence was narrow and enclosed, the companionship too unvaried, gossiping rife—at Cape Coast Castle, according to Westgate, conversation seldom turned on anything other than scandal—incidents were magnified out of proportion, and friendships were precarious.[2]

Brew's personal relations, uncertain and fluctuating as they were, substantiate this. The good terms he maintained with Westgate were temporarily interrupted by a dispute over claims on the partnership, after Westgate had returned to the coast, and were then restored.[3] With the British and Dutch in the forts there were constant stormy passages throughout the years, although this did not preclude business transactions and a measure of friendship with Richard Miles, and with Jan Woortman, who was in command at Kormantin.[4] But sometimes a quarrel reached the point of bordering on violence. During an argument at Castle Brew with Horatio Smith, Brew lost his temper and struck him. Smith eventually refused to live in the house and stayed at Cape Coast Castle before returning to England to report the matter to the assignees.[5] Wrangling between Brew and his nearest neighbour, Governor Charles Bell of Anomabu fort, over a slighting remark in 1774 about the state of Brew's credit, almost culminated in a duel at the beginning of the next year. Bell, who suspected that his neighbour had shaken a cane at him in a 'menacing posture' as he walked under his awning

---

[1] Committee to Governor and Council, Cape Coast Castle, 7 Aug. 1759, T. 70/29, f. 179.

[2] Thomas Westgate to Richard Brew, 10 Aug. 1770, T. 70/1536, pt. 2.

[3] See pp. 66–7 above.

[4] Thomas Westgate to Richard Brew, 28 Oct. 1768, T. 70/1536, pt. 2 and see pp. 74, 97 above and 105 below.

[5] Richard Brew to Samuel Smith's assignees, 30 March 1776, T. 70/1534 and see p. 90 above.

at the fort, offered 'that satisfaction which one gentleman owes another in such cases'. Brew accepted the challenge, the time and weapons to be Bell's own choice. Only an apology by the Governor for the offence he had given prevented them from settling their differences in combat.[1]

In spite of such incidents, it would be wrong to suppose that coastal society was entirely devoid of humane qualities. At Castle Brew, glimpses can be obtained of a day-to-day existence that had harmonious as well as fractious aspects, and they reveal the interdependence of a minority far removed from its home environment. Between Brew and his neighbours, whether at Anomabu, Cape Coast, Tantumkweri, or Winneba there was frequent communication, primarily by letter which a messenger would deliver, although occasional visiting took place. At times of illness or emergency, assistance would be offered or sought. Hence Westgate suggested to Brew, who had been unwell, that he should convalesce by taking a sea trip down to Winneba, and there was an appeal for help to Miles when Castle Brew suffered damage in the rainy season and Brew needed labour to repair it.[2] Inquiries and advice about health were exchanged. Brew was told that he ought to have more exercise and avoid indigestible foods such as yam, and he and Westgate reminded each other not to neglect the daily dose of bark, a preventive against fever.[3] Gifts of food were made, and the loan of books, newspapers, and magazines requested. For a Christmas present in 1773, Westgate received a sheep and a turkey from Brew, and warned the donor in his letter of thanks to beware of 'Xmas. gambols' with the Dutch factor, Jan Woortman, who by reputation 'used to foil even the Danes Parson at his own weapons—brandy and latin'.[4] The arrival of a ship on the coast bringing fresh supplies and perhaps a consignment of

[1] Correspondence between Richard Brew, Charles Bell and David Mill, 19 and 20 Dec. 1774, T. 70/1532; correspondence between Richard Brew and Charles Bell, 5 and 6 Jan. 1775, T. 70/1533.
[2] Thomas Westgate to Richard Brew, 10 Aug. 1773, T. 70/1536, pt. 2; Richard Brew to Richard Miles, 14 June 1776, T. 70/1534.
[3] Thomas Westgate to Richard Brew, 25 June and 10 Aug. 1773, T. 70/1536, pt. 2; Richard Brew to Thomas Westgate, 2 June 1774, T. 70/1532. For a discussion of the use of chinchona bark, see P. D. Curtin, *The Image of Africa* (Madison, 1964), pp. 192–5.
[4] Thomas Westgate to Richard Brew, 7 and 18 Aug. 1770, 14 Oct. and 28 Dec. 1773, T. 70/1536, pt. 2.

newspapers from Europe was always a welcome event. Twenty hampers of 'fine potatoes' were landed at Cape Coast in October 1775. They were intended for the provisioning of another vessel, the *Peggy*, due shortly, but Governor Mill 'made free to break one', and offered a supply to Miles and Brew if they would send over a canoe.[1]

A settler's personal life, never far removed from business matters, could not pursue a solely European course. The African environment exerted influence, and with Brew to a degree that drew him into Fanti affairs more intensively than any of his contemporaries. Central to this was his relationship with John Currantee of Anomabu, and with John Currantee's family.[2] When and in what circumstances the relationship began is not known. But by 1756, after a spell as a private trader at Mumford to the east of Anomabu, Brew was already considered, in European circles, to exercise the 'remarkable ascendant' over John Currantee's mind that justified his appointment as Governor of the new fort.[3] Aided by a knowledge of the vernacular, an extremely useful attribute, and of Fanti custom, he retained this reputation of unusual standing in indigenous society, even after the caboceer's death. There is little doubt that his position owed much to the fact that he took as his 'wench' Effua Ansah, one of John Currantee's daughters, and sister, therefore, to William Ansah, who had been prominent in the fort-building negotiations of the early seventeen-fifties.[4] By contracting a suitable local 'marriage', and strengthening his personal links with a source of power, Brew added to the tactical advantages he enjoyed among European traders.

The role of 'wenches' on the coast at this time requires emphasis as an important social aspect of Afro-European relations. While fleeting liaisons were sometimes contracted, there were few resident traders, lacking white female company, who did not enter into a more settled relationship with a local woman. This was a form of 'marriage' which might persist as long as the trader remained in West Africa.[5] Responsibility was often

---

[1] Richard Brew to Thomas Eagles, 10 Nov. 1774, T. 70/1532; David Mill to Richard Miles, 20 Oct. 1775, T. 70/1534.   [2] See pp. 13–15 above.
[3] See pp. 43–4 above.   [4] See pp. 20–1 and 40 above.
[5] For a nineteenth-century account of 'country marriage', see G. E. Brooks Jr., 'The Letter Book of Captain Edward Harrington' in *Transactions of the Historical Society of Ghana*, vol. VI (1963), pp. 76–7.

assumed for the 'wench' and for her offspring, and the 'country marriage' was treated seriously as a regular feature of the coastal way of life. Bequests were made in wills. One bequest was worded thus: 'in consideration of her strict attention and attendance on me during the three years we have lived together the sum of £20 sterling to be paid her in gold dust at the rate of four pounds sterling per ounce ... together with 2 gold rings which belong to me as a token of remembrance'.[1]

Nor did interest necessarily end when the trader left the coast. In 1778 Richard Miles passed on the news to ex-Governor-in-Chief Petrie that his 'little family' were all well. In Accra his 'wench' was still pursuing her 'old trade of bead stringing', while his mulatto daughter had made him a grandfather. Education in England for offspring was sometimes envisaged and put into effect. Miles spoke of plans for bringing Petrie's son, Bob, with him when he returned home; his subsequent remarks in a letter shortly after arrival in London can be taken to refer to Miles's own children. Harry had arrived 'quite hearty and well', he wrote to a coastal correspondent, and would go next week to a boarding school at Hillingdon where some of the younger branches of the Miles family had been educated, and where he would certainly be well looked after. More unusual was the intention Miles expressed of having 'Sal' with him in England. 'You may tell the mother but as I am not yet settled I let her remain. Should I go to the Coast next year I can bring her of [sic] with me.'[2]

Richard Brew's association with Effua Ansah was one that secured local recognition. In origin it may date from the early seventeen-fifties when he was at Tantumkweri and Mumford, or possibly even earlier; there is no decisive way of knowing. Certainly she was well established during the Castle Brew era. He had children by her: a mulatto daughter who was given the name Eleanor, and another, who was called in Fanti fashion, Amba. They were baptized in 1767 by the Reverend Philip Quaque at their father's 'earnest desire', although how old they

<hr>

[1] Copy of Wills, Committee of Merchants trading to Africa, 1792–1829, ADM. 1/705 (G.N.A.).
[2] Richard Miles to Gilbert Petrie, 16 July 1778 and 10 Aug. 1779, T. 70/1483, ff. 130, 225; Richard Miles to a coastal correspondent, 10 Nov. 1780, T. 70/1483.

were then is not apparent.[1] Brew named these two daughters
and their mother as beneficiaries in his will, and it was their
claims which Richard Miles thought would have to be met
because of the support they would receive from Effua Ansah's
relative Amonu Kuma, chief caboceer of Anomabu. The executors further acknowledged them as members of Brew's family
by a gift of four gallons of rum with which to celebrate his
funeral custom in accordance with local practice, the cost of
this being charged to the estate.[2] It is interesting to note that
earlier in 1776, when Effua Ansah's mother had died, Brew
then accepted responsibilities within the social framework of
Fanti by making that contribution to the deceased's funeral
expenses incumbent on family and friends, and obtained 'Blue
Bafts' for the purpose.[3]

Whether or not Effua Ansah was also the mother of his sons
Richard and Harry, the former for a time clerk in the business,
and the latter the perpetuator of the Brew line in Fanti, is unknown; the boys do not figure in their father's will. They were
given an English education, from which they returned in 1768,
and it can be assumed that they were older than Eleanor and
Amba and would have been born during Brew's first years on
the coast. Unless his relationship with Effua Ansah goes back
as far as this, another 'wench' must have been their mother.[4]

At Castle Brew over the years, there was accordingly a mixed
household, the family—to whom Westgate sent compliments
in his letters—trading associates such as Webster and Horatio
Smith, and a domestic staff including a cook, a principal
servant, and house slaves.[5] The visitors received there were
similarly mixed. Ships' captains from Liverpool and Rhode
Island were among them, combining business with the pleasures

---

[1] Philip Quaque to the S.P.G., 7 March 1767; Richard Brew's will, 3 Aug.
1776.

[2] Richard Brew's will, 3 Aug. 1776; Executors' Accounts, entry dd. 5 Aug. 1776,
T. 70/1504; Richard Miles and Jerome Bernard Weuves to Committee, 10 Sept.
1776, T. 70/32, f. 38 and see pp. 18–19 above. Effua Ansah's name appears as
'Ephiansa' in the will, and as 'Ephuansah' in the Executors' Accounts.

[3] Richard Brew to S. Gwyther, 7 May 1776, T. 70/1534.

[4] Thomas Westgate to Richard Brew, 28 Oct. 1768, T. 70/1536, pt. 2. There is
mention of 'Attah', a wench of Mr. Brew's, in 1751, when he was at Dixcove; entry
dd. 19 April 1751, T. 70/1467, f. 118.

[5] Thomas Westgate to Richard Brew, 7 Aug. and 8 Sept. 1770, T. 70/1536, pt.
2; Executors' Accounts, T. 70/1504. See also pp. 65, 69–70 above.

of Brew's table, bringing new arrivals to West Africa, information from the outside world, and perhaps a particular item—shoes, slippers, or trinkets—which Brew had ordered in England or had had repaired there.[1]

Among African visitors one must be singled out for special mention: the Reverend Philip Quaque, who was for half a century chaplain at Cape Coast Castle. A Fanti educated in England, and the first African to be ordained in the Anglican Church, Quaque began his mission at Cape Coast in 1766. He visited Anomabu for the first time on 2 January 1767, and stayed for one week in Castle Brew on the 'kind Recommendation' of Samuel Smith whom he must have met in London through the African Committee. On Sunday he held divine service in its 'most noble Hall', and read prayers and preached a sermon to a 'very good Audience . . . both White and Black'. It was after the service that he baptized Brew's mulatto daughters and three others, giving them certificates before his departure.

He described his host, on this occasion, as behaving 'in the most polite manner imaginable'. Subsequently, however, there was a rift and some 'trifling words'. Brew expressed his annoyance, according to Quaque, by telling the Govenor of Anomabu that he would never come to Cape Coast 'to be Subservient to and to sit under the Nose of a Black Boy to hear Him pointing or laying out their faults before them'. But harmony was eventually restored. On Trinity Sunday 1770 the Cape Coast chaplain again conducted evening service at Castle Brew, during which he baptized the infant child of Captain Ebenezer Price, one of Brew's close trading acquaintances, in the presence of 'several Liverpool Captains and others'.[2] Between the Brew and Quaque families a marriage connection was also formed through Harry, Richard's son. This was significant for the future. From it there sprang the Brew family, notable in the history of nineteenth-century Fanti.[3]

[1] Thomas Westgate to Richard Brew, 28 Oct. 1768, T. 70/1536, pt. 2; Philip Quaque to the S.P.G., 27 Sept. 1770.
[2] Philip Quaque to the S.P.G., 7 March 1767, 1767 [sic], and 27 Sept. 1770 and see p. 21 ff. above. Richard Brew and Horatio Smith also attended a service at Cape Coast Castle in 1775; Philip Quaque to the S.P.G., 30 July 1775.
[3] Thomas Westgate to Richard Brew, 24 Sept. 1770, T. 70/1536, pt. 2 and see p. 119 ff. below.

At his Anomabu residence, too, Brew conducted the flamboyant excursion into African politics that illuminates so clearly the nature of his local connections.[1] Through influence, liberal gifts, bludgeoning tactics, and manœuvring, he was able to intervene in disputes between the Ashanti and Fanti, and secure for himself the diplomatic asset of custody of one of the King of Ashanti's close relatives. On first entering Fanti territory in 1765 in pursuit of the Akim, Osei Kojo had guaranteed peaceful intentions towards his Fanti allies by handing over a member of his family as hostage. Later, when friction and fighting developed with the Fanti, he despatched emissaries in an attempt to discover the grounds of their hostility. The emissaries, too, were retained on the coast and not allowed to return. Between 1765 and 1772, when rumours of another invasion from inland periodically disturbed the European forts, Osei Kojo continued to stipulate the return of the hostages, of whom his own relative was the most important, as the essential condition of a settlement to end prevailing discord.[2]

During the negotiations of the coastal and interior states, which were rendered more tortuous by European mediation, Brew gave ample demonstration of the strength of his foothold among the Fanti. The earliest instance of this occurred when they handed over to him the royal hostage, Osei Kojo's 'cousin german, a fine young fellow of about 20. . . . This young man the Fanty Caboceers and Punins . . . deposited in Castle Brew, in preference to Cape Coast or Elmina. As for Anomabu fort, it was never thought of', wrote Brew with pride. The guardianship, it should be observed, had devolved on him through the medium of John Currantee's family.[3] Next he induced the Fanti to allow him charge of further Ashanti prisoners. He then despatched an embassy to Osei Kojo submitting peace proposals and offering his services as an intermediary with Fanti. The connivance of one or two Fanti caboceers enabled

---

[1] See pp. 73–4 and 93–4 above.
[2] Priestley, 'Richard Brew: an eighteenth century trader at Anomabu' in *Transactions of the Historical Society of Ghana*, vol. IV, pt. I (1959), pp. 38–42 and 'The Ashanti Question and the British: eighteenth century origins' in *Journal of African History*, vol. II, no. 1 (1961), pp. 42–53.
[3] J. P. T. Huydecooper to William Mutter, 28 Aug. 1765, C.O. 388/53; Donnan, *Documents Illustrative of the Slave Trade to America*, vol. II, p. 528.

the embassy to proceed into the interior, although others were said to have been ignorant of the episode.[1]

Three years later, in 1768, Brew achieved the most signal of his diplomatic triumphs over the British establishment. This was at a cost to himself, according to Governor Petrie, of £1,200, since the Fanti were very quick to take advantage of three rival negotiators and very willing to elongate the process of settlement. Informing Petrie that they were prepared to exclude the Dutch from a share in peace-making, they suggested that he should join forces with Mr. Brew in bringing it to a conclusion. Brew rejected 'with the utmost disdain' the Governor's proposal to associate him in a subordinate capacity. When the elders of Anomabu appealed to the Fanti Oracle, their highest counsel, for guidance on the return of the hostages to Osei Kojo,[2] the outcome turned eventually in Brew's favour. They were instructed to deliver the hostages to Cape Coast Castle for repatriation. But 'Mr. Brew's profusion prevailed over the power of the Deity'. Instead the elders directed *him* to send one back to Ashanti and to keep the other until such time as the maintenance expenses, which he now audaciously claimed from its King, had been met.

In consequence, Osei Kojo's relative remained at Castle Brew until 1771, and was only released then under pressure from the Fanti who agreed to stand security for the claim. Needless to say, it never received any satisfaction, and the lengthy detention of the hostage incurred strong disapproval in London, where it was regarded as the cause of another invasion scare in 1772.[3] By way of concrete results, Brew's expensive diplomatic adventure had achieved little. Its significance lies in the evidence it affords of his Fanti role and of European entanglement, for commercial reasons, in the politics of the Gold Coast.

A final assessment of Brew must stress the fact that he exemplifies, in well-defined form, many of the characteristics of eighteenth-century coastal existence. Not least of these was the

---

[1] Richard Brew and William Webster to William Mutter, 14 Sept. 1765 and Mutter's comments on the letter, C.O. 388/53; William Mutter to Committee, 14 Dec. 1765, T. 70/31, f. 154; Gilbert Petrie to Committee, 21 Oct. 1678, ibid. f. 312.   [2] See p. 11 above.

[3] Priestley, 'Richard Brew: an eighteenth century trader at Anomabu' in *Transactions of the Historical Society of Ghana*, vol. IV, pt. I (1959), pp. 40–2.

intermingling of the European and African ways of life, with the African way often imposing its pattern. In so far as Brew was unusual, it was in scale rather than in kind, in the extent of his integration with Fanti, the magnitude of the trading empire he envisaged, and the degree of bravado which his methods reveal. There was a touch of the feudal lord about his behaviour and mode of living, the result perhaps of an Irish background. Castle Brew symbolizes this. In temperament, he was an extreme individualist, a tough but not uncultured adventurer with a capacity for adapting to a different environment—hence his thirty years on the west coast. Like other settlers, Brew hoped to return home in due course well endowed materially, and he enlarged at times on the difficulties besetting him in West Africa. The Fanti, long adept at striking a hard bargain, came in for their full share of European criticism here.[1] But the statement made by a ship's captain in the seventeen-forties, after being stationed for over a year at Anomabu, must also have been applicable in the case of Brew: 'I plainly find the Coast has a greater power over me than ever.'[2] Not only in the eighteenth century has this proved to be so.

Immersed as he was in the slave trade, there is little in his attitude to suggest anything other than the acceptance of it typical of both European and African participants. Its joint operators viewed it as an economic concern. Brew's comment in one letter that he was 'a friend to Liberty', and mortally hated 'logs and chains' although living in the midst of slavery, must not be interpreted to mean condemnation of the trade. Rather is it a reference to the need to free himself, in a business sense, from the Smith partnership by paying his share of the debts.[3] Along with the European approach to slavery went a relative absence of racial or religious superiority. Settlers came to trade, not to colonize or convert, and Brew would appear to have been very representative. That the impact he made on coastal affairs was of considerable force becomes apparent from British and Dutch remarks in 1776 after his death. This event

[1] Richard Brew to Richard Miles, 22 Feb. 1776, T. 70/1534; Priestley, 'The Ashanti Question and the British: eighteenth century origins' in *Journal of African History*, vol. II, no. 1 (1961), p. 50.

[2] Gill, *Merchants and Mariners of the Eighteenth Century*, p. 84.

[3] Richard Brew to William Devaynes, 2 May 1770, T. 70/1531 and see pp. 62–5 above.

had 'occasioned no small Revolution' at Anomabu, wrote the Governor-in-Chief from Cape Coast Castle, while at Elmina the Dutch looked forward to an era of peace now that one so 'notorious' had left the earthly scene.[1] Yet the name of Brew was not to be eliminated from the coast. The subject himself of acculturation, a line of descendants emerged who would achieve prominence in Fanti society as harbingers of change and modernization, and it is to these descendants that attention must next be directed.

[1] P. Woortman to Assembly of the X, 26 Sept. 1776, W.I.C. 119; David Mill to Committee, 19 Oct. 1776, T. 70/32, f. 41.

PART THREE

The Fanti Brews

CHAPTER I

Richard Brew's Descendants

Among educated African families on the Gold Coast during the nineteenth and early twentieth centuries, the Brews of Fanti are notable for the part they played in trade, law, and public affairs. Centred on Cape Coast and Anomabu, and connected by marriage with families of like kind, the Brews reflect, over several generations, the changing economic, political, and social scene on the west coast. Their oldest members today provide links with the last decades of the nineteenth century and are a source of family tradition.[1] Combining this with written records, it becomes possible to trace lines of descent over a hundred and fifty years, and to reconstruct, in their main features, the careers of some outstanding Brews. In no single case is the material as detailed and evocative as for their eighteenth-century Irish progenitor. The setting and circumstances are those of African society, and the records mainly official and legal rather than personal. Yet despite these limitations, and the fact that the picture does not lend itself, in all aspects, to equal precision of treatment, impressions can undoubtedly be formed of a number of distinctive personalities.

The interest and value of Brew family tradition lies more in the general atmosphere it conveys, and the evidence of integration in African society, than in detailed information. Elderly members of the family, one of them born in 1880, constantly express regret that memories now are so limited, and those who were knowledgeable about the past no longer alive. Every New Year's Day, they say, at gatherings of the family, the elders used to recount its history, but nothing was ever written down.

The attempt to penetrate the past through the present brings

[1] I am much indebted to members of the Brew family and to others in Ghana who have kindly provided information used in this and subsequent chapters.

difficulties, too, because of the similarity of the Brew naming pattern. From the late eighteenth century to the twentieth, the Christian names Richard, Harry, and Samuel have been used with such regularity as to cause confusion,[1] and it is often far from easy to establish which particular person is under discussion as 'the old man' or 'old Brew'. Information about one predecessor may be remembered with much more clarity than about another of the same period. Earlier relationships tend to be defined loosely by generation rather than by precise kinship terms—a characteristic of the Fanti extended family[2]—and the time sequence is often hazy and telescoped. Among the Brews, there is both an awareness of and a pride in their family history. This history, however, is 'corporate' rather than strongly individualist in nature.

On one point of tradition, all consulted have been in agreement—namely that the Brews stem, on the male side, from a European ancestor. But the details about him are now blurred with the passage of time. 'We are all descended from Europeans' (*akrampafu*), commented an old lady in the vernacular; the *akrampafu*, modelled on European lines, was the special military company in Cape Coast to which mulattos and their descendants and servants belonged.[3]

An interesting view, expressed on more than one occasion, is that the first Brew came from Scotland. The origins of this may lie in attempts made by the family, probably during the early part of the present century, to trace their ancestry; the investigator's attention, it is said, was directed to Scotland, although he died before being able to complete the inquiry.[4] Frequently stressed, too, is the fact of merchant origin and of trading activity in the family, with the Christian name of the ancestor and the moment of his arrival in West Africa from Europe, subjects of uncertainty. Henry and Collins are suggested as possibilities, never Richard, and the white forebear whose local marriage brought the Brew family into existence is accorded a place in a timeless past. The Akan setting has predominated, and the

[1] See Appendix (a) and (b), pp. 199–200.

[2] Christensen, *Double Descent among the Fanti*, p. 20.

[3] J. C. de Graft Johnson, 'The Fanti Asafu' in *Africa*, vol. V (1932), pp. 310, 321 and see p. 18 above.

[4] The reference here is to J. E. Casely Hayford. His uncle, James Hutton Brew, is also said to have been interested in Brew ancestry; see p. 102 n. 4 above.

Brews who probed their European ancestry were at the same
time in the forefront of the Fanti cultural movement.[1] Yet
emphasis on the male line of descent, in a matrilineal society,
has certainly contributed to the growth of more westernized
elements in the family structure.[2]

To reconstruct a family history over several generations from
the patchwork of present memories alone would not be feasible;
fortunately, written records provide further clarification. In the
main, these records fall into the official rather than the private
category. Little is available in the way of family papers beyond
the occasional letter, Bible, and birthday book, and the docu-
mentation, sometimes of a genealogical nature, connected with
legal cases and arbitration.[3]

On the official side, the legal records are the most fruitful
as a source of information, not only for relationships but for
chronology, insight into the activities of different Brews, and
trends of development in society. Especially important and
revealing are the reports of property disputes in the nineteenth
and early twentieth centuries.[4] Genealogy becomes extremely
significant when inheritance is at stake, and although during
the court evidence it was largely memory that was being tapped,
this was at closer range to the relevant events and personalities
than it would be today. A very elderly witness in the first
decade of the twentieth century, for example, could recall a
Brew who had been born in the seventeen-seventies and had
died about 1849, and she herself was the repository of much
family history from her grandmother.[5] Social change, in-
tensifying after two world wars, had not as yet seriously
weakened traditional channels of communication.

When the extensive legal material is used for genealogical

[1] See p. 118 n. 4 above and p. 190 below.
[2] See p. 182 ff. below.
[3] Among private records, the papers of J. E. Casely Hayford, a grandson of
Samuel Collins Brew, form a major exception. These papers still await investigation.
It is possible that they contain material relevant particularly to James Hutton
Brew, Casely Hayford's uncle, and closely associated with him in journalism.
[4] Considerable use has been made of the extensive and varied Records of the
High Court, Cape Coast (abbreviated hereafter as H.C.C.C.) for Part 3 of this
study. These Records are contained in the Ghana National Archives, Accra.
[5] Sarah Wood v. Kwamina Buachee and others, 14 Feb. 1908, H.C.C.C.
323/52. The reference is to Richard Brew, grandson of the Irish trader. See pp.
125–6 below.

purposes and Brew origins traced back to the eighteenth century, Harry, and not his father Richard, appears as the founder of the family. Richard receives no mention at all.[1] The end of the eighteenth and early part of the nineteenth century must be regarded as the period of greatest obscurity in Brew history, a time when the lineage was establishing itself in Fanti, against a background that was economically and politically disturbed as a result of the abolition of the slave trade in 1807 and the Ashanti coastal invasions.[2] Indeed, even in the circumstances of more sharply defined memory some decades ago, an element of doubt had existed about Harry Brew. Had he been a European or a mulatto? Two versions of the family tree, in private hands today, conflict on this point. In one, he is given as a 'mulatto', a word which is then crossed out and replaced by 'European'. In the other, exactly the reverse applies.[3] During the first years of the twentieth century, lawsuits generally portray him as a white man, but the evidence of a leading witness, born in 1822 and praised by the court for her remarkable memory, seems at least on one occasion to be ambiguous.[4] Both from the angle of present-day family tradition, and of recorded genealogy, there is a distinct lack of precision about the European ancestry of the Fanti Brews.

In working out a Brew line, considerable significance attaches, therefore, to Harry, son of the Irish Richard. Sporadic though the information is about Harry Brew, a link can be made between the material of the nineteenth and twentieth centuries and that of the eighteenth century. Although the 'Brew line' implies a non-Akan approach in tracing ancestry back to a male forebear,[5] it is from the matrilineal side of the family, as a result of Harry Brew's marriage, that the vital clues of relationship

---

[1] The following cases are particularly useful in establishing Brew genealogy: Mansah v. Thompson, 1 Sept. 1904, H.C.C.C. 320/52; Sarah Wood v. Kwamina Buachee and others, 14 Feb. 1908, H.C.C.C. 323/52 (this includes a Brew family tree); Sarah Wood v. Mrs. Maud Thompson, 18 Dec. 1908 in P. A. Renner, *Cases in the Courts of the Gold Coast Colony and Nigeria*, vol. I, pt. 2 (London, 1915), pp. 802–4; Sarah Wood v. Kwamina Buachee and others. 11 Dec. 1909, H.C.C.C. 324/52. See also n. 3 below, which refers to versions of the family tree.

[2] See p. 129 ff. below.

[3] I am grateful to Mr. P. J. Bartels for access to these documents.

[4] Sarah Wood v. Kwamina Buachee and others, 14 Feb. 1908, H.C.C.C. 323/52 and see n. 1 above.

[5] See pp. 17–18 above.

are derived. Of central importance is the fact that Harry's wife, Abba Kaybah, the mother of his children, belonged to the same family, along the female line of descent, as did the Reverend Philip Quaque. During the nineteenth and twentieth centuries, property disputes involving the Brews occasioned references in the court evidence to Quaque, who was described as their 'uncle'. These disputes also caused the Brews to be traced back, over several generations, to the union of Abba Kaybah and the 'white man', Harry Brew.[1]

Turning to the eighteenth-century records, attention must be drawn to a description of Harry Brew, Richard's son, as a relation of 'Parson Quaque'.[2] The source of this important comment, which was made in 1770, was Thomas Westgate, Richard's former partner, now back on the Gold Coast and corresponding with his old friend at Anomabu;[3] it can be assumed that marriage underlay the Brew–Quaque relationship to which he referred. Also to be noted is the fact that in 1792 'Henry Brew' was appointed linguist at Cape Coast Castle, a post once held by Cudjo Caboceer with whom Philip Quaque had had kinship ties.[4] This would suggest that through his wife's family, Harry Brew was brought into contact with the most influential trading circles of Cape Coast. Combining these various strands of evidence, it seems justifiable to consider Harry Brew, the son of Richard and a relation of Philip Quaque, Henry or 'Harry' Brew, linguist at Cape Coast Castle, and the Harry Brew who married Abba Kaybah as one and the same person.

Of the four known children of the Irish Richard—Eleanor, Amba, Richard Junior, and Harry—only through Harry can a chain of descent be established. Nothing further is heard about Brew's daughters, Eleanor and Amba, after their mention in connection with their father's will and the settlement of his estate.[5] In the case of Richard, Junior, possibly the elder of the two boys, contemporary documents give rather more information.

[1] See, for example, G. E. Hooper v. H. Brew, 11 Jan. 1881, H.C.C.C. 287/52 and p. 120 n. 1 above.
[2] Thomas Westgate to Richard Brew, 24 Sept. 1770, T. 70/1536, pt. 2.
[3] See pp. 65–6 above.
[4] Entry dd. 12 June 1792, T. 70/153, f. 205 and see pp. 15–16, 21–2 above.
[5] See p. 86 above.

Richard differed from his brother, Harry, in that he failed to secure an established place in local society, and his career was decidedly a chequered one. Receiving a 'liberal education' in England, he returned to West Africa in 1768 and entered the Castle Brew concern as a clerk. Later he was disowned, because he 'gave himself up so entirely to all Kinds of Debauchery, that his Father was under the Necessity of turning him out of Doors, after which he lived like a Vagabond amongst the Natives'. A period of poverty ensued. He was then employed in the service of the African Committee at Anomabu fort as a gunner, and in 1781 at Cape Coast Castle as a writer, where his accounting abilities received special mention from the Council.[1] Richard's ultimate fate is not known. He may have been the 'English deserter Richard Broûw' whose death was reported by the Dutch at Elmina on 14 June 1782, in the circumstances of Anglo-Dutch conflict during the War of American Independence.[2]

Perpetuation of the Brews accordingly stems from Harry and his children by Abba Kaybah in the late eighteenth century, the scene, Anomabu and Cape Coast with their busy trading communities. Harry must have been born about 1750 or perhaps a little earlier, and it was almost certainly he who was educated in England along with Richard, Junior. The sons rejoined their father on the west coast in 1768.[3] By September 1770, according to Thomas Westgate's comment, Harry must have been married, since the Quaque link was then in existence.[4] It should be observed that the Reverend Philip Quaque had first visited Castle Brew from Cape Coast in 1767 on the recommendation of Samuel Smith, and that he was there again in 1770.[5]

A gap of twenty-two years follows before further information comes to light about Harry Brew, and he is then found on the Cape Coast Castle establishment. The appointment of a mulatto writer, 'Henry Brew', to be assistant linguist there dates from 1 April 1792.[6] During the interval, Harry probably engaged in

[1] Thomas Westgate to Richard Brew, 28 Oct. 1768, T. 70/1536, pt. 2; entry dd. 22 Dec. 1780, T. 70/145, ff. 13-14; entry dd. 2 July 1781, T. 70/152, f. 109.
[2] Elmina Journal, entry dd. 14 June 1782, W.I.C. 990.
[3] Thomas Westgate to Richard Brew, 28 Oct. 1768, T. 70/1536, pt. 2.
[4] See p. 121 above.
[5] See pp. 109 above.   [6] Entry dd. 12 June 1792, T. 70/153, f. 205.

trade, and moved to Cape Coast from Anomabu where his father had died in 1776.[1] These facts, of course, imply that he did not enter the Committee's service until his forties, whereas the post of writer was one frequently sought after by younger men, European, African, and mulatto. The special duties that attached to it in this instance must be noted, however. For the position of linguist, age would certainly be an advantage, and the Council's description of Henry Brew as 'the best Interpreter' to be found in the country,[2] suggesting fluency in English and the vernacular, is further evidence of his qualifications for the job.

Other circumstances convey the impression of a man of mature years. After the death of Aggrey, the chief linguist, in 1793,[3] Henry Brew's importance increased. Designated 'Mr. Brew' in a British report, he was the bearer of messages from Cape Coast Castle to powerful chiefs such as Amonu Kuma of Anomabu, and his application for a rise in salary from £60 to £80 per annum was supported by the Governor and Council on the grounds of his attentiveness to duty.[4] When a smallpox epidemic caused his death on 4 March 1796, the Castle authorities regarded the event as a public loss. He had allowed all his family to be inoculated by the surgeon—numbers of Africans received this treatment at Cape Coast—but could not be persuaded himself to take advantage of the facilities.[5] Had it not been for inoculation, the 'Brew dynasty' in Fanti might have come to an untimely end.

Counting Harry as the first-generation descendant of Richard, a family tree extending over six generations can be built up, growing in complexity from the second half of the nineteenth century.[6] Among its special features are the Christian names adopted from one generation to the next; their European

[1] See p. 81 above.
[2] Entry dd. 12 June 1792, T. 70/153, f. 205.
[3] See p. 19 above.
[4] Archibald Dalzel to Committee, 15 May 1795, T. 70/33, f. 474; Secretary, Cape Coast Castle to William Douglas, 4 Aug. 1795, ADM. 1/702 (G.N.A.); entry dd. 4 Aug. 1795, T. 70/1067; Committee to Governor and Council, Cape Coast Castle, 3 Dec. 1795, T. 70/71, f. 167. The African Committee refused the increase on the grounds of shortage of funds. According to the Garrison Ledger for Cape Coast Castle, Henry Brew's salary was £40 p.a.; see T. 70/1369, f. 26.
[5] Archibald Dalzel to Committee, 12 March 1796, T. 70/33, f. 500.
[6] See Appendix (a) and (b), pp. 199–200.

rather than their Fanti names are those by which the Brews are
generally denoted in the records. 'Richard', for example, has
been persistently used up to the present, as among the Brews
of County Clare during the eighteenth and nineteenth centuries.[1] 'Harry', too, figures with like frequency, but in this case
without an Irish parallel. The name first occurs when Richard
Brew's mulatto son was so called. 'Samuel' belongs to the
second generation of descendants, and was the name given by
Harry to one of his sons. The other was called 'Richard'. Thus,
before the end of the eighteenth century, 'Richard', 'Harry',
and 'Samuel' were already in use among the Fanti Brews.
Other family names were introduced in the nineteenth century,
notably 'James', together with additional surnames such as
'Collins' and 'Hutton'. A composite version then indicated the
particular branch of descent, for example, Samuel Collins Brew,
Richard Collins Brew, James Hutton Brew, Samuel Henry Brew,
and Richard Henry Brew. In the case of daughters, a less regular
pattern seems to have been followed, although 'Maria' recurs,
and also 'Elizabeth' and 'Henrietta'.

These names often have a significance, now sometimes
difficult to determine, in connection with Brew family history.
'Richard' is self-evident, since it comes from the first inhabitant
of Castle Brew. 'Harry', 'Samuel', and 'James' are less easy to
explain, although 'Samuel' lends itself to an interesting line of
speculation. It was bestowed by Harry Brew on one of the sons
he had by Abba Kaybah, and may have been taken from his
wife's family. The existence there of a mulatto called Samuel
Smith, the same name as Richard Brew's London partner, is
on record.[2] Among other Brew names, 'Collins' and 'Hutton',
the former of Irish association, were derived from traders on the
coast. On the female side, 'Maria' can be associated with Eccua
Maria, the mother of Samuel Smith and an important figure in
the family to which Abba Kaybah belonged.[3]

The union of Harry Brew and Abba Kaybah, crucial as it
was in the development of a Brew dynasty, resulted in three
children—two sons, Richard and Samuel, and a daughter,

[1] See pp. 31–2 above.
[2] Sarah Wood v. Kwamina Buachee and others, 14 Feb. 1908, H.C.C.C. 323/52
and see p. 59 ff. above. Samuel Smith is described in the law case as a 'white son'
of his mulatto mother.
[3] See n. 2 above and Renner, op. cit. vol. I, pt. 2, p. 802.

Eyaapah. Only Samuel, commonly known as Sam Kanto, was survived by issue,[1] and for two generations after the Irish trader, continuance of the Brew line hung on a slender thread. With the third generation, two distinctive and identifiable branches fan out through Sam Kanto's sons, Harry Brew and Samuel Collins Brew, born in the first years of the nineteenth century.[2] From Harry, the second of the Brews to be called this, were descended Richard Henry and Samuel Henry and their successors of the same name. From Samuel Collins, whose wives and progeny were considerable in number, arose almost a dynasty in itself, James Hutton Brew, William Ward Brew, and J. E. Casely Hayford being three noted personalities who were closely related to him.

With this fourth generation—the offspring of Harry and of Samuel Collins—the family tree becomes more complex. Marriage of Brew daughters, for example, into such families as the Bannermans and the Hayfords, during the second half of the nineteenth century, created important links between western-educated groups in coast society.[3] Indeed, to trace all subsequent Brew relationships with familes in Cape Coast and Accra would be a mammoth task. Of necessity, a selective approach has been adopted in the present work, determined partly by directness of descent, the impact made on affairs by different individuals, and the availability of information.

Five generations of Fanti Brews, starting with the first Harry, son of the Irish trader, and ranging over a hundred and fifty years are included within the scope of this study. Some merit particular attention because of their part in establishing descent or the prominence of their contemporary role. A case in point, from the former angle, is Richard Brew, the elder son of Harry Brew and Abba Kaybah. His frequent mention in legal records, and the fact that there was still personal memory of him at the beginning of the twentieth century, make him a valuable link in the genealogical chain. One of the descendants of Richard's matrilineal family, who asserted a property claim against the

[1] Renner, op. cit. vol. I, pt. 2, p. 802.
[2] Their exact date of birth is not known. Samuel Collins Brew died in 1881, and Harry Brew in 1890; both were old men. See Acting Puisne Judge to District Commissioner, Saltpond, 17 Feb. 1881, H.C.C.C. 204/52, f. 296; Brew v. Brew, 15 Jan. 1900, H.C.C.C. 310/52.
[3] See p. 186-7 below.

Brews in 1908 when she was eighty-six years old, reported that she had known him in her youth as 'an old man with grey hair'. He had been born in 1778, she said, and had died about 1849.[1] The date of birth, it should be noted, accords well with the assumption, based on eighteenth-century evidence, that his father Harry had married by the seventeen-seventies.[2] This nineteenth-century Richard Brew, who lived to the age of seventy, inherited considerable property subsequently much in dispute. He can be placed at one end of the time-scale in relationship with the Reverend Philip Quaque, his maternal uncle,[3] and at the other end with great-nephews whose lives extended into the present century.

The second angle of approach, prominence of contemporary role, is well illustrated by three successive Brews. They are Sam Kanto Brew, his son Samuel Collins Brew, and Samuel Collins's son, James Hutton Brew, whose deaths occurred in 1823, 1881, and 1915 respectively. Each, during his lifetime, was at the forefront of significant coastal events.

Sam Kanto, the younger son of Harry Brew and Abba Kaybah, belonged to the disturbed period between Britain's abolition of the slave trade in 1807 and the growth of legitimate commerce, when illicit slave trading and Anglo-Ashanti relations were interconnected.[4] Very little about him survives in present-day family tradition, and the main evidence for his activities comes from official documents, with legal material establishing the genealogical links.

The life of his son, Samuel Collins Brew, covered about three-quarters of the nineteenth century. A dominant personality in the age of legitimate commerce and African participation in public affairs, Samuel Collins is more sharply defined than many of the Fanti Brews.[5] The fact that two of his grandchildren are still alive provides a link with the past, while the numerous lines of descent from him open up other avenues of inquiry. Written records, too, add usefully to the picture.

Especially important is the fact of his marriage into the stool family of Abura Dunkwa. An offspring of this marriage was

---

[1] Sarah Wood v. Kwamina Buachee and others, 14 Feb. 1908, H.C.C.C. 323/52.
[2] See p. 121 above.
[3] G. E. Hooper v. H. Brew, 11 Jan. 1881, H.C.C.C. 287/52; Sarah Wood v. Kwamina Buachee and others, 14 Feb. 1908, H.C.C.C. 323/52.
[4] See p. 129 ff. below.   [5] See p. 143 ff. below.

James Hutton Brew, active in Gold Coast politics and journalism during the first two decades of the colonial era, and a herald of west coast nationalism.[1] The name of James Hutton Brew is one widely remembered in modern Ghana.

Over a long period of time, the Brews were among those who experienced the impact of western education. Although the details are often slight, it is clear that the place and level of education, in their case, varied from one generation to another. During the seventeen-sixties, the Irish Richard sent his mulatto sons overseas;[2] the next known instance of this occurred almost a hundred years later. In the early part of the nineteenth century, Richard and Sam Kanto, the sons of Harry Brew, belonged to the small minority known as 'scholars', those who were literate and at least able to read and write. Richard, however, who was designated a 'half scholar', could read only; he and his brother may have acquired these qualifications at the school run by their uncle, Philip Quaque, in Cape Coast Castle.[3]

In the mid-nineteenth century, another Brew received his education in England. This was James Hutton Brew, the son of Samuel Collins, who went there at the age of eight. James Hutton returned to the Gold Coast after several years and practised from 1864 as an attorney.[4] Later, two of his nephews, J. E. Casely Hayford and William Ward Brew, qualified in England as barristers. A professional élite, often trained outside the country, was now beginning to emerge in West Africa and to this the Brews added their quota.

Under missionary influence, the educational facilities inside the Gold Coast also expanded, and secondary education began to develop with Cape Coast as the leading centre.[5] During the eighteen-eighties, James Hutton's relative, Samuel Henry Brew, was educated at the Wesleyan High School, Cape Coast, the prelude to a notable career in government service and to

---

[1] See p. 158 ff. below.

[2] See p. 122 above.

[3] Sarah Wood v. Kwamina Buachee and others, 14 Feb. 1908, H.C.C.C. 323/52 and see pp. 22–3 above.

[4] Acting Chief Justice to J. H. Brew, 30 May 1864, H.C.C.C. 202/52, f. 391; M. J. Sampson, *Gold Coast Men of Affairs* (London, 1937), p. 91.

[5] See Foster, *Education and Social Change in Ghana*, especially pp. 48–106. A number of Gold Coast Africans were also educated in Sierra Leone—at Fourah Bay College, Freetown, founded in 1827.

scholarly activities, particularly of a linguistic kind. In 1904, when a scheme was drawn up for establishing schools in Fanti through private investment in a limited company, Samuel Henry gave it his support, a fitting commentary on the link the Brews had had with education for almost a century and a half.[1]

Once they have been disentangled from the confusion caused by repetitive naming, and have been placed in a genealogical frame of reference, the Brews form a fruitful subject of investigation. In an area whose rich family history is little explored, they throw useful light on some of the long-term effects of European trading settlement.

[1] See pp. 176–8 below.

CHAPTER II

Sam Kanto Brew:
Abolition and the Ashanti Question

Early in the nineteenth century, Fanti experienced two events whose consequences would be profound—abolition of the slave trade by Great Britain, and Ashanti's invasion of the seaboard, the latter expected since the second half of the eighteenth century.[1] Both occurred in 1807, and foreshadowed an era of economic and political disturbance during which the Afro-European relationship of the slave-trading epoch underwent subtle but significant changes. Abolition removed the old *raison d'être* of the British settlements, and over the following decades the need for their continued existence was often called in question. Yet in the process of adjustment to a new pattern of economic activity and to a different balance of power on the coast, the settlements increased rather than diminished their involvement in African affairs.

Termination, by parliamentary enactment, of the slave-trading exchange between African and British merchants was the climax of a movement, dating back to the late eighteenth century, in which the humanitarian element had been strong. But abolition alone was not the sole objective. It was believed that slave trading must be replaced by legitimate commerce as a positive way of drawing Africa into the orbit of the civilized and Christian nations of the world.[2] This view originated at a time when British industrialization necessitated expanding markets for manufactured goods, and evangelical pressure stressed Christian obligation towards Africa. Legitimate commerce thus fulfilled the requirements of both economics and morality. In

[1] See p. 12 above.
[2] See Curtin, *The Image of Africa*, especially pp. 259–86.

practice, however, it was to encounter many difficulties during
the early decades of the century, and to have unforeseen
results.

Foremost among these difficulties was the gulf that existed
between the passage of law at Westminster and its effective
implementation on the west coast. From the standpoint of
Africa, abolition of the external slave trade proved an extremely complex undertaking. Economically, it threatened the
main source of West African wealth, disrupting the network
that linked coastal middleman and inland supplier. Both parties
were closely affected, and naturally reluctant to abandon an
age-old and lucrative practice. Futhermore, it soon became
obvious that despite the British action, slaving outlets still
existed on the coast, through the dealers and shippers of other
nations. In their attempts to establish new forms of exchange,
the British had to counter this European activity, and inside
West Africa, to persuade the middlemen and slave producers
of coast and interior that the African economy must be re-
oriented.

If the goal of legitimate commerce caused local upheaval and
drew the British more deeply into African affairs, so the Ashanti
coastal invasion of 1807 and its aftermath had the same effect.
The possibility of an Ashanti-Fanti clash had long been realized
in the settlements. In 1807 the event occurred, together with a
brief attack by Ashanti on Anomabu fort.[1] Over the next
decade, further invasions altered the political scene in the
maritime area and brought the Fanti states under Ashanti
control, presenting the British with the problem of new relationships at a time of economic revolution on the coast.[2]

As in the eighteenth century, neutrality and trade were
their objectives, but in practice the British faced a dilemma.
They had a long-standing commercial tie with Fanti, in whose
territory the major settlements were to be found. A limited
degree of protection and of commitment to the Fanti cause
might therefore be expected of them.[3] On the other hand,

[1] Col. Torrane to Committee, 12 June and 20 July 1807, T. 70/35.
[2] See G. E. Metcalfe, *Maclean of the Gold Coast* (London, 1962), especially pp.
35–9, and A. A. Boahen, 'Asante, Fante and the British, 1800–1880' in *A Thousand
Years of West African History* (Ibadan, 1965), pp. 341–58.
[3] Priestley, 'The Ashanti Question and the British: eighteenth century origins'
in *Journal of African History*, vol. II, no. 1 (1961), pp. 49–59.

Ashanti's value as a source of gold and ivory, a market for manufactured goods, and a gateway to the interior weighted opinion strongly in favour of developing amicable relations after the 1807 descent on the coast. It was of the 'utmost importance' to be on good terms with the Ashanti King, wrote the African Committee ten years later.[1] During the era of legitimate commerce, the role of Ashanti was to be crucial, as a slaving power with trade potentialities now of a different kind, and as a major political force—a threat to Fanti, where the British had an important sphere of influence.

From the early years of the nineteenth century, the settlements had to adapt to these conditions. The process, a prolonged one, was accompanied by a series of administrative changes. First to be affected was the Company of Merchants trading to Africa, which had existed since 1750. In 1821 it was abolished and the Crown took over responsibility for the settlements. Seven years later, in 1828, they reverted to mercantile control which lasted until 1843, when the Crown resumed direction. After thirty years, in 1874, the settlements and surrounding Protectorate became the newly created Gold Coast Colony, despite earlier reluctance on the part of the home government to increase West African commitments, and its near-abandonment at times of already existing ones. Legitimate trade and Ashanti seaboard incursions had both contributed to the deeper involvement of the British on the coast, where their *de facto* authority preceded the government's formal declaration of colonial status.

Two members of the Brew family, father and son, provide an insight into different aspects of a situation that can be defined in terms of trade and the Ashanti question. Each was himself a trader and their lives spanned the period up to 1881; considering the Brews' ancestral origin, it was only to be expected that mercantile activity would remain a family occupation. Sam Kanto Brew,[2] the elder of the two and a grandson of the first Richard, lived at the turn of the century. He died in 1823, shortly after the Company of Merchants had been dissolved and the forts had been taken under Crown control. Interwoven

[1] Committee to Lord Bathurst, 22 May 1817, T. 70/74, f. 207.
[2] Also known as Samuel Husband Brew, according to copies of the family tree; see p. 120 n. 3 above.

with his life was firstly, the abolition of the slave trade, and secondly, Ashanti pressure on the coastal states, implicating the British as this had done earlier, in the time of Richard Brew.

Between Sam Kanto and his grandfather, many similarities can be detected, notably in their large-scale business, their mode of behaviour, and their dealings with the administration at Cape Coast Castle. Sam Kanto was a son of Harry Brew, linguist at the Castle in the last decade of the eighteenth century,[1] and he was described by the British Governor as 'a turbulent and refractory character, defying all authority, and living in open violation of the laws'.[2] The opinions expressed about him and the impact he made on affairs both call to mind his Irish predecessor. Literate,[3] and by virtue of his origins well placed for commercial opportunity, he belonged to the old-established world of Fanti middlemen whose livelihood was undermined by the parliamentary legislation of 1807. That he should have been among those who sought alternative buyers for the slaves supplied by Ashanti in highly organized exchange with the seaboard is hardly surprising. To the British at Cape Coast Castle, endeavouring to grapple with the new situation of legitimate commerce and a close relationship with Ashanti, Sam Kanto seemed to epitomize the difficulties consequent thereon.

He was born in Cape Coast, where his family lived, and he traded in slaves along the coast as far east as the Accra region, and inland with the Fanti state of Abura, an important link in the chain of communication that led to Ashanti.[4] At Mouri, on the seaboard a few miles from Cape Coast, Brew maintained a nineteenth-century counterpart to Castle Brew. The Dutch had once had a public settlement at Mouri, Fort Nassau, which they had now abandoned. With a bravado reminiscent of his grandfather, Sam Kanto occupied the fort and hoisted the Spanish

---

[1] See pp. 122–3 above.

[2] John Hope Smith to William Hutchison, 7 Nov. 1817, T. 70/41.

[3] Sarah Wood v. Kwamina Buachee and others, 14 Feb. 1908, H.C.C.C. 323/52.

[4] John Hope Smith to William Hutchison, 7 Nov. 1817, T. 70/41; Henry Adamson to John Hope Smith, 9 Nov. 1817, ADM. 1/704 (G.N.A.); Daendels's Journal, entry dd. 19 Feb. 1818 (Furley Collection, Balme Library, University of Ghana); personal communication.

flag. Aided by Spanish sailors, he used Fort Nassau as a base for the delivery of slaves to Spanish ships.[1]

By the time he made a mark on coastal events in the period 1817–23, Sam Kanto's business had reached proportions that caused the British to refer to him as a 'powerful mulatto slave trader' and a 'great slave trade merchant'. In scale of undertaking he was perhaps the greatest, and certainly the most prominent of a group of mulattos so engaged at Cape Coast.[2] In order to stop all the leeward traffic, wrote the British Resident in Kumasi, it would be necessary to prevent Brew from carrying on his nefarious trade. He had available a constant supply of slaves, it was said, ready to ship out to vessels anchored some distance offshore for fear of capture.[3]

Britain's illegalization of the export of slaves certainly did not result in its immediate diminution in West Africa. Other nations were ready and willing to continue as purchasers, notably the Spanish, Portuguese, and Brazilians, while the King of Ashanti was ready to continue as supplier. It was the Spanish, sometimes acting on behalf of American merchants,[4] with whom Brew established a firm business relationship in the decade following abolition, and who gave him practical assistance during the course of his clashes with Cape Coast Castle. In September 1817, for example, after the appointment of Governor Hope Smith, a strong anti-slave trader, British headquarters attempted to organize Brew's capture at Mumford.[5] The intention had been to secure him in the nearby fort at Tantum, with the help of some of the local population,[6] before his removal to Cape Coast in an armed canoe. Assisted by Spanish sailors, as well as by the inhabitants of Mumford, Brew succeeded in evading the Tantum people, who were allies

[1] Daendels's Journal, entries dd. 19 and 28 Nov. 1817, 19 Feb. 1818; 'A New Check List of the Forts and Castles of Ghana' in *Transactions of the Historical Society of Ghana*, vol. IV, pt. I (1959), p. 62.

[2] John Hope Smith and others to Committee, 21 Feb. 1818, T. 70/36; Daendels's Journal, entry dd. 19 Feb. 1818; T. E. Bowdich, *Mission from Cape Coast Castle to Ashantee* (London, 1819), p. 339. Also mentioned in Daendels's Journal as a mulatto slave trader is Samuel Smith; see p. 124 above.

[3] William Hutchison to John Hope Smith, 11 Oct. 1817, T. 70/41.

[4] Bowdich, op. cit. p. 339.

[5] Richard Brew had set up as a private trader at Mumford in 1754; see pp. 37–8 above.

[6] Also known as Tantumkweri. Richard Brew had been Governor of the fort for a time; see pp. 36–8 above.

of the British, and escaped in a Spanish ship sailing towards
Accra; both sides experienced casualties in the fray. Some weeks
later, he returned to the Mumford district, once again in a
Spanish schooner, and received the honour of a ship's salute as
he went on shore.[1]

What gave special significance, from the British point of view,
to Sam Kanto's activities as an illicit slaver in Fanti, was his
commercial tie with the King of Ashanti, a situation which
Richard Brew had hoped to effect in the eighteenth century.[2]
Speedy response from Ashanti to Britain's change of heart in
1807 was hardly to be expected, since abandonment of the slave
trade threatened the economic structure of the inland producer
just as much as that of the middleman states. If the consciences
of other European buyers were not affected in the same way,
then Osei Bonsu, the King of Ashanti, saw little reason why
they should not continue to be supplied. Sam Kanto entered
into the picture here, to quote the British, as the main support
of Ashanti's trade with the coast. He passed on its slaves to Spanish
merchantmen in return for powder and firearms, which were
then despatched inland, and were sometimes accompanied by
Spanish gifts for the King.[3]

That Brew had managed to set himself up as an important intermediary between Ashanti and the coast is obvious. One channel
through which this operated was Abura, in the Fanti hinterland. In Abura there was an Ashanti Resident and allegiance
was owed to Osei Bonsu. Brew had fled there during the quarrel
with Cape Coast Castle in 1817. Subsequently, a number of
Ashanti from Paintree's croom (Abura Dunkwa),[4] an active
centre of slaving transactions, tried to exact an assurance from
the pro-British caboceers at Tantum that they would not assist,
at any time, in Brew's capture. When the Tantum caboceers

[1] John Hope Smith to Henry Adamson, 11 Sept. 1817, ADM. 1/704 (G.N.A.);
Henry Adamson to John Hope Smith, 24 and 28 Sept., 9 Nov. 1817, ibid.; Sec-
retary, Cape Coast Castle to Henry Adamson, 26 Sept. 1817, ibid.; John Hope
Smith to William Hutchison, 21 Nov. 1817, T. 70/41.

[2] See pp. 73–4 above.

[3] Thomas Bowdich to John Hope Smith, 29 Aug. 1817, T. 70/40, f. 138; William
Hutchison to John Hope Smith, 11 Oct. 1817, T. 70/41.

[4] Paintree was an Abura caboceer who had close ties with Ashanti, and whose
'croom' or village was much frequented by slave traders. He was killed at Mouri
in 1821, when troops from Cape Coast Castle carried out a punitive expedition
there.

refused to comply, the Ashanti threatened to burn the town and British fort.[1]

Of even greater import than Abura Dunkwa's support for Brew was the interest displayed by King Osei Bonsu at Kumasi in his affairs, and especially in his dispute with Cape Coast Castle. Sam Kanto, already an embarrassment to the British on the commercial front, thus became a central figure in early Anglo-Ashanti discord.[2]

For an understanding of this situation, it is necessary to refer back to the Ashanti break-through to the coast in 1807 and the clash with Anomabu fort. These events were followed by a series of invasions over the next decade which altered the balance of power along the seaboard, and subjected the Fanti states to inland control. The British were now faced with the decision as to what policy they should adopt in view of the conquest of the maritime region. Ashanti's commercial potentialities, however, caused the African Committee in London to urge upon the coastal administration the desirability of friendship.[3]

In 1817, direct contact between Cape Coast Castle and Kumasi was opened up by the Bowdich Mission, and a treaty was signed in September of that year with Osei Bonsu. One member of the Mission, William Hutchison, remained behind in Kumasi as Resident. The treaty established formal amity between the contracting parties, and Osei Bonsu agreed that the Governor-in-Chief of the British settlements should act as his intermediary in certain maritime towns when disputes arose there involving Ashanti. But practical implementation of the treaty, and not least, the extent of the King's authority over Cape Coast where the British had their headquarters, were to lead to difficulties, aggravated by Ashanti reluctance to end the slave trade. These difficulties soon coalesced around the person of Sam Kanto Brew.

Running through the conflict between Brew and British headquarters was a problem well demonstrated by Richard in

---

[1] Henry Adamson to John Hope Smith, 4 Nov. 1817, ADM. 1/704 (G.N.A.); John Hope Smith to William Hutchison, 7 Nov. 1817, T. 70/41; William Hutchison to John Hope Smith, 20 Dec. 1817, ibid.

[2] See E. Collins, 'The Panic Element in Nineteenth-Century Relations with Ashanti' in *Transactions of the Historical Society of Ghana*, vol. V, pt. 2 (1962), pp. 79–138 for a discussion of Anglo-Ashanti relations centring on the Bowdich Mission, 1817. [3] See p. 131 above.

the eighteenth century, namely the relationship between fort and private trader, complicated now by the fact that the trader was African and a slave dealer, and Cape Coast within the Ashanti orbit of power. In 1817, soon after he assumed office, Governor Hope Smith had ordered Brew's arrest on the grounds of his disrespectful behaviour towards the Castle authorities. Brew escaped from Cape Coast and resisted capture, thanks to the assistance he received from his Spanish clients and the people of Mumford.[1] He refused the deposit of gold as security for good behaviour that had been Hope Smith's condition for his return to Cape Coast, and remained thereafter at large.[2] Through the medium of a special messenger, Brew caused the King of Ashanti to direct his attention to a quarrel that centred on a maritime town in Fanti.

In October 1817 Osei Bonsu sent for Hutchison, the British Resident in Kumasi, about the Brew episode.[3] The ensuing correspondence and discussions lasted for several months. According to the report of Sam Kanto's special messenger in Kumasi, his master had been attacked by the Cape Coast townspeople when he was escaping arrest because of a European debt, and they had sought to kill him. The King thereupon decreed that Brew should be summoned to Cape Coast for a palaver on the subject before an Ashanti captain; whoever had broken the law—Brew or the Cape Coast people—would be required to pay a fine in gold to the King. Osei Bonsu's standpoint was that the recent agreement empowered the British to deal with any wrongdoing committed by people living under the shadow of the forts, but that in the bush it was he, the King, who exercised jurisdiction. Brew was obviously placed in the latter category.[4] Osei Bonsu also added the statement, most objectionable to the British, that the Cape Coast people, and indeed all the Fanti, must be considered as his 'slaves'.[5]

Significant about the Sam Brew incident was that it touched

[1] John Hope Smith to William Hutchison, 21 Nov. 1817, T. 70/41 and see pp. 133–4 above.

[2] John Hope Smith to William Hutchison, 7 Nov. 1817, T. 70/41.

[3] William Hutchison to John Hope Smith, 11 Oct. 1817, T. 70/41.

[4] Sam Kanto Brew was living near Winneba in October 1817; William Hutchison to John Hope Smith, 11 Oct. 1817, T. 70/41.

[5] William Hutchison to John Hope Smith, 11 and 26 Oct. 1817, T. 70/41; the King of Ashanti to the same, 25 Oct. 1817, ibid.

a most sensitive point in Anglo-Ashanti dealings at this time—
the position of those Fanti living around the settlements now
that Ashanti had subjugated the coastal region. For his part,
Hope Smith considered that Brew fell within the British sphere
of influence; Osei Bonsu, he said, must surely know the im-
propriety of interfering there. Hutchison was instructed to tell
the King clearly that Brew's differences were with the Governor,
not with the people of Cape Coast, that it was the Governor
who had ordered his capture, and that there was no intention
of harming him. Also to be deprecated officially in Kumasi was
the Ashanti attempt, under threat of damage to Tantum town
and fort, to stop the caboceers there from helping in the seizure of
Brew, should he return to their area. For this insult from Abura,
Hutchison was to demand formal satisfaction of the King.

During Hutchison's interview with Osei Bonsu, the King
denied that he had had any knowledge, until very recently, of
the Tantum affair. Nevertheless, Hutchison insisted on a letter
of apology to the Governor. In reply to some 'offensive ob-
servations' by one of the Ashanti chiefs, he said that if it was
their intention to invite Brew to Kumasi, the British government could make no objection, but he himself would apply to
be recalled.[1]

In the course of diplomatic exchanges over Sam Kanto Brew,
the strongest emotions of all were aroused in Hope Smith
by Osei Bonsu's reference to the Fanti as his 'slaves', in Akan,
the same word as that for 'subjects'. Never could the Cape Coast
people and others under British protection be included in that
'most degrading title', the Governor told Hutchison, with
orders that this must be made quite plain to the King.[2] Undoubtedly it was Osei Bonsu's connection with a practice and
a form of trade now regarded as abhorrent, and an obstacle to
Anglo-Ashanti accord, that gave added point to the Brew
episode. In the opinion of Hope Smith, the King possessed
great merit and was favourably disposed towards the British,
but under the influence of evil advisers he had sponsored the
cause of Brew, his intermediary with Spanish slavers. According

---

[1] John Hope Smith to William Hutchison, 7 and 21 Nov. 1817, T. 70/41;
William Hutchison to John Hope Smith, 20 Dec. 1817, ibid. and see pp. 134-5
above.
[2] John Hope Smith to William Hutchison, 21 Nov. 1817, T. 70/41.

to Hope Smith, Brew had managed to persuade Osei Bonsu that it was he who was responsible for the presence of so many buyers off the coast; he had represented himself as persecuted by the British because of his 'zealous attachment' to the trade, and had sought royal protection in order to set up a regular system. Writing to the African Committee in February 1818, Hope Smith said that once Brew was captured, he intended to transport him from the country as a very dangerous person.[1]

Ultimately, in 1823, deportation was to be the slave trader's fate, although the Governor then was Sir Charles Macarthy with headquarters in Sierra Leone, and the West African settlements had passed from the Company of Merchants to the Crown.[2] Brew's final irruption into public affairs and its sequel were not without elements of the dramatic, in keeping with the earlier pattern of his life. The setting, too, was familiar—Anglo-Ashanti relations—deteriorating, however, to the point of imminent warfare. But a different factor was that Brew, once the declared antagonist of Cape Coast Castle, appeared now as its ally against Ashanti, a change of front not unlike the flexible attitude of Richard Brew towards authority in the eighteenth century.[3]

Anglo-Ashanti friction in 1823 had its basic cause in the recurrent problem of responsibility for the Fanti in the vicinity of British settlement. Three years after the 1817 treaty, another one had been negotiated by Joseph Dupuis, the first consul in Kumasi to be appointed directly by the Crown. This treaty had acknowledged the King of Ashanti's rights over the whole of Fanti country. Strongly opposed by the authorities at Cape Coast Castle, it was never ratified on the British side, and when the Crown assumed control of the settlements in 1822, Anglo-Ashanti relations, bedevilled by misunderstandings, had reached breaking point.[4]

An incident in Anomabu precipitated matters. During an altercation between a Fanti sergeant at the fort and an Ashanti trader, the Governor and the King of Ashanti each came in

---

[1] John Hope Smith to William Hutchison, 21 Nov. 1817, T. 70/41; John Hope Smith and others to Committee, 21 Feb. 1818, T. 70/36.

[2] Sir Charles Macarthy's Governorship dated from 1822; the Act abolishing the Company of Merchants was passed in the previous year; see p. 131 above.

[3] See p. 97 above.

[4] Metcalfe, op. cit. pp. 38–9.

for abuse. The offending sergeant was captured at the instigation of the Ashanti and taken to Abura Dunkwa, where he
was executed in February 1823, several months after the initial
incident. Troops thereupon left Cape Coast Castle, on a night
march, to punish the Ashanti captain in Abura Dunkwa. They
would have reached their destination early the next morning,
had they not fallen into an ambush, where surprise enemy
attack resulted in British casualties. The guide who had led
them there was Sam Kanto Brew.[1]

That Brew should have supported the Ashanti against Cape
Coast Castle is not surprising, in view of his old link with Abura
Dunkwa in the slave-trading network. Also, the Ashanti captain
on this occasion was the one who had intervened on his behalf
at Tantum in November 1817.[2] Much more unusual is to find
Sam Kanto acting in a position of trust for the British. Administrative change, and the replacement of Hope Smith by Sir
Charles Macarthy based on Sierra Leone, may have had something to do with it. According to Mrs. Bowdich, the widow of
T. E. Bowdich who had led the Mission to Ashanti, Brew
exercised considerable influence over Macarthy, and was able
'so to infatuate the new Governor, that he consulted him on
various occasions'. Despite warnings from other coastal residents
about Brew's 'real character', this confidence was continued,
Mrs. Bowdich says, until events showed it to have been extremely misplaced.[3] Family tradition, too, it should be noted,
still recalls Sam Brew as 'Macarthy's right-hand man'.[4]

The Governor's version, on the other hand, was that he encouraged Brew in 'lawful commerce, agriculture and every
species of honest industry',[5] following the recent forgiveness of
his misdeeds by Hope Smith. Whatever illusions Macarthy may
have had that this would mean a fresh start for Brew were

---

[1] H. I. Ricketts, *Narrative of the Ashantee War* (London, 1831), pp. 13–20; C. C.
Reindorf, *History of the Gold Coast and Asante* (Basel, 1895), pp. 179–81; Crooks,
Records relating to the Gold Coast Settlements, pp. 168–71; Metcalfe, op. cit. pp. 39–40.

[2] See pp. 134–5 above.

[3] R. Lee, *Stories of Strange Lands* (London, 1835), pp. 190–1. Mrs. Bowdich
(Mrs. R. Lee) mistakenly describes Brew as the 'betrayer' of Sir Charles Macarthy,
who was killed, of course, in hostilities against the Ashanti in 1824. See also p. 27
n. 1 above.

[4] Personal communication. There was, however, some confusion here between
Sam Kanto Brew and Samuel Collins Brew, his son.

[5] Sir Charles Macarthy to Lord Bathurst, 4 Aug. 1823, C.O. 267/58.

certainly dispelled by the time the Governor reported to the Secretary of State about the Dunkwa episode.

After troops had marched from Cape Coast Castle on the evening of 25 February, he wrote, Brew had voluntarily offered his services, along with sundry followers, and had earnestly requested ammunition. This was granted, whereupon Brew purposely misdirected the British forces into an ambush, having previously warned Ashanti's Fanti allies of the intended attack. Such was the behaviour of one supposedly zealous in the British interest, the Governor continued, 'a most dangerous character' who had carried on the slave trade under the old Company, only four miles from Cape Coast Castle, and who had openly shown allegiance to the King of Ashanti.[1]

On the expedition's return, Macarthy ordered Brew to be confined to the Castle and instituted an inquiry. Although the illness of the magistrate rendered this inquiry incomplete, it left no doubt in the Governor's mind about the accused man's guilt. But the question of what form of punishment to adopt was an extremely difficult one, Macarthy said, in view of Brew's Ashanti link, the importance of his family connections in Cape Coast,[2] the widespread personal enmities he had aroused, and the fact that there was no British court of justice on the Gold Coast to try such cases. Macarthy decided, therefore, to deport him to Sierra Leone or the Gambia until such time as peace with Ashanti was restored; in these new surroundings he could

---

[1] Sir Charles Macarthy to Lord Bathurst, 17 May and 4 Aug. 1823, C.O. 267/58. At a dinner given on the coast on St. Patrick's Day, 1823, a song was sung entitled 'The Gold Coast Volunteers', in which there was mention of Brew. One verse contained these lines:

> Let's drive from this country, the trait'rous Brew,
> And down with the power of O'Saii Tootoo.

In view of Brew's part-Irish ancestry, there was some irony in the situation! See entry, 12 July 1823, in *The Royal Gazette and Sierra Leone Advertiser* (Freetown), vol. V, no. 268 and p. 27 n. 1 above. I am indebted to Professor Ivor Wilks for drawing my attention to this reference.

[2] Macarthy's statement here is borne out by a comment of the Governor in 1806 that Sam Brew and his brother Richard were 'of the first Family in Town'. This is doubtless a reference to their relationship with the Rev. Philip Quaque, who was connected with Cudjo Caboceer and the ruling dynasty of Cape Coast. Family tradition today associates Sam Kanto Brew and Philip Quaque as contemporaries. See Col. Torrane to Committee, 4 Apr. 1806, T. 70/34, f. 328 and pp. 21–2, 121 above. I am indebted to Mr. R. Porter for this reference.

be left at liberty without danger. Even his friends were glad that he had been removed, the Govenor added.[1]

Deportation, the sequel to Brew's involvement with the Ashanti, brought the unexpected consequence of his death while on the way to Sierra Leone, in circumstances that were indicative of suicide. On 16 May Macarthy sent him on board H.M.S. *Cyrené*, where he shared a cabin with the ship's carpenter. Orders were given that every attention was to be paid to his comfort and no restraint placed on his movements. In the early hours of 24 May Brew was found dead, his throat cut with a razor belonging to the carpenter. Shortly before this, its owner said in his deposition, Brew had disturbed him by groping about the cabin near the razor case and whispering that someone wanted to kill him. After being assured that this was not so, and that the sounds he heard were made by people coming below to shelter from the weather, he had mixed himself a glass of rum and water, said good-night, and retired to bed. An hour later, the carpenter had heard the noises that accompanied the discovery of Brew's body.

Another deposition taken was that of the ship's surgeon. He reported being called shortly after four o'clock in the morning to attend to the deceased. According to him, the wound which was the cause of death had certainly been self-inflicted. Forwarding these depositions and his report to London on 4 August 1823, Macarthy expressed the opinion that Brew, who combined European dress and language with 'the very grosest [*sic*] superstition, idolatry and *fetish*', had acted 'under a momentary impression of his belief in the latter'.[2]

Knowledge that Brew's end was tragic has survived into the present century. In a law case heard during the first decade, an elderly witness made reference to the manner in which he had died, while at the present day, it is said that he was suspected of betraying the administration and taken 'for a ride' on the high seas.[3]

A colourful personality like Richard Brew, Sam Kanto belonged to the world of Afro-European slave trading in which

[1] Sir Charles Macarthy to Lord Bathurst, 17 May 1823, C.O. 267/58.
[2] Sir Charles Macarthy to Lord Bathurst, 17 May and 4 Aug. 1823, C.O. 267/58.
[3] Sarah Wood v. Kwamina Buachee and others, 14 Feb. 1908, H.C.C.C. 323/52 and personal communication.

Richard had been prominent half a century earlier. The old commercial pattern persisted, and Fanti and Ashanti activities had not yet been diverted into channels consistent with the dictates of British economics and morality. In one respect, however, the nineteenth-century world *had* changed—by the irruption of Ashanti into the maritime region and its conquest of Fanti. This conquest posed the British with the problem of maintaining commercial enclaves on the coast and fostering inland markets at a time of considerable political turbulence. As in the eighteenth century, European trade and African politics interacted, with the Ashanti theme even more dominant than before; during the lifetime of Sam Kanto Brew's son, further interesting developments would take place.

CHAPTER III

Samuel Collins Brew:
Legitimate Trade and Pax Britannica

The long and active life of Samuel Collins Brew (*c.* 1810–81), the younger son of Sam Kanto,[1] saw the Afro-European partnership of slave-trading origin reach a climax on the Gold Coast and begin to decline. By the middle decades of the century, legitimate commerce was at last overtaking its stubborn rival, and in the new economy African merchants, for a while, were still to be prominent. They were also to play an important part in settlement administration, now extending its range from commerce to justice, with the object of fostering stable local conditions to benefit the growth of trade. A merchant and public official, Samuel Collins Brew's career impinged on Gold Coast affairs at the moment when African participation in the European sphere was at its height. But already the seeds of a different relationship were being sown. By the time that he died in 1881, the parting of the ways had taken place. Its consequences would soon make themselves felt.

Legitimate commerce, as an instrument for the 'civilizing' of West Africa, aimed at encouraging Africans in 'lawful commerce, agriculture and every species of honest industry', to quote Governor Macarthy's words about Sam Kanto Brew.[2] First, however, it proved necessary to attack the foreign slave trade in which Fanti middlemen, like Sam Kanto, had been

[1] Renner, *Cases in the Courts of the Gold Coast Colony and Nigeria*, vol. I, pt. 2, p. 802. The date 'circa 1810' for Samuel Collins Brew's birth is based on the fact that by the eighteen-forties, he was a substantial merchant, and advanced in years when he died in 1881. One of his wives, who died on 6 Oct. 1851 at the age of thirty-five, would have been born in 1816. There is a memorial tablet to her in the ruins of his house at Anomabu; see p. 189 below.

[2] See p. 139 above and Curtin, *The Image of Africa*, pp. 259–86.

deeply engaged.[1] This was done through a network of diplomacy and an extensive naval patrol along the coast, although the process of undermining a tenacious trade was an extremely lengthy one.

In positive terms, the most important economic innovation during the nineteenth century was the growth of West Africa's palm-oil trade. Among exports, palm-oil achieved pride of place in response to increasing European demand. Gold and ivory, two of West Africa's staple products, continued to be exported, while on the import side, little change occurred from the earlier pattern of textiles, spirits, and tobacco, except that British cotton goods gained in popularity over Indian manufactures.[2]

The firm establishment of a new form of commerce, however, did not depend only on stopping foreign outlets for slave dealing. There was an essential internal corollary—peaceful relations between the African states so that the trading paths might be kept open and goods flow freely between coast and interior. During the eighteenth century, closure of the paths through inter-state discord had frequently led to stagnant trade on the coast. During the nineteenth, the same situation applied, and West Africa's exports showed marked annual fluctuations in volume.[3] In the case of the Gold Coast, the crucial factor was Ashanti-Fanti relations. They affected, in particular, the availability on the seaboard of gold and ivory, now the inland kingdom's main commodities for export.

As with his father, Ashanti exercised considerable influence upon the circumstances of Samuel Collins Brew's life. Especially was this so during the thirties and forties of the century, an important formative period in Ghana history, and one characterized by interesting developments in the Anglo-Ashanti-Fanti relationship. Central to these developments was the greater tranquillity that reigned between coast and interior, and the renewal of inland trade, which had been dormant since the disturbances of the early twenties. For this improvement, credit must go to George Maclean, President of the mercantile admini-

[1] See pp. 132–5 above.
[2] W. K. Hancock, *Survey of British Commonwealth Affairs*, vol. II, pt. 2 (London, 1942), pp. 158–9; Metcalfe, *Maclean of the Gold Coast*, pp. 116–17.
[3] D. Kimble, *A Political History of Ghana, 1850–1928* (Oxford, 1963), p. 4.

stration at Cape Coast Castle after 1830.[1] 'Nominee and agent of business-men', Maclean saw that intertribal warfare was an impediment to trade and prosperity, and devoted himself to the urgent task of stopping it.[2]

As the first step towards a *modus vivendi* between Ashanti and the coastal states, it was necessary to bring about peace. Anglo-Ashanti hostilities had resulted in the death, in battle, of the British Governor, Sir Charles Macarthy in 1824, followed in 1826 by an Ashanti defeat.[3] Soon after assuming office, Maclean laid the essential foundation stone of his work, a treaty with the Ashanti, which he concluded in 1831. By the treaty, they abandoned political control of the coastal peoples, a disputed matter since 1817 as the Sam Kanto Brew episode had shown,[4] and in return gained unrestricted commercial access to the seaboard, without the need, as before, to deal through middleman tribes. Inaugurating 'a revolution in the trade relations of the coast', this section of the treaty gave practical recognition to one of the main objectives of the Ashanti since the eighteenth century—their right to conduct trade themselves in the area of European settlement.[5]

Peace not only had to be made, however, it had to be kept, and coastal incidents likely to result in disturbance and to impede the free movement of Ashanti traders avoided. In a society where actions were linked not with individuals but with collective groups, and where the old economic structure had been dealt a serious blow causing inevitable instability, it was easy for minor disputes to develop into major ones, extending, perhaps, beyond the bounds of a single state. Maclean therefore made it a special point of his policy to create a strong arbiter on the coast in the shape of the British mercantile administration. His aim was to establish 'a system of public law over and above the law of the tribe', in the words of the 'Bond' of 1844—'moulding the custom of the country to the general principles of British law'.[6]

[1] See Metcalfe, *Maclean of the Gold Coast*, on which this and the following two paragraphs are based. See also p. 131 above.
[2] Metcalfe, op. cit. Preface, p. ix.
[3] Macarthy was killed in 1824 in hostilities with the Ashanti near the village of Adamanso. The Ashanti were defeated in 1826 at Katamansu; see Metcalfe, op. cit. pp. 41–4.   [4] See pp. 135–8 above.   [5] Metcalfe, op. cit. pp. 89–90.
[6] Metcalfe, op. cit. pp. 90–1, 307 and see p. 152 below.

Herein lay the most distinctive and far-reaching part of his work, achieved with remarkably few resources and through the exercise of personal influence—the network of British justice that radiated out from the settlements, gradually embracing more and more of the Fanti peoples. By an *ad hoc* exercise of power, and in response to the needs of the situation, as he saw them, Maclean thus developed an informal judicial 'Protectorate' in the maritime region between the river Pra, west of Cape Coast, and the river Densu, west of Accra, after the 1831 treaty had been signed and Ashanti overlordship withdrawn. Its object was the preservation of peace over as wide an area as possible.

The improvement in relations between coast and interior during the thirties, and the spread of *Pax Britannica*, form the background to the establishment of Samuel Collins Brew as a successful Fanti merchant. Like Richard Brew in the eighteenth century, Samuel Collins's business centre was Anomabu, not Cape Coast, his family town. After suffering depopulation as a result of the Ashanti attack in 1807, Anomabu had eventually recovered some measure of its eighteenth-century trading prosperity, and Samuel Collins had moved there from Cape Coast when he was a young man, probably in his twenties or early thirties.[1] At Anomabu, he built a substantial house. Its ruins are still visible at a spot known as 'Sam Brew *kukwadu*' (Sam Brew's hill).[2] In position and architecture, the house differed from Castle Brew, which had been sited much closer to the fort.[3] But like Castle Brew, it was the home of a commanding personality —one of the 'merchant princes' of the time as a grandson later described him, a 'proper money man' in the words of an elderly descendant today.[4]

Unfortunately, due to lack of sources, far less is known, in detail, about the trading concerns of Samuel Collins Brew than

---

[1] He was well established in Anomabu by the early eighteen-forties, and according to a later lawsuit, looking for a place there to build a house. George Blankson, another prominent Anomabu merchant, said in 1874 that he had known Brew for some forty-three years, which would suggest that Brew arrived in Anomabu in the early eighteen-thirties; Quow Amokoo of Anomabu v. Samuel Brew of Anomabu, 15 July 1872, H.C.C.C. 256/52; George Blankson of Anomabu v. Quassie Eddoo and others, 4 Nov. 1874, H.C.C.C. 258/52.

[2] Personal communication.   [3] See pp. 57–8 above.

[4] J. E. Casely Hayford, *Gold Coast Native Institutions* (London, 1903), p. 95 and personal communication. A 'proper money man' means a rich man.

about those of his European ancestor, and only the broadest outlines of the picture can be given. His business at Anomabu was built up, perhaps in association with a brother, Harry Brew,[1] during a period of expanding trade and prosperity when Maclean's policy was beginning to pay dividends; in 1836, Gold Coast merchants formally expressed their gratitude to the President for the improvement that had taken place in the country's condition.[2] On the export side, Brew's business depended principally on the Ashanti connection. According to his account, he traded in gold and ivory, but not in palm-oil,[3] and the significance to him of good relations with Ashanti is shown by the fact that in 1848, along with Harry Brew, he signed a letter praising Governor Winniett's attempts at amelioration after a renewal of inland difficulties.[4]

As a coastal trader operating on his own behalf, Brew dealt with British firms engaged in importing and exporting—with Hutton and Sons of London and especially with Forster and Smith, one of the major participants in West African commerce.[5] From them he received goods on credit, cloth, rum, and tobacco pipes, to be sold in the stores which he maintained at Anomabu and at other points along the coast. These stores were often in the charge of a wife, of whom Brew had several, some of them acting as his agents.[6] In 1851, when one wife applied for a divorce, he brought a case against her for the balance of a trading account.[7]

By the eighteen-forties, Samuel Collins Brew ranked among the small group of substantial Gold Coast traders, African as well as European, who were involved in legitimate commerce, the two-way exchange between Britain and West Africa that was now replacing the triangular slave trade. His business concerns were described at the time as 'extensive'; for this reason, it was doubted in 1848 whether he and another well-known Anomabu merchant, George Blankson, would be able to spare

---

[1] See n. 4 below.
[2] Metcalfe, op. cit. pp. 202–3.
[3] In petition of W. H. Selby re George Blankson, 3 July 1872, H.C.C.C. 284/52.
[4] Letter to Cdr. William Winniett, 4 Dec. 1848, ADM. 1/450 (G.N.A.).
[5] In matter of insolvent estate of Samuel Collins Brew, 11 Jan. 1867, H.C.C.C. 413/52; Kimble, op. cit. p. 4.
[6] Personal communication.
[7] Adjuah [?] v. S. C. Brew and S. C. Brew v. Adjuah [?], 26 Feb. 1851, H.C.C.C. 248/52.

the time to carry out their duties as the executors of a particular estate and collect in the debts due to it.[1]

Similar testimony about Brew's position comes from John Duncan, a British traveller to West Africa. Duncan visited Anomabu in November 1844, a place of 'considerable trade' as he described it. He 'experienced great kindness . . . from the merchants . . . both English and native' there, and enjoyed the hospitality of 'Mr. Brewe, a very respectable and enterprising merchant'. Accompanied by a wife, Brew took his guest on a tour of neighbouring Fanti towns and villages. In one, he introduced Duncan to the chief with whom he was well acquainted; in another, the local inhabitants, gathered around the new arrivals in the market-place, were much intrigued by Brew's musical box.[2]

The mid-century undoubtedly saw the peak of Samuel Collins's business career. During the sixties, he entered upon a less satisfactory phase, with financial difficulties and consequences similar to those which the slave trader Richard had experienced a hundred years earlier while in partnership with Samuel Smith.[3] Prominent in the situation that underlay Samuel Collins's altered fortunes was the revival of disturbances between coast and interior. In 1844, when Maclean ceased to be President of the Council at Cape Coast Castle, the Ashanti-Fanti relationship once more ran into troubled waters. Despite the 1831 treaty, there was closure of the paths, and obstacles were raised to the free movement of inland and coastal traders.[4] Furthermore, following the Maclean epoch, vacillation and uncertainty in British policy regarding the settlements, which were now back under Crown control, only served to aggravate local instability. These were not conditions conducive to the prosperity of men like Samuel Collins Brew, dependent on the inland route. In 1863, Ashanti again invaded the coastal states, and the ensuing disruption of trade brought serious results.

Along with other African merchants, Brew became insolvent during a decade of unsettlement, and in 1867 his case was heard before the Chief Magistrate in Chambers. Forster and Smith of

[1] Letter from F. Swanzy, 28 Dec. 1848, H.C.C.C. 197/52.
[2] J. Duncan, *Travels in Western Africa in 1845 and 1846*, vol. I (London, 1847), pp. 39–50, 61. I am indebted for this reference to Professor J. D. Fage.
[3] See pp. 63–5 above.
[4] Metcalfe, op. cit. pp. 330–1.

London, the shipping firm with whom he had been doing business since 1853 or 1854, were his main creditors. According to Brew's version of affairs, his difficulties had started about ten years after this, when the trade with Ashanti in gold and ivory was interrupted because of another military descent on the coast. He had been unable, therefore, to meet his commitments in the normal fashion, and when Forster and Smith exerted pressure, through their agents, for the payment of a balance of between £8,000 and £9,000, he had surrendered his property to them, including the house at Anomabu, in order to settle the debt.[1] It will be recalled that a not dissimilar fate had once befallen Castle Brew.[2]

Apart from Ashanti-Fanti unrest, the general trend of economic development on the Gold Coast must be taken into account when considering merchant embarrassment during the sixties and seventies. There had recently been a period of growing African participation in overseas trade and an expansion of the credit network. Responsible for this development was the steamship, and the introduction, in 1852–3, of regular sailings between Liverpool and West Africa, offering quick, cheap services. The result was an increase in the number of independent traders, including Africans, who were engaged directly, although often on a small scale, in importing and exporting.[3] As independent traders multiplied and the credit system spread, so the complications of adjusting European-type business activity, individualist in approach, to the collectivism of the clan became more marked.[4] Corporate ownership of property and wide kinship obligations were not easily reconciled with an impersonal economic relationship focused on Europe, and cases of inability, on the part of traders, to meet their debts occurred with greater frequency. British firms began to be more cautious about advancing goods on credit to independent traders, and to show a growing preference for working through paid agents on the coast, some of whom also received commission.[5]

[1] In matter of insolvent estate of Samuel Collins Brew, 11 Jan. 1867, H.C.C.C. 413/52; In petition of W. H. Selby re George Blankson, 3 July 1872, H.C.C.C. 284/52.   [2] See pp. 64–5 above.   [3] Kimble, op. cit. pp. 4–5.   [4] See p. 17 above.
[5] Kimble, op. cit. p. 5; H. J. Bevin, 'The Gold Coast Economy about 1880' in *Transactions of the Gold Coast and Togoland Historical Society*, vol. II, pt. 2 (1956), pp. 79–80.

How far economic and social factors of this kind contributed to Samuel Collins Brew's insolvency, perhaps limiting his capacity to withstand the Ashanti upheaval, it is impossible to say. The actual size of his business remains unknown, and there are no trading records. But evidence of other kinds suggests that it was quite considerable, judged by the standards of the time. His connection with Forster and Smith, dating from the early eighteen-fifties when a steamship service began, may well have led to its expansion—possibly even to some over-extension. From Brew's outstanding balance of account with this firm of £8,000 to £9,000, it can be inferred that he received a large quantity of goods on credit for the benefit of various trading stations.[1] There is evidence, too, that during his career, Brew was himself the plaintiff in a number of cases concerned with debt. In one case, heard in 1859, he claimed the balance of a Bill of Exchange of £525 from a fellow African businessman.[2] Indeed, coast credit and its internal ramifications may well have been the preliminary to his later troubles.

Nor is there any doubt that his position in Fanti society must have meant heavy commitments and responsibilities, as befitted a merchant with a large establishment of wives, children, and domestics;[3] descendants of Brew's domestics still live close to his ruined house in Anomabu. This house had cost him £4,000, he said, and was mortgaged for £2,400 to Forster and Smith before they foreclosed and sold.[4] In Cape Coast, too, his native town, he possessed another one, 'Brew House', later to become the family residence of descendants, including his son, James Hutton Brew.[5]

[1] In petition of W. H. Selby re George Blankson, 3 July 1872, H.C.C.C. 284/52.
[2] Samuel C. Brew of Anomabu v. Thomas Hughes of Cape Coast, 18 Nov. 1859, H.C.C.C. 274/52.
[3] For domestic or dependent status in a family, see Sarbah, *Fanti Customary Laws*, pp. 6–10, 102 ff.
[4] In petition of W. H. Selby re George Blankson, 3 July 1872, H.C.C.C. 284/52; Quow Amokoo of Anomabu v. Samuel Brew of Anomabu, 15 July 1872, H.C.C.C. 256/52.
[5] J. E. Casely Hayford to his kinsmen, 26 May 1929. I am indebted to Mr. S. H. F. Brew of Freetown for access to this letter. Samuel Collins Brew valued his Cape Coast house at £1,500. He said that he had bought it in 1853; In matter of insolvent estate of Samuel Collins Brew, 11 Jan. 1867, H.C.C.C. 413/52; Sam v. Albert Brew and others, 26 Sept. 1905, H.C.C.C. 321/52 and see p. 189 below. After Brew's death, his estate was valued at about £580; In matter of the estate of Samuel Collins Brew, 10 April 1882, H.C.C.C. 287/52.

By the close of Brew's life, the problem of creating 'a race of *native capitalists*'[1] who would bring the benefits of legitimate commerce to society had been demonstrated as profound. Conditions in the West African mercantile world favoured bigger units, and, in general, the future lay with large-scale firms.[2] To what extent there had been European pressure on the African merchant must await further elucidation of the economic history of the Gold Coast during the nineteenth century.[3]

Association of the Brews with commerce certainly did not come to an end with Samuel Collins. One of his sons, for example, Richard Collins, traded along an extensive area of the Gold Coast from Apam to Axim, and further afield, in the Ivory Coast.[4] But it is significant that Richard operated as the factor and commission agent of a European firm,[5] a sign that the age of independent African exporters, of whom his father had been representative, was passing.

Trade was not the sole activity in which Samuel Collins Brew engaged. Like other merchants, African and European, he served the British administration on the Gold Coast—in his case, for at least twenty years, from 1857 until 1879, shortly before he died. This service was at first on a voluntary basis and then, from 1868, the year following his insolvency, he held a salaried appointment.[6] It seems highly probable that during the last decade of his life, if not before, trade ranked as second in importance with him to public affairs.

The particular mould in which Brew's duties were cast was judicial, and linked him with the Maclean era when the relationship between the British settlements and the African peoples had entered a new phase. Trading administration then expanded into the administration of justice, although earlier, during the slaving period, arbitration by fort authorities in disputes between Africans as well as between Africans and

[1] Kimble, op. cit. p. 5, quoting from *The African Times*.
[2] See Hancock, op. cit. vol. II, pt. 2, chap. II, section 3, especially pp. 206–8 and Kimble, op. cit. pp. 6–7. Hancock draws attention to the long-term conflict of individualism and combination in West African trade.
[3] A considerable study of this subject is being undertaken by Mr. H. J. Bevin.
[4] R. C. Brew v. James Nelson, 23 April 1872, H.C.C.C. 271/52 and personal communication.
[5] R. C. Brew v. J. H. Capper, and Company of African Merchants v. R. C. Brew, 10 Aug. 1872, H.C.C.C. 284/52.
[6] *Gold Coast Blue Book, 1868*, p. 82.

Europeans had not been unknown. Antedating Maclean, too, was the office of justice of the peace, which became the pivot of the British judicial system on the Gold Coast. Its introduction dated from the eighteen-twenties, when for a few years the settlements were under Crown control; the intention had been that justices should confine themselves primarily to trading disputes in which Europeans were involved.[1]

But Maclean's emphasis on *Pax Britannica* as a means of enforcing peace with Ashanti and improving trade, led to the growth of magistrates' functions both territorially and in kind. They concerned themselves increasingly with African justice, especially with cases of debt, panyarring,[2] violence, and theft over a widening orbit of the coastal region beyond the settlements. Coldly received in Colonial Office circles as an unauthorized extension of British commitment, Maclean's system eventually gained official acceptance in 1843, when the settlements reverted to Crown control. A new post, that of Judicial Assessor, came into being, while Parliament gave legal sanction to the exercise of jurisdiction outside 'Her Majesty's Dominions', in this case equated with the settlements. On the coast, a number of Fanti chiefs voluntarily recognized British judicial authority by the 'Bond' of 1844; their people submitted 'not as subjects, but as independent nations, in alliance with, and protected by, the United Kingdom'.[3]

Integral to the judicial process as it evolved under Maclean was the fusion of English law and practice with the customary law of African society. On the one hand was the justice of the peace, on the other hand, the Fanti chief and his elders, key figures in the situation. During the early stages, in particular, it was necessary for the European system to work through channels traditionally concerned with the dispensation of justice. A literate African acted as intermediary, and bridged the two worlds. Here was a role for which the Brews were well

---

[1] Metcalfe, op. cit. pp. 170–1. A difficult legal problem had been raised by Sam Kanto Brew in the Dunkwa episode of 1823. It was resolved by deporting him to Sierra Leone; see pp. 138–41 above.

[2] 'Panyarring' was the seizure, for an unpaid debt, of a person connected, even if remotely, with the debtor; see Sarbah, *Fanti Customary Laws*, pp. 115–16.

[3] J. A. B. Horton, *West African Countries and Peoples* (London, 1868), p. 243 quoted in Kimble, op. cit. p. 195. See also Metcalfe, op. cit. especially pp. 306–307.

equipped, western-educated as they were, and with an influential position in Fanti through family connections.[1]

Samuel Collins Brew's uncle, Richard, brother of Sam Kanto, set the pattern in the mid-forties. Richard was a family elder, able to speak and read English although not to write it. He acted as interpreter to the Judicial Assessor's Court at Cape Coast, and among his tasks was the investigation of cases 'in a country fashion' to establish innocence and guilt, before the two parties faced a European legal officer. This is an interesting example of the use made of customary procedures.[2] By the end of the next decade, British justice on the Gold Coast had become more formalized and more entrenched,[3] and its functionaries included Samuel Collins Brew. An elder in Fanti,[4] like his uncle, he served in the capacity of magistrate, together with other prominent residents, African and European.

Brew's period of office lasted from the late eighteen-fifties until 1879, and coincided with a series of important events. These included the Ashanti invasion of the seaboard in 1863, pressure in Britain for the abandonment of the settlements, and a Fanti move, which the British rejected, to strengthen and modernize the indigenous political system.[5] Following another Anglo-Ashanti war in 1873, the British government eventually accepted the fact of a colonial situation on the Gold Coast, with certain consequences for those in the position of magistrate.

Samuel Collins Brew's official career seems to have begun in the year 1857, when he held the Queen's Commission of the Peace at Anomabu.[6] He assisted the civil commandant of the fort in the dispensation of justice, and sometimes deputized for him, as in 1864.[7] Four years later, in 1868, Brew was appointed

[1] See p. 140 n. 2 above and pp. 174–5 below.
[2] Cases dd. 10 Dec. 1844, 1 Jan. 1845 and 15 July 1845, H.C.C.C. 246/52; Thomas Hutton v. William Jacobs, 24 Oct. 1845, ibid.; Sarah Wood v. Kwamina Buachee and others, 14 Feb. 1908, H.C.C.C. 323/52.
[3] Kimble, op. cit. pp. 68, 195–8. See F. Agbodeka, 'The Fanti Confederacy, 1865–69' in *Transactions of the Historical Society of Ghana*, vol. VII (1965), pp. 82–123 for an account of protests against British jurisdiction.
[4] George Blankson of Anomabu v. Quassie Eddoo and others, 4 and 18 Nov. 1874, H.C.C.C. 258/52.
[5] See pp. 160–1 below.
[6] W. Z. Coker to S. C. Brew, Esq., J.P., Anomabu, 3 Nov. 1857, H.C.C.C. 201/52, f. 206. It is possible, of course, that Brew acted as a J.P. before this.
[7] W. C. Fynn to S. C. Brew, Esq., J.P., Acting Civil Commandant, Anomabu, 24 March 1864, H.C.C.C. 202/52, f. 359.

to the post of stipendiary magistrate at Anomabu, for which he received £100 per annum and quarters in the fort.[1] It was as a salaried official that he resigned from government service eleven years after this, on account of ill health and advanced age.

These years had seen the Gold Coast transformed, in effect, into a colony, and corresponding changes in the machinery of justice. The civil commandant became a district commissioner, magistrates' courts were abolished and district commissioners' courts replaced them.[2] There was no necessary replacement of African personnel, however; like his European colleagues, Samuel Collins Brew now exercised the wider powers that were one result of formal colonialism. In 1875 he was Acting District Commissioner of Saltpond, a town in Fanti not far from Anomabu, on a salary of £200 per annum supplemented by free quarters and a hammock allowance of £45 to cover transport on official business.[3] In 1877 the Governor appointed him District Commissioner at Saltpond, and at the beginning of 1878 transferred him to Winneba, near Accra, where Brew remained until his resignation from the service in November 1879.[4]

Whether as justice of the peace, stipendiary magistrate, or their direct descendant, district commissioner, Brew's most frequent cases, debt, violence, and obstruction to trade, show considerable continuity with the Maclean era. In the late eighteen-fifties, he and his fellow justice of the peace, George Blankson, also an African merchant, maintained close touch with the Judicial Assessor at Cape Coast, who sent them instructions during the absence of a civil commandant at the fort. In 1858, for example, Brew was requested to despatch four prisoners from Anomabu to Cape Coast, to release a man who had been detained two days beyond his time, and to treat with indulgence a chief imprisoned because of debt and now sick, accepting security for repayment if he considered that further confinement would endanger the debtor's life. Other tasks that came his way were acting as official administrator when a trader died intestate, presiding over a meeting of creditors in the case

---

[1] *Gold Coast Blue Book, 1868*, p. 82.   [2] Kimble, op. cit. p. 304.
[3] *Gold Coast Blue Book, 1875*, p. 96.
[4] Entry dd. 4 April 1877, *Government Gazette, 1877*, no. 3; entry dd. 10 January 1878, *Government Gazette, 1878*, no. 1 and see pp. 155-6 below.

of an insolvent debtor, and dealing with a situation in which murder had been committed.[1]

After 1874, as a district commissioner, Brew's role was still primarily a judicial one. But there were procedural changes. His powers were more formally defined and linked with the political arrangements of the newly established colony. In future, it was from Government House, Accra, that certain of his instructions would come, and the Colonial Secretary there to whom official correspondence would have to be addressed. Replying to a letter which Brew had written to judicial headquarters in November 1877, the court registrar pointed out that Accra was the centre for direction and advice.[2]

Government House despatches, while Brew was at Winneba, provide an insight into his duties and reveal once again a familiar pattern. Thus, on 13 October 1879, official surprise was expressed that Brew had not reported on the matter of a stoppage of palm-oil down to the coast to which his attention had earlier been directed. He was told that the Executive must be notified of any interruption to trade in his district and of the persons concerned in it. On this occasion, armed African police were sent from Accra because of general disturbance in the Winneba area. Their commanding officer was instructed to investigate the matter of the palm-oil stoppage with Brew, and with the agent of the trading firm involved, Messrs. Swanzy, and to inform all kings and chiefs in the district, before as large a gathering as possible, that no one must be prevented from bringing anything down to the coast, on pain of severe punishment by the Governor.[3] As in the thirties and forties, under Maclean, free trading access between seaboard and interior was given high priority by the British colonial administration.

Shortly after the palm-oil stoppage, Brew resigned his position. The correspondence relating to this throws some light on the view held of him in official quarters. His departure was

[1] Robert Clarke to S. C. Brew, Esq., J.P., 9 Nov. 1857, 19 April 1858, 21 April, 9 May, and 19 May 1858, H.C.C.C. 201/52; W. C. Fynn to the same, 23 Aug. 1858, ibid.; the same to the same, 24 March 1864, H.C.C.C. 202/52, ff. 359–60; Regina per S. C. Brew v. others, 24 Aug. 1868, H.C.C.C. 277/52.

[2] Thomas Hughes to Samuel Collins Brew, 24 Nov. 1877, H.C.C.C. 204/52, f. 129.

[3] Thomas Woodcock to Samuel Collins Brew, 13 Oct. 1879, ADM. 1/758, ff. 237–8 (G.N.A.); the same to Asst. Inspector Wilton, J.P., 13 Oct. 1879, ibid. ff. 239–40.

set in motion by a government proposal, early in November 1879, that he should be transferred from Winneba to Dixcove. Brew thereupon requested three months' leave, on the grounds of health, before moving to his new station. His request was not granted. On 22 November 1879, Brew wrote a letter of resignation to the Acting Colonial Secretary in Accra, saying that 'advancing years and failing health' had made this action necessary, and that he was now unable to carry out efficiently the duties of his office. His resignation was accepted. Brew then sought, on 5 December, to withdraw it. But official processes could not be reversed. The matter had been reported to the Secretary of State for the Colonies, and another officer, also an African but younger, appointed.[1]

The reasons behind Brew's change of attitude in the space of a fortnight can only be surmised. Possibly he had written the initial letter during a moment of pique and may not have expected the Governor to accept it. In any event, he was elderly—in the late sixties, at least—and by 1881, just over a year after resignation, he was dead. For some twenty years, office of one kind or another had come his way. It is very likely that during the latter part of his life, official business proved too onerous. Writing to the Secretary of State on 1 December 1879, the Governor, H. T. Ussher, confessed himself 'much relieved' by the resignation, since according to him, Brew's actions had brought discord between powerful chiefs and 'had set the District in a blaze'.[2] These words have a strangely familiar ring and might well have been written in the eighteenth century of Richard. Samuel Collins certainly followed in the footsteps of his great-grandfather and of his father, Sam Kanto, two other strong personalities. Like them, he incurred official disapproval, although for different reasons and in different circumstances.

When Brew died, his funeral was celebrated in a manner appropriate to one who had been at the forefront of the Anomabu trading community. Memories of the celebration, and of the

---

[1] Acting Colonial Secretary to Samuel Collins Brew, 6 Nov. 1879, Establishment Files (G.N.A.); Samuel Collins Brew to Acting Colonial Secretary, 8 Nov. 1879, ibid.; Samuel Collins Brew to the same, 22 Nov. 1879 and subsequent minutes, ibid.; H. T. Ussher to Sir Michael Hicks-Beach, 1 Dec. 1879, ADM. 1/469, f. 187 (G.N.A.).

[2] H. T. Ussher to Sir Michael Hicks-Beach, 1 Dec. 1879, ADM. 1/469, f. 188 (G.N.A.).

traditional Akan custom, have persisted up to the present. Liberal calabashes of rum, for instance, are said to have been placed at various points of the town for all and sundry, including Brew's customers from up-country, to enjoy.[1] Nor was Christian symbolism neglected, and the Methodist Cemetery at Anomabu today contains a large stone monument, still cared for by the descendants of his domestics, and marking the place where he is buried.

Yet by the eighteen-eighties, the age of African 'merchant princes'[2] and merchant officials was drawing to a close. They were the products of another age, when trade between equals had been the dominant feature, uncomplicated by questions of humanitarianism or of religion. From legitimate commerce and *Pax Britannica* a new relationship would emerge, and its sequel would be colonialism. Brew's working life shows clearly one of the distinctive characteristics of this colonialism—its imposition on a society where there was already a small, educated African élite participating in trade and administration.[3] In the future the élite role would change, and educated Africans seek careers less in trade, where large European firms had the advantage, and increasingly in the professions and government service. But in the case of government service, the opportunities open to the educated would be decidedly narrower than they had been for Samuel Collins Brew, and the African district commissioner disappear eventually from the scene until almost the middle of the twentieth century.[4]

[1] Personal communciation. It is interesting to note that large sums for funeral expenses were claimed by James Hutton Brew, the administrator of his father's estate; Acting Puisne Judge to J. H. Brew, 24 March 1883, H.C.C.C., 205/52.

[2] See p. 146 above.

[3] For a wide-ranging discussion of the role of the western-educated élite in Africa, see *The New Elites of Tropical Africa*, ed. P. C. Lloyd (London, International African Institute, 1966). A paper by the present writer, 'The Emergence of an Elite: a Case Study of a West Coast Family', pp. 87–100, deals with the Brews.

[4] See pp. 180–1 below.

CHAPTER IV

James Hutton Brew:
Conflict with Colonialism

The growth of colonial authority on the Gold Coast was a devious process. British activity in West Africa was sometimes in conflict with official attitudes at home,[1] and the centre of political gravity shifted but slowly from African to European. The involvement of the British in law and order, however, brought a chain of repercussions. Not the least of these was the progressive weakening of chieftaincy in the exercise of its vital powers. On the Gold Coast, a vacuum was created which sooner or later would have to be filled. Commerce and humanitarianism notwithstanding, the home government had no planned intention of taking on the task. The inadequate pittance meted out to the settlements and the recurrent cry during the nineteenth century for limitation or even for withdrawal from West Africa are proof of this. Yet in 1874, informal colonialism was cloaked in legality by the British, and a decisive step was taken towards resolving an anomalous situation.

Among the forces that drew Britain, politically, into the Gold Coast, the long interplay between the settlements and the Akan must be singled out as crucial. On the coastal Akan, in particular, the consequences of European impact were most immediate and far-reaching. Both integrating and disruptive in their effects, the settlements brought trading wealth to the maritime region. They stimulated the growth of towns such as Cape Coast and Anomabu, increased the contact between them and provided an economic basis for the expansion of Fanti

---

[1] Consider, for example, the attitude of the Colonial Office as expressed by James Stephen in the eighteen-forties; R. Robinson and J. Gallagher, *Africa and the Victorians* (London, 1961), p. 16. See also Metcalfe, *Maclean of the Gold Coast*.

influence along the seaboard.[1] They were also a channel for the modernizing influence of new skills and new ideas which, under the pressure of later events, might have helped to counteract Fanti separatism.[2]

Disruptive in the long-run, however, was European involvement in Akan quarrels. The Fanti had not been averse to British support and had hoped to use it to maximum advantage. But military defeat by Ashanti early in the nineteenth century, together with the economic upheaval following abolition of the slave trade seriously weakened Fanti's bargaining position, and ushered in the voluntary Protectorate associated, in origin, with George Maclean.

As this Protectorate developed, changes took place in the Anglo-Fanti relationship, and the balance of power began to swing in favour of the British. From the chrysalis of trading and judicial administration, a political structure gradually emerged, although the principle of African co-operation and consent continued for some time. In 1850, when the Gold Coast settlements were separated administratively from Sierra Leone and given their own constitutional arrangements, a Legislative Council was established. Over the next few years its members included African merchants. One of them was Samuel Collins Brew, who served on the Council between 1864 and 1866.[3]

Shortly after the new constitution had been introduced, Cape Coast Castle sought African co-operation for an experiment in direct taxation. The object was to raise revenue for wider social tasks such as the provision of schools and the building of roads. When the plans were being made in November 1851, the Governor approached a number of educated Africans, of whom Samuel Collins was one. He asked them to support a moderate house tax in the coast towns and to explain to their countrymen the reason for its imposition.[4] But the taxation experiment proved markedly unsuccessful. Unable to obtain sufficient funds by this method, and with little financial support from home, the

---

[1] See pp. 12–17 above.

[2] See pp. 19–23 above and 162–6 below.

[3] Kimble, *A Political History of Ghana*, pp. 168, 455–6. George Blankson, friend and contemporary of Samuel Collins Brew, also served on the Legislative Council. See p. 160 n. 2 below, however.

[4] Colonial Secretary to Messrs. Blankson, Brew and others, Anomabu, 20 Nov. 1851, H.C.C.C. 198/52 and see Kimble, op. cit. pp. 169–81.

coast government operated under very severe difficulties. Its
entanglement in local affairs was eroding established authority
while at the same time stopping short of effective substitution.

It is not surprising that crisis point should ultimately have
been reached, and that renewed Ashanti pressure on the coast
should have helped to precipitate it. The economic effects of
another invasion from inland in 1863 have already been noted;
what this invasion also revealed was the deficiency of Cape Coast
Castle, despite its broadening authority, as the military pro-
tector of Fanti.[1] In Britain, reluctance to continue the West
African involvement came to a head when the 1865 Select
Committee appointed to inquire into coast affairs, recommended eventual British withdrawal from all territory, except
probably Sierra Leone.[2] The fate of the settlements now hung
precariously in the balance, adding further to an uncertain
local situation, and to the growing discontent among the indigenous population.

Moves to end the stalemate came from within Fanti itself,
and took the form of an attempt by the chiefs and educated
élite to strengthen and modernize traditional government on
the seaboard. Hence arose the Fanti Confederation movement
of 1867–72; its origins were traceable, in part, to the protests
by chiefs, from the mid-sixties, against alien encroachment on
their powers.[3] The movement culminated in proposals in
1871–2 for a written constitution, and offered the Cape Coast
government the possibility of recognizing and encouraging a
process of internal reform.

While holding back themselves from the exercise of full
sovereignty, the British disapproved nevertheless of this show of
independence on the part of their voluntary Protectorate, and
reactions to the Confederation were decidedly unfavourable.
After another Anglo-Ashanti war had been fought, in 1873–4,
and the Ashanti had been defeated on their own territory by a
British army, the consequences of 'protection' of the coastal

[1] See p. 148 above. British action on this occasion was negligible; see Kimble,
op. cit. p. 199.
[2] Kimble, op. cit. pp. 205–9. In 1866, Sierra Leone again became the seat of
government and the judicial centre for the West African settlements; Kimble, pp.
214–15.
[3] See Agbodeka, 'The Fanti Confederacy, 1865–69' in *Transactions of the Historical Society of Ghana*, vol. VII (1965), pp. 82–123.

peoples were at last accepted. When Gold Coast colonialism began its official life, therefore, counter-response among Africans had already been evoked, a fact which must always be remembered in the subsequent history of the nationalist movement.

This early drive for 'self-government' was characterized by the support it received from both the old and the new élite. In ideas and leadership, the Fanti Confederation Scheme owed much to educated Africans, who were themselves the product of settlement westernization. Traditional chiefs, however, made a notable contribution too, and no social gulf divided one group from the other. The 'new man' of the coast town, while acting as European magistrate, might occupy a senior position in Akan society, and carry the responsibilities of family elder, as Samuel Collins Brew had done.[1] He might also intermarry with the traditional élite; Samuel Collins Brew's wives had included Amba Opanwa of the stool family of Abura Dunkwa.[2] One of the offspring of this union between a merchant official and a 'royal' was James Hutton Brew, who was to be outstanding in the Fanti Confederation movement. Pioneer politician and journalist, and for many years a vigorous critic of the colonial administration, James Hutton Brew set a course in West African nationalism which would later be followed by other descendants, and notably by his nephews, J. E. Casely Hayford and William Ward Brew.[3]

He was born at Anomabu on 13 July 1844,[4] and belonged to a generation of literate Africans who saw their opportunities in the European power structure declining at a time when recent precedent had aroused different expectations. James Hutton received his education in England where he was sent at the age of eight. After returning to the coast, he took up the practice of law; in 1864, at the age of twenty, he was licensed as one of the

[1] See p. 153 ff. above.
[2] Sampson, *Gold Coast Men of Affairs*, p. 91. There are various spellings of Brew's mother's name. That used here is taken from a document, dated 6 Sept. 1882, in which she appears as 'Ambah Oppanwah'. I am indebted to the *Ohene* of Abura Dunkwa for access to this and other papers.
[3] See Appendix (b), p. 200. William Ward Brew was the son of Albert Cruickshank Brew, full brother of James Hutton Brew. Both Ward Brew and Casely Hayford were barristers, had distinguished public careers and received the M.B.E.; see Sampson, op. cit. p. 91 and p. 173 below.
[4] Entry in Family Bible in the possession of the *Ohene* of Abura Dunkwa.

first Gold Coast attorneys. This profession as yet required no formal training but a sufficient acquaintance with British procedures to be able to represent clients in court.[1] Brew continued in practice until 1880. His clients included his father, Samuel Collins Brew, during the insolvency proceedings of 1867, and the agent of Forster and Smith when they brought an insolvency petition in 1872 against George Blankson of Anomabu.[2] Brew's connection with the law rather than with trade[3] reveals an interesting occupational trend among the western-educated on the coast, and shows that the spread of British jurisdiction had repercussions of a professional kind.[4] Politically, too, it is a point of some importance that the new currents of activity in West Africa after the middle of the nineteenth century should have drawn so much strength from the attorneys and British-trained lawyers who succeeded them.

In James Hutton Brew's long career as an innovator—at least twenty-seven years were spent thus—the Fanti Confederation movement of 1867–72 stands out as a decisive landmark influencing his ideas and his future course of action.[5] Within a short time of commencing legal practice and while still in his twenties, he became deeply immersed in the constitution-making of 1871–2. Exactly how this link with the Confederation began is not clear. Brew may have been present at its first meeting in January 1868, a particularly disturbed period on the coast. The Fanti chiefs, assembled at their historic centre,

[1] Acting Chief Justice to J. H. Brew, Esq., Anomabu, 30 May 1864, H.C.C.C. 202/52, f. 391; Sampson, op. cit. p. 91; Kimble, op. cit. pp. 68–70.

[2] In re estate of Samuel Collins Brew, 10 Jan. 1867, H.C.C.C. 499/52; In petition of W. H. Selby re George Blankson, 3 July 1872, H.C.C.C. 284/52. Brew was suspended from practising in 1880 on account of his conduct in a particular case; Robert Pobee v. J. H. Brew, Robert Hayford v. J. H. Brew, F. E. Korsah v. J. H. Brew, 14 Sept. 1880, H.C.C.C. 287/52. For other cases of suspension, see Kimble, op. cit. pp. 68–9.

[3] See, however, p. 172 below.

[4] The first Gold Coast African to be called to the English bar (1887) was John Mensah Sarbah, author of *Fanti Customary Laws* and *Fanti National Constitution*; Sampson, op. cit. p. 213. See also p. 161 n. 3 above.

[5] For the Fanti Confederation movement, see Kimble, op. cit. pp. 222–63 and Agbodeka, art. cit. p. 160 n. 3 above. The details of James Hutton Brew's political career given in this chapter have been drawn primarily from Kimble. Documents relating to Brew and the Fanti Confederation are printed in G. E. Metcalfe, *Great Britain and Ghana, Documents of Ghana History, 1807–1957* (Ghana, 1964), pp. 338–40, 342–6 and C. W. Newbury, *British Policy towards West Africa, Select Documents, 1786–1874* (Oxford, 1965), pp. 324–6.

Mankessim, had then set up a government with three 'Presidents of the Fantee Nation' and a Council.[1]

During this early phase, the Confederation had a pronounced military aspect as an alliance among the Fanti to resist arbitrary transfer of certain British forts to the Dutch. The latter were disliked because of their Ashanti leanings, and hostilities against them and their Elmina coastal allies ensued.[2] Eventually, the Dutch decision to withdraw from all their Gold Coast settlements removed the immediate cause of difficulty, but not the fundamental reason behind Confederation—the need for a strong government in the maritime region.

A further meeting held at Mankessim in October and November 1871 dealt with the political aspects of Confederation, definable in general terms as 'the improvement of the country at large'.[3] James Hutton Brew now came to the forefront of the picture. According to his own account, he went to Mankessim at the invitation of the kings and chiefs of the country, and was asked to help in framing a constitution that would embody their resolutions concerning the permanent welfare of Fanti.[4] At Cape Coast Castle, too, he was regarded as a leading draftsman of the constitution,[5] and the role was certainly an appropriate one for an attorney to undertake.

The 1871 constitutional proposals aimed at giving Fanti a more effective central government, within the general framework of the traditional order. Provision was made for an elected King-President and an Executive Council, a nominated representative assembly to deal with legislation, and a National Assembly of chiefs that would meet once a year for the purpose of electing the executive and generally reviewing business. At its first meeting, the National Assembly appointed the rival kings of two leading Fanti states, Mankessim and Abura, to carry out jointly the duties of King-President, while the office

[1] Kimble, op. cit. pp. 224–5 and see pp. 11, 12 above.
[2] See D. Coombs, *The Gold Coast, Britain and the Netherlands 1850–1874* (London, 1963).
[3] Kimble, op. cit. p. 248.
[4] The Local Government v. James Hutton Brew, 7 Dec. 1871, H.C.C.C. 270/52.
[5] Kimble, op. cit. p. 252. It was also thought that Dr. Africanus Horton, the Sierra Leonian doctor and writer on political and medical subjects, had influenced it. Horton held a medical appointment in the Gold Coast. He was attending James Hutton Brew professionally in the early eighteen-seventies; Dr. A. B. Horton v. J. H. Brew, 23 May 1874, H.C.C.C. 271/52; Kimble, op. cit. p. 230.

of Under-Secretary of the Executive Council went to James
Hutton Brew.[1]

As a result of this office, Brew became a spokesman for the
Confederation in its negotiations with Cape Coast Castle, and
experienced his first clash with British authority. In drawing
up their constitution, the Fanti had had no thought of ter-
minating the British link. On the contrary, they hoped for the
assistance and approval of their 'benefactors on the Sea Coast'
in taking positive steps towards the good government and
development of the country.[2] On 30 November James Hutton
Brew, accompanied by the Vice-President of the Executive
Council, W. E. Davidson, called on C. S. Salmon, the Acting
Administrator at Cape Coast Castle. They presented him with
an explanatory letter from the National Assembly for the
Governor-in-Chief, together with a copy of the constitution for
the benefit of the Secretary of State in London.

Salmon, however, reacted violently. He considered Fanti's
attempt at unity and self-improvement to be a conspiracy
against the government, and Brew himself 'a penniless lawyer,
with an *awful* private character (a half caste)'.[3] Orders were
given for the arrest of the executive, and Brew was consequently
among those who appeared in court on 7 December to answer
a charge of conspiracy brought by the local government. Like
his fellow defendants, he was released on bail. But prosecution
never took place, for Salmon's precipitate action had incurred
the disapproval of the Colonial Office.[4]

The prospects for agreement over constitutional change improved markedly when J. Pope Hennessy, another Adminis-
trator-in-Chief and a man whose racial views were distinctly
progressive, came to the west coast.[5] Again James Hutton Brew
played a major part in events. On 11 April 1872, as one of a
deputation, he visited the new Governor, recently arrived from
Sierra Leone, to explain the views about Confederation. This
time the reception encountered was different and the personal
assessment of Brew more favourable; Pope Hennessy minuted

[1] Kimble, op. cit. pp. 247–9.   [2] Kimble, op. cit. p. 249.
[3] Kimble, op. cit. pp. 249–52.
[4] The Local Government v. James Hutton Brew, 7 Dec. 1871, H.C.C.C.
270/52; Kimble, op. cit. pp. 249–54.
[5] See Pope Hennessy, *Verandah* for an account of Sir John Pope Hennessy's
eventful career in different colonial territories. See also p. 27 n. 1 above.

that he had listened with much interest to Brew's 'clear and able statement'.[1] It would be a pity, the Governor said, to discourage any legitimate attempt by the Fanti at an improved form of government, although consultation with the protecting power would have to be an essential part of the process. He expressed complete agreement with sections of the scheme which the deputation had described to him that day, and promised to send the whole of it, when received, to the British government for consideration.

Shortly after this, a document reached him, signed by James Hutton Brew and entitled a 'Scheme to be submitted to His Excellency Governor J. Pope Hennessy and to the Home Government for their approval as regards the Fanti Confederation'. Among other things, it proposed that further members, 'natives or residents of the Gold Coast', should be added to the Legislative Council, and that British as well as Fanti courts of law should continue to operate, the former hearing appeals. In financial matters, an annual expenditure of £20,000 on official stipends, education, and other services was envisaged. The Confederation was to raise the funds in part itself, but half would be provided, it was hoped, by the authorities at Cape Coast Castle. Failing British support for these 'self-government' recommendations, Brew's document put forward, as the only practical alternative, that Her Majesty's Government should 'take over the whole country', ruling it vigorously, however, and not 'in the shameful and neglectful way' of the past.[2]

Not until October 1872, after several months' delay, did Pope Hennessy finally send the 'Scheme' to London. Aware of the need for change, and unlike his predecessor careful to emphasize the respectability of the Confederation and its supporters, he nevertheless advocated the second line of action—full colonial government.[3] The parting of the ways between Britain and Fanti had been reached, and the moment lost when a policy of modernization might have been encouraged on the coast, in co-operation with educated Africans and traditional chiefs. Colonial authority henceforth would favour the latter at the expense of the former, and would regard 'scholars' as an

[1] Crooks, *Records relating to the Gold Coast Settlements*, pp. 423–4.
[2] Crooks, op. cit. pp. 424–8; Kimble, op. cit. pp. 256–8.
[3] Kimble, op. cit. p. 259.

undesirable influence on the illiterate. Already this was a strand
in official thinking at Cape Coast Castle, where 'scholars' had
been held responsible for the sequence of events ever since
King Aggrey of Cape Coast had challenged British jurisdiction
in the mid-sixties. Brew became the epitome of 'half-educated
schemers', and the local government clearly thought of him as a
prime instigator of the Mankessim meetings, although he himself denied all knowledge as to their origin.[1] But whatever views
officialdom might hold to the contrary, there was very much more
to be explained in 1867–72 than the manœuvrings of a politically
minded attorney. For the future, James Hutton Brew would be
in a position of opposition, not alone, but at the centre of a small
group of coastal intelligentsia who were developing new ideas
and employing new tactics.

After 1874 and Britain's assumption of sovereignty, Brew's
main purpose was to secure the recognition of African rights.
To this end, he exerted pressure on the colonial administration
through organized channels. Indeed, for the first twenty-five
years of its existence, the Gold Coast Colony had no more
forceful critic than James Hutton Brew, who carried on his
activities both from Cape Coast and from London, where he
lived between 1888 and 1915, the year of his death. There were
few major questions during that period, whether of constitutional structure, Ashanti or colony land, with which he was
not personally concerned as a spokesman of the indigenous.

Brew's role among the educated, coastal élite was combined
with emphasis on his traditional status. In the line of succession
to the Abura Dunkwa stool, he made much of this aspect of his
life. In 1878, for example, he announced to the Governor that he
had been placed on the stool as 'Prince Brew of Dunquah and
Abracrampa', a title which he used frequently when in England,
and in 1887 he described himself as a chief who held courts.[2]

[1] The Local Government v. James Hutton Brew, 7 Dec. 1871, H.C.C.C.
270/52; Kimble, op. cit. pp. 192–221, 228–9, 252–60.
[2] Acting Colonial Secretary to Prince Brew of Dunquah and Abracrampa, 5
Feb. 1879 (papers in the possession of the Ohene of Abura Dunkwa); Brew v.
Swanzy, 16 Dec. 1887, H.C.C.C. 296/52. The evidence about James Hutton Brew
and the stool is conflicting. It is said in Abura Dunkwa today that he was in
England when it became vacant, and was therefore unable to succeed. In 1895,
however, replying to official inquiries about Brew's use of the title, the district
commissioner reported that Brew had been appointed Chief of Dunkwa, but was
not entitled to call himself 'Prince' as there had never been a king; District Com-

The image of a community of interest between western-educated leaders and Gold Coast chiefs, fostered for tactical reasons, was not without considerable reality in the later decades of the nineteenth century.

Of great importance to Brew, once the Fanti Confederation Scheme had collapsed and colonialism had taken official root, was his campaign for political reform. In this, he showed remarkable modernity, and aimed at a representative form of government which would allow more scope than the prevailing regime for the expression of African opinion; as at the time of the Confederation, total severance of the British connection was never envisaged. The most advanced statement of his views came in the mid-eighties, when he proposed an elected Legislative Council exercising sovereign power in the country and to which the British Governor-in-Chief would be responsible. Distinctly unusual for the period was Brew's suggestion that all groups in society, from illiterates to Europeans, should have representatives in the Council.[1] Behind this progressive demand there lay a belief that the colonial government had insufficient knowledge of the needs and aspirations of Gold Coast Africans, an omission for which constitutional remedies must be found.

James Hutton Brew advocated a political solution well ahead of his time, and one that looked beyond the immediate confines of Fanti. His methods as well as his aims were innovatory. Two must be singled out for special mention—journalism and deputations, as means of influencing opinion and demonstrating to the metropolitan government the strength of local feeling.

Brew, who has been described as 'the pioneer of West African journalism',[2] founded a succession of newspapers in Cape Coast after the breakdown of Confederation. First came *The Gold Coast Times* in Cape Coast, and then from 1885, *The Western Echo* followed by *The Gold Coast Echo*. The editor of *The Gold Coast Echo* was J. E. Casely Hayford who previously had been Brew's assistant. 'With all his ability, I never knew a humbler man . . .', wrote Casely Hayford some years later, about his

missioner, Cape Coast to Colonial Secretary, 5 July 1895, Bd. 19/1 S.C. (G.N.A.). I am indebted to Professor P. D. Curtin for this reference.

[1] Kimble, op. cit. p. 413.

[2] C. F. Hutchison, *The Pen-Pictures of Modern Africans and African Celebrities*, vol. I (London, n.d), p. 53.

uncle. 'Never did he pass an article to the head printer without first reading it aloud to us, and inviting our free criticism. The "Owl" column of *The Western Echo* is spoken of to this day.'[1] Through the medium of his newspapers, Brew emphasized the Gold Coast's distinctive African culture, described the short-comings of the coast government and carried on his movement for political reform, especially in 1886. Copies of *The Western Echo* were then sent regularly to the Colonial Office and to influential circles in Britain, with the object of bringing African grievances into greater prominence.[2]

Above all, he used the columns of the press to urge that there should be a deputation to the Colonial Office on the subject of representative government. Financed by a local subscription, this group would bring direct pressure to bear on the British government. The scheme, forerunner of others relating to West African affairs, was first mooted in *The Gold Coast Times* on 26 August 1882, and received much publicity from *The Western Echo* during the eighteen-eighties. It was Brew's opinion that coastal agitation alone would not be sufficient if the territory was ever to advance beyond its present backward condition and secure a type of government that would reflect African interests. He considered the Governor's policy a serious obstacle to improvement, and a personal approach to the home government essential.

Detailed arrangements for the deputation were made, and public meetings held. Both the traditional leaders of society and the western-educated were associated with the plans for its financing and organization; in Accra, for example, Brew had his friend, fellow attorney and relative by marriage, Edmund Bannerman, as organizer.[3] But the first flush of enthusiastic support was not sustained. Funds proved difficult to raise, the chiefs by no means wholeheartedly in favour, and co-operation between the Fanti and Ga regions an uncertain quantity. In spite of a rallying cry from *The Western Echo*— 'Now or Never! If this opportunity is let slip . . . we deserve the doom and fate of slaves'—the deputation scheme had disap-

---

[1] Kimble, op. cit. pp. 409, 412 and n. 6, 417–18; Sampson, op. cit. p. 95.
[2] Kimble, op. cit. p. 412.
[3] James Hutton Brew's sister Elizabeth, daughter of Samuel Collins Brew by another wife, married Edmund Bannerman; see pp. 186–7 below.

peared from the realms of possibility by 1887, and *The Western Echo* itself had ceased publication.[1] Yet the activity centring on Brew was not entirely devoid of result, even if slight, in terms of increased representation of opinion. In 1886, the Governor restored unofficial members, including Africans, to the Legislative Council and subsequently increased their numbers.[2]

Despite the failure of his immediate project, Brew's political career had not come to an end, nor had the Colonial Office heard the last of him. After 1888 and until his death twenty-seven years later, he lived in England.[3] From this vantage point and for at least a decade, he was a leading figure still in the West African pressure group. Two major questions occupied him during this time, the future of Ashanti, and Crown Land policy. Both resulted in deputations and in the extension of ideas earlier made manifest by the Fanti Confederation.

The deputation from Ashanti, which reached London in the summer of 1895, was inspired by a fear, soon to be justified, that Britain's growing interest in the interior was the first step towards establishing a Protectorate. Led by John and Albert Ansah, relatives of the Asantehene, the deputation had the active support of James Hutton Brew as its London spokesman and associate. Indeed, Brew wrote in advance to the Colonial Office to ask if it would be received there. Nor did a negative response prevent him from notifying officialdom of its arrival, and repeating his request, again unsuccessful, for an interview.[4] The practical consequences of the deputation might be negligible and the issues involved multifarious, but Brew's interest in the fate of the traditional enemy of Fanti was not without significance. In some measure it foreshadowed the expanding horizons to which Casely Hayford would shortly give literary expression in his study of Akan institutions, when he emphasized

[1] Kimble, op. cit. pp. 410–18.
[2] Kimble, op. cit. pp. 415–18.
[3] Jacob Sey, a Cape Coast business man, engaged him and a Freetown lawyer, Sir Samuel Lewis, as counsel in a lawsuit heard in the English High Court. Brew never returned to West Africa thereafter; J. D. Hargreaves, *Life of Sir Samuel Lewis* (London, 1958), p. 15; Sampson, op. cit. p. 95.
[4] Kimble, op. cit. pp. 285–9. According to present-day family tradition, Prince Brew and his brother Albert Cruickshank Brew were personal friends of the King of Ashanti. For the marriage between Brew's nephew (the son of Albert) and the daughter of an Ashanti chief, see pp. 187–8 below.

the cultural unity of the Akan, impelling 'the fusion of the Fantis and the Ashantis into one people'.[1]

At the same time as Ashanti independence hung in the balance, Brew flung himself into that most burning of all West African questions—the Crown Lands Bill. The Bill was introduced in various forms by the Gold Coast government from 1894, and was an attempt to control speculative concessions for gold-mining and timber, an economic development that dated back to the eighteen-seventies. No measure aroused more profound and widespread opposition than the proposal that all land should be owned or at least administered by the Crown. Whatever the scheme's merits or demerits on practical grounds, it was damned from the outset. Since land was regarded as a cornerstone of the tribe and held deep religious significance, the Bill seemed to attack the indigenous structure, and to infringe the relationship by which land had remained in African hands. On the coast, chiefs and the western-educated élite joined forces in protest meetings, petitions, and telegrams to London where their ally, James Hutton Brew, took up the cause in yet another battle with the Colonial Office. In an interesting statement, dated 22 March 1895, Brew advanced his line of argument, much of it irrefutable. The Gold Coast Protectorate, he said, was unusual in kind and had not been the result of 'conquest, cession, or treaty'; governmental powers, therefore, did not extend to rights over land.[2]

Two years later, political life in West Africa, with which Brew had been concerned for over a quarter of a century, reached a further milestone when the Gold Coast Aborigines' Rights Protection Society was founded in Cape Coast. The Society was deeply involved from the outset with opposition to the Crown Lands Bill, and aimed at keeping 'the acts of the Government' under critical review, an objective very close to Brew's heart. Its main support came from Fanti, where an educated group assumed leadership backed by numbers of chiefs. 'It was the Confederation all over again . . . the noblest embodiment of the nation', a Fanti lawyer has written.[3] In

[1] Casely Hayford, *Gold Coast Native Institutions*, p. 241, quoted in Kimble, op. cit. p. 529.

[2] Kimble, op. cit. pp. 330–8. See also Metcalfe, *Great Britain and Ghana*, p. 475.

[3] Kimble, op. cit. p. 340 ff. and especially p. 355, quoting from J. W. de Graft Johnson, *Towards Nationhood in West Africa* (London, 1928), pp. 31–2.

1898, a deputation, organized by the Society and consisting of three Cape Coast merchants, was able to obtain an audience at the Colonial Office, where it successfully made known the views of Africans on the vital Land Bill.[1]

Although James Hutton Brew continued to live in London until his death in Camberwell on 14 April 1915,[2] the climax of his political career appears to have come in the last decade of the century. Thereafter, he exercised influence on members of the Gold Coast intelligentsia who went to England for their training, often of a legal kind. Any assessment of Brew's place in the movement of national awakening must give due emphasis to his highly developed sense of political strategy, in part reflecting long Afro-European interaction on the Gold Coast. His aptitude was such that it served only to strengthen official views that the 'educated native' was 'the curse of the West Coast', a malign influence on illiterate chiefs, responsible for all the disturbances and challenges to authority since before the Fanti Confederation.[3] Personal motives, too, were often called in question. Hence officialdom considered that the real aim of Brew and Bannerman in proposing a deputation on representative government in the mid-eighties had been to secure funds for the purpose of a private visit overseas.[4]

The question arises as to how far the condemnatory appraisal of James Hutton Brew as a self-seeking adventurer of doubtful character is an accurate representation of the facts. British officials, with the occasional exception, sought the worst possible interpretation in every case—unprincipled scheming—and gave an unfavourable slant to personal circumstances which otherwise might have been ignored.[5] Motives are extremely hard to establish now and certain aspects of Brew's life rather

---

[1] Kimble, op. cit. pp. 349–55.

[2] James Hutton Brew's death certificate (Somerset House, London). The date of his death is given in the Family Bible at Abura Dunkwa, where it is also noted that a Memorial Service was held at the Jubilee Chapel, Cape Coast on 22 May 1915; see p. 161 n. 4 above.

[3] Kimble, op. cit. p. 91.

[4] Kimble, op. cit. pp. 410–18, especially p. 414. Brew was also said to be in debt (see Kimble, p. 418) and a number of cases involving him do appear in the legal records (G.N.A.). But debt was by no means an uncommon state of affairs on the coast in the nineteenth century, as the records reveal.

[5] Brew's private life came under attack, for example; see Kimble, op. cit. p. 252 n. 6 and p. 418. Pope Hennessy, however, did not join in the general denunciation; see pp. 164–5 above.

obscure. It would be very interesting, for example, to know more
about his last fifteen years in England. That he had personal
as well as political objectives in mind throughout his career
seems undeniable. It was a many-sided career. Family tradition
today describes him as a merchant and a diplomat,[1] as well as
a lawyer, and the business side of his activities, were fuller
details available, might well prove illuminating.

One important piece of evidence is supplied by Brew's death
certificate, issued in London, on which his occupation is given
as 'Land Company Promoter'.[2] He must be counted among
those Africans who filled a new middleman role from the later
nineteenth century—as the intermediary between chief and
European in land concessions for gold-mining. For instance,
Brew had connections with the Gold Coast Native Concession
Purchasing Company, Ltd., founded in 1882.[3] To what extent
business interests were a major concern of his it is impossible to
say. But his desire to visit London, his association with the cause
of Ashanti, a gold-producing area, and his opposition to the
Crown Lands Bill which sought to regulate concession granting
might all have been influenced by them, at least in part. To
assume, however, as colonial authority usually did, that *no*
genuine public issues bound together the innovating and
traditional elements in coast society was very wide of the mark,
as the effective opposition to the Crown Lands Bill demonstrates.

James Hutton Brew had been born during the halcyon days
of African merchants on the Gold Coast. He died during the
early stages of a world catastrophe that was to have repercussions on the self-government movement in West Africa. Looking
back to his forebears and especially to the Irish trader, it seems
possible to discern family traits. One of these was a highly independent attitude towards authority. There are definite re-
minders, too, of Richard in James Hutton's fluent pen and
outspoken literary style. His bombardment of the Colonial
Office, in 1895, with 'voluminous documentary evidence' on
the subject of the Ashanti embassy recalls the 'very voluminous

---

[1] It states, too, that he went to England to become the first Gold Coast representative in Parliament.
[2] James Hutton Brew's death certificate (Somerset House).
[3] Kimble, op. cit. p. 343.

production' on coastal trading administration that had emanated from Richard's pen in 1770.[1]

Looking ahead, it can be said that James Hutton Brew opened up paths which would be explored further by a younger generation of educated Africans, including his lawyer nephews, J. E. Casely Hayford and William Ward Brew. In their time, West African nationalism entered a new phase, extending its range from the Gold Coast and Ashanti to Nigeria, Sierra Leone, and the Gambia. Casely Hayford, journalist, writer, and politician, was a major figure in this, and in the National Congress of British West Africa, which was formally established in Accra in 1920. He was President of it from 1923 until his death in 1930, while Ward Brew was one of the founder members.

Lineally descended from the Fanti Confederation and the Aborigines' Rights Protection Society, the Congress reproduced, on an interterritorial plane, the principles of constitutional change, local development, and African advance for all British West Africa. It stressed the elective element in government and the need for indigenous control of land.[2] Casely Hayford was heir to the mantle of James Hutton Brew in this, and, like him, an innovator who also gave prominence to the intrinsic value of the African heritage.[3] But during the Congress period, a new departure was made with the assertion that the *western-educated* were the natural leaders of the people, and spoke on their behalf in the matter of West African unity. This attitude brought about tension between the chiefs and the educated that had not been obvious earlier, revealing the growing complexity of political patterns on the Gold Coast.[4]

[1] Kimble, op. cit. p. 289 and see p. 96 above.
[2] Kimble, op. cit. especially pp. 381–9, 399–400 and plate 5a facing p. 436.
[3] See p. 190 below.
[4] Kimble, op. cit. especially pp. 381–96.

CHAPTER V

Samuel Henry Brew and Ebenezer Annan Brew: Africans in Government Service

Ever since trading settlements had been established within the maritime states, some form of European administration had existed on the Gold Coast employing a small number of literate Africans. During the slave-trading period, these Africans were an influential minority, a channel through which 'strangers' conducted their business in an alien social and political environment. Legitimate commerce and *Pax Britannica* during the middle decades of the nineteenth century at first extended rather than diminished the African role, and carried it into the sphere of justice, where the indigenous merchant reached his apogee as a guardian of Her Majesty's peace.[1]

The growth of British political power, however, especially after 1874, brought a scaling-down of African opportunities in the service of the colonial government. As the quantity and range of government business increased, the administrative structure moved away from its trading origins and the merchant official was gradually replaced by a professional. Africans then found that there was a much greater differentiation within the service, and that they themselves were restricted, in general, to junior-level posts.

At each stage of administrative development from the eighteenth to the twentieth centuries—mercantile, judicial, and colonial—members of the Brew family are to be found serving in capacities for which a degree of western education was essential. First came Harry Brew, linguist at Cape Coast Castle in

---

[1] James Bannerman, for example, a justice of the peace for many years, was Lieutenant-Governor of the Gold Coast Settlements in 1850–1; Kimble, *A Political History of Ghana*, p. 65.

the seventeen-nineties, and spokesman for British headquarters when slave trading predominated.[1] Under the judicial Protectorate, Harry Brew's son, Richard, and grandson, Samuel Collins Brew, both held important positions. During the mid-eighteen-forties, Richard was interpreter to the Judicial Assessor's Court at Cape Coast, which was attended also by the chief of Cape Coast and by justices of the peace, while in Samuel Collins Brew, a magistrate and district commissioner, the African official is seen at his height, on a par with the European.[2]

Colonial status did not immediately bring about deterioration in prospects. Samuel Collins, for example, remained a district commissioner until his resignation in 1879, and by 1883, nine out of forty-three senior posts were still in African hands.[3] But from the later nineteenth century, as colonial authority concerned itself with a widening span of affairs, greater specialization developed in government service, stiffer entry qualifications were adopted, and the structure became more formalized and hierarchical.[4]

The colonial service on the Gold Coast, by the beginning of the present century, staffed both a political administration and professional departments. The former centred on the Governor's Secretariat and district commissioners were its key officials 'in the field'. The latter held responsibility for matters such as education, agriculture, and medicine. Each had junior and senior grades, reflecting the general pattern of the British civil service, and it was the junior grades to which Africans were now confined.

At a time when standards of western education on the Gold Coast were rising, and families like the Brews had known positions of influence, the new élite thus encountered frustrating obstacles to their entry into the top posts. It is hardly surprising

[1] See pp. 122-3 above.
[2] See p. 153 ff. above. In the eighteen-fifties, another Brew acted as clerk of Anomabu Court. This was Samuel Henry Brew, nephew of Samuel Collins Brew and father of Samuel Henry Brew, the civil servant referred to in this chapter; William C. Fynn to Samuel H. Brew, Clerk of the Court, Anomabu Fort, 16 Dec. 1858, H.C.C.C. 201/52.
[3] Kimble, op. cit. p. 94. Seven of the district commissioners were African. On the general subject of Africans in government service, see Kimble, pp. 65-7, 93-109.
[4] Kimble, op. cit. pp. 98-9, 101.

that the nationalists, of whom Casely Hayford was one, should have taken up the civil service cause in their struggle for indigenous rights.[1] Casely Hayford's own cousins, Samuel Henry and Ebenezer Annan Brew, were themselves affected by the barriers, although Ebenezer Annan, the younger of the two, ultimately benefited from new departures after the First World War.

No better example could be found of the divergence between growing educational achievement on the part of Africans and their restricted opportunities for advancement in government service at the close of the nineteenth century than in the case of Samuel Henry Brew. Born on 15 December 1865,[2] Samuel Henry was a government official for over thirty years, one of the few to reach the top of the ladder in his grade. A keen interest in education distinguished him, and his marked scholarly qualities are still commented on by those who remember him personally. Three generations earlier, Richard Brew, interpreter to the Court at Cape Coast, had been a 'half-scholar' able to read but not to write.[3] Samuel Henry, however, received his education at the Wesleyan High School in Cape Coast.[4] As a member of the local intelligentsia, he presented papers to the Gold Coast National Research Association, founded by his relative, Casely Hayford,[5] while his publication of a Fanti grammar symbolized the cultural renaissance that was accompanying African nationalism. In 1904, he backed a local venture, the Fanti Public Schools Company Ltd., for the promotion of education, a means—to quote his own words—of assisting 'the elevation and advancement of a nation'.[6] Teaching, in fact, occupied him for six years of his youth, between 1881 and 1887, and again after his retirement from government service in

[1] Kimble, op. cit. especially p. 107.

[2] Establishment Files (G.N.A.). I am grateful to the Establishment Secretary, Government of Ghana, for permission to consult the Personal Files of Samuel Henry Brew and Ebenezer Annan Brew.

[3] See p. 127 above.

[4] Establishment File: S. H. Brew. The Wesleyan High School for Boys was opened in 1876, the first instance on the Gold Coast of a more advanced educational institution. Ultimately it had to close through shortage of funds, but was re-opened and later named Mfantsipim School, achieving considerable success; Foster, *Education and Social Change in Ghana*, p. 102.

[5] Kimble, op. cit. p. 525.

[6] Samuel Henry Brew to the Governor's Private Secretary, 12 April 1904, Establishment File: S. H. Brew; Kimble, op. cit. p. 513 n.4.

1920.[1] But it was in government service that he made a note-worthy career for himself, within the limits of promotion then open to an African.

Samuel Henry first entered the colonial service in April 1887, at the age of twenty-one, when he became a clerical assistant in the Governor's Office with a salary of £40 per annum.[2] From this humble beginning, he advanced steadily upwards through the ranks of junior clerk and first grade clerk to a confidential post of high responsibility in the Secretariat—that of Assistant Chief Clerk, later designated Native Chief Clerk. This was the position which he held in 1912, after twenty-five years' service, and for which the salary scale was £250 to £300 per annum.[3]

In 1914, shortly before the outbreak of war, Brew made further progress. He applied to fill a Special Class appointment as Chief Clerk in the Medical Department, following the death of a European officer, and was transferred on the Acting Governor's recommendation. Brew remained Chief Clerk until his retirement on 16 June 1920. By this time, his salary had risen to £360, a substantial amount for the period, and during two years of retirement, he received an annual pension of £217. He died on 6 June 1922.[4]

Had circumstances been different, Samuel Henry Brew would almost certainly have achieved a rank in the hierarchy more senior than that of Chief Clerk, important though this undoubtedly was. Throughout his life, the quality of his work earned him frequent praise in official circles[5] and a considerable degree of trust was placed in him. He was often among those

[1] Establishment File: S. H. Brew and personal communication.
[2] Establishment File: S. H. Brew.
[3] Establishment File: S. H. Brew.
[4] Establishment File: S. H. Brew; *Gold Coast Government Gazette, July–December 1920*, p. 885; *Gold Coast Colony Blue Book, 1921*. Brew was also receiving a war bonus of £36 per annum when he retired; S. H. Brew to Colonel Sir Matthew Nathan, 21 June 1920, Samuel Brew dossier (Birmingham University Library). I am grateful to Professor Ivor Wilks for drawing my attention to this manuscript.
[5] W. Brandford Griffith to Acting Colonial Secretary, 29 April 1892, Establishment File: S. H. Brew; Colonial Secretary to Governor, 3 Dec. 1892, ibid.; Governor's minute dd. 17 April 1896, on Brew's application for leave of absence, ibid.; Governor's minute dd. 5 Aug. 1910 supporting Brew's application for appointment in the Gambia, ibid. Brew was described in 1889 as the only government shorthand writer in the colony; Governor to Secretary, Board of Education, 28 June 1889, ibid.

clerks who accompanied the Governor on journeys from Accra, and on several occasions between 1905 and 1914, while in the Secretariat, he acted in place of the European Chief Clerk when the latter had leave. After one instance of this, in 1907, the Governor expressed appreciation of 'the thoroughly efficient manner' in which Brew, as deputy, had performed his duties.[1] Special tasks also came his way, for example, as Secretary to a Committee of the Legislative Council.[2] From a working angle, there was ultimately little distinction between him and a junior European officer. The difference lay in the nature and extent of their prospects.

It is reasonable to surmise that as a result, Brew experienced some disappointment and frustration. In 1909 he requested six months' leave from the Secretariat with full pay and a free passage to England, in order to take a part of the African Tropical Service Course, which had recently been introduced for European officials. The Governor, in reply, regretted that he was unable to support the application. The following year, affected perhaps by the set-back, Brew applied for appointment in the Gambia. This time, he *did* have the Governor's backing as 'a very efficient officer', but it transpired that there were no vacancies. In 1911 came his petition for a personal allowance of £50 per annum. In this petition, Brew drew attention to his twenty-four years' service, the favourable recommendations he had been given and his periods of deputizing for the European Chief Clerk, with gratuities between 1905 and 1911 totalling less than £48—facts that speak for themselves.[3] His salary range then increased, and his appointment in 1914 as Chief Clerk to the Medical Department represented some advance. But it had come slowly, and the contrast with European colleagues who were able to move into a higher, non-clerical grade must have occasioned feelings of restlessness even in one of whose 'faithful service' the Governor made mention in his obituary notice.[4]

---

[1] Governor's minute dd. 12 Oct. 1907, Establishment File: S. H. Brew; *Gold Coast Government Gazette, 1898*, p. 318; ibid. *1899*, p. 253; *Gold Coast Colony Blue Book, 1906;* ibid. *1912.*

[2] Establishment File: S. H. Brew.   [3] ibid.

[4] Establishment File: S. H. Brew. The obituary notice also mentioned the fact that Brew received the 1895–6 Ashanti Star, and the medal and clasp for service in the 1900 Ashanti campaign.

Gold Coast government service, like many other fields of activity, felt the impact of change in the immediate post-war years, a consequence of manpower shortage and the general pressures for innovation. The change was particularly apparent during Sir Gordon Guggisberg's enlightened Governorship between 1919 and 1927. This period coincided with the National Congress movement in which Casely Hayford was so prominent and in which educated opinion was the motivating force.[1] A number of senior appointments in the service were then thrown open by Guggisberg to African candidates; Samuel Henry Brew, after official retirement, hoped that it might be possible for him to hold one of them in Cape Coast—his native town, whence he had returned from Accra.[2] The real beneficiary, however, was to be a brother, younger by twelve years, Ebenezer Annan Brew, who made his mark in the Agricultural Department, where entry into higher grade posts now became possible.

Ebenezer Annan was born at Cape Coast on 15 February 1878.[3] Like Samuel Henry, he displayed both ability and application. When he was eighteen he joined the Posts and Telegraph Department as a learner, but was soon selected, under a new scheme, for agricultural training at Hope Gardens in Jamaica. He spent two years there, after a preliminary year at the Botanical Station, Aburi, near Accra, and in August 1901, returned to Aburi as Garden Assistant on a salary of £50 per annum.[4]

Progress henceforth was slow and steady and the returns limited until the nineteen-twenties. In 1908, after six and a half years, he was promoted to be Native Travelling Instructor with a salary range of £100 to £150 per annum. He held this post for twelve years, a period that included the First World War. From 1916 he was in charge of an agricultural sub-station,

<hr />

[1] Kimble, op. cit. especially pp. 102–9, 381 ff., and see R. E. Wraith, *Guggisberg* (London, 1967), especially pp. 167–77, 213–42.

[2] S. H. Brew to Colonel Sir Matthew Nathan, 21 June 1920, Samuel Brew dossier (Birmingham University Library). Brew requested Sir Matthew Nathan, an ex-Governor of the Gold Coast, to approach Guggisberg on his behalf. Nathan did so, and Guggisberg promised to see what could be done. Brew's years of retirement, however, were spent in teaching in Cape Coast, not in government service: it is possible that this was a result of Guggisberg's influence.

[3] Establishment File: E. A. Brew.

[4] Establishment File: E. A. Brew; *Gold Coast Government Gazette, 1898*, p. 106; *Gold Coast Colony Blue Book, 1901*.

where cocoa, coffee, fruit, and ginger were cultivated and far-
mers came to receive advice. During this time, he too, like his
brother, took part in Cape Coast's intellectual activities, and
contributed weekly notes on agriculture to the journal, *The
Gold Coast Nation*.[1]

More rapid progress, the result of Governor Guggisberg's
forward-looking measures, characterized Ebenezer Annan's
latter years in the service. In 1920, he became Native Assistant
Inspector for which the scale was £240 to £336; he was thus
approaching the salary his brother had known before retirement. Only two years later, Ebenezer Annan moved into the
senior rungs of the Agricultural Department as African Assistant
Superintendent, beyond a level that had been accessible to his
brother; the scale here was £400 to £780 per annum. Ill
health unfortunately cut short an extremely promising career,
and compelled his premature retirement in 1926 when he was
only forty-nine years old.[2]

By the nineteen-twenties, then, the government machine
had made some accommodation to the fact that a small group
of able and educated Africans existed on the Gold Coast;
Ebenezer Annan Brew's career reflects a trend, slow but inevitable, towards greater Africanization. Yet despite Guggisberg's
reforms, certain key offices long remained barred to Africans,
such as that of district commissioner. By origin a judical
post, the district commissioner was now the Governor's chief
link with outlying parts, and a political as well as an administrative figure. Not until 1942 would an African again hold the
kind of appointment that Samuel Collins Brew and others up to
the turn of the century had done.[3] With the onset of colonialism
and the hardening of opinion against Africans in anything other
than the junior ranks, there was especial opposition to their

[1] Establishment File: E. A. Brew, especially E. J. P. Brown to E. A. Brew, 8
March 1916 and subsequent correspondence; *Gold Coast Agricultural Report, 1916* et
seq.
[2] Establishment File: E. A. Brew; *Gold Coast Colony Blue Book, 1926–7*. See also
p. 177 above. Ebenezer Annan died on 22 May 1932 at the age of fifty-five. Both
he and William Ward Brew were unofficial members of Cape Coast Town Council;
ibid. *1931–2* and *1932–3*. An obituary notice was published in *The Gold Coast
Farmer*, vol. I, no. 2 (June 1932).
[3] In 1883, there were seven African district commissioners. By 1899, there
were three and in 1908, none; Kimble, op. cit. pp. 94, 99 n. 1, 100 n. 1, 122, 123
n. 1.

presence in the upper strata of the sensitive political administration.

Considering government service as a whole, it could not be
said that under colonialism the western-educated were without
openings. The difficulty was that these openings were subordinate ones, did not go far enough, and seemed a reversal of the
past when an African had even held the rank of Lieutenant-
Governor of the settlements.[1] While circumstances and needs
had changed since the days when there was a merchant-
controlled administration, local nationalists could justifiably
point to the absence of Africans at the top, whether as civil servants or as legal officers. Yet from the point of view of long-
term Africanization, much would be gained from the stock of
experience and tradition that had been built up, at the junior
levels of government service by families such as the Brews over
a period of several generations.

[1] See p. 174 n. 1 above.

CHAPTER VI

The Brews in Society

Part-European in origin and western-educated, the Brews stand out as distinctive figures in the Fanti maritime towns of the nineteenth century. Their activities were affected by the Ashanti problem, and were linked with the expanding orbit of power of the European settlements. It remains to consider them from the angle of society on the Gold Coast, where African and European cultures had long had a meeting point. Springing in the first instance from trade, innovating elements had been introduced into Fanti; the Brews illustrate some of the effects upon traditional patterns of life there.

Of fundamental importance to the investigation is family structure, which was bound up with the matrilineal clan, bedrock of the social order.[1] The Brews, it has been seen, belonged to the matrilineal family of the Reverend Philip Quaque, as a result of marriage in the eighteenth century between Harry, son of the Irish trader, and Abba Kaybah. European blood thus found its way into an important Fanti kinship group in Cape Coast.[2]

From descendants of the matrilineal family, much information can be derived about relationships and ancestry, particularly in the context of property disputes during the nineteenth and twentieth centuries. The matrilineal family regarded the Brews as forming part of their lineage, through Abba Kaybah, and elderly members of the line in present-day Cape Coast take a similar view. During past law cases, the Brews, too, made mention of their connection with Quaque, and they refer today to his descendants 'on the other side of the family'. Yet a difference of emphasis is discernible. The Brews think of *themselves* as a distinct and corporate group, with a strong pride in their

[1] See pp. 17–18 above.   [2] See above, pp. 120–1 and 140 n. 2.

forebears, and from this point of view, their matrilineal ancestry receives considerably less attention than does the male
line of descent.

Discernible through the Brews, therefore, is a trait present in
Akan coastal society under European influence, namely emphasis on patrilineal descent as an important determinant of
family structure. The present work has traced them, throughout, along the male line from father to son, a non-Akan concept
of family that nevertheless had definite validity in the Fanti
maritime towns. In this sense, a 'Brew family' certainly existed,
and displayed many of the attributes of one traced matrilineally, with the difference that lineage stemmed from a man.

Hence the Brews attached prominence to father and sometimes to grandfather, particularly in the case of Samuel Collins
Brew. One of his grandsons, J. E. Casely Hayford, whose
mother had been a daughter of Samuel Collins, clearly assumed
a Brew family of male descent. Writing to his kinsfolk in 1929,
Casely Hayford referred to their 'family unity' and 'notable
ancestry' with his late grandfather in mind. When visiting
England, he began to trace Brew origins on the European side,
a matter in which his uncle, James Hutton Brew, is also said to
have shown interest.[1] Two of Samuel Collins's surviving grandchildren display the same awareness of family at the present day,
and can recall annual meetings of the elders, held in the New
Year, when they were told its history. Descended from him
through his sons, they think of themselves as belonging to the
paternal line and recognize, although without knowing precise
details, that this began with a European ancestor.[2]

The emergence of a family pattern oriented towards the
father is also seen in the inheritance process, where the changes
taking place through European contact were linked with a
different attitude towards property. Under the traditional
order, inheritance was regulated matrilineally. Property was
owned collectively by the clan and the concept of unrestricted,
individual, private ownership was exceptional.[3] But Afro-
European commerce brought new opportunites for the African
middleman. These were demonstrated by the Fanti goldtaker

[1] J. E. Casely Hayford to his kinsmen, 26 May 1929 and personal communication.
[2] See pp. 117–18 above.   [3] Sarbah, *Fanti Customary Laws*, pp. 61–2.

who had 'acquired his property chiefly by trading with Europeans', and whose house was 'more splendidly furnished than those of any of his neighbours'.[1] Property acquired in this way took on the different connotation of association with a person rather than with a group, and rights of disposal tended to be viewed accordingly. In such circumstances, it became not uncommon for a father to think of his own children as heirs. This was a limitation of kinship claims that could easily give rise to friction, and pointed the way towards family units focusing, to a greater extent, on parents and their offspring.

Evidence of changing views is brought to light by the Brews in frequent litigation from the mid-nineteenth century. The disputes arose over both the 'ancestral property' of the matrilineal family, and the 'self-acquired property' of the Brews, to which the matrilineal family ultimately asserted a right of possession. Many complex issues were involved, turning on marriage, domestic or dependent status within a family, and relationship between branches of the lineage often very hard now to disentangle.[2]

In broad terms, the conflict grew out of an interpretation of property rights that narrowed the field of kinship claims, and introduced a concept of individualism outside the pattern of strict customary law. Indicative of this was the use of the Will in oral and ultimately written form for the disposal of property, a practice which was 'of modern growth', according to J. M. Sarbah, the nineteenth-century authority on Fanti law.[3] Examples of testamentary disposition and of the consequences that might ensue from it are to be found among the Brews.

Particularly noteworthy was a lawsuit brought by a descendant of their matrilineal family in 1908 against the paternal line. It related to property that had earlier come into the possession of the Brews, and had been transmitted subsequently by

---

[1] Adams, *Remarks on the country extending from Cape Palmas to the River Congo*, pp. 18–19.

[2] According to the plaintiff in Sarah Wood v. Mrs. Maud Thompson, 18 Dec. 1908, the Brews were dependants of her family because of the status, several generations back, of Abba Kaybah, the wife of Harry Brew; Renner, *Cases in the Courts of the Gold Coast Colony and Nigeria*, vol. I, pt. 2, p. 802 ff. Domestic status was very common in Fanti and arose for a variety of reasons; it certainly did not necessarily imply a condition of complete slavery. Marriage with domestics of the family was common, and in some circumstances, domestics might be in the line of inheritance; see Sarbah, op. cit.   [3] Sarbah, op. cit. pp. 95–7.

will. This property, known as Brabadzi land, a few miles from Cape Coast, was 'of very considerable extent and value',[1] and had first been acquired by Sam Kanto Brew, the early nineteenth-century slave trader. It belonged, therefore, to the category of private or self-acquired property that originated in individual not corporate family effort, and it was symbolic of the new forms of wealth existing on the coast as a result of Afro-European trade. When Sam Kanto died in 1823, the land passed to his uterine brother Richard, ultimately described as 'a very rich man'.[2] In 1849, on Richard's death, it then passed by Richard's testamentary disposition to his nephew Henry, the eldest son of Sam Kanto; there was no female line since Richard's sister had died without issue.

The significant fact here was the retention of substantial landed property within a Brew sub-lineage through the procedure of Will, and by inheritance along the male line of descent, excluding the matrilineal kinship group. In accordance with customary law, this group might well consider Brabadzi to be 'family property', after the failure of a Brew line of inheritance through females in 1849. Over half a century later, in 1908, a Cape Coast descendant of Abba Kaybah's family claimed ownership of Brabadzi from the Brews. By that stage, the land was under the control of a niece of Henry Brew, his sister's daughter. An interesting legal case followed, including an appeal by the plaintiff to the High Court. The case ended in 1910 with both parties agreeing that the land be divided.[3]

Brabadzi proceedings show the conflict between newly developing practice and customary laws of inheritance; on this occasion, it was the wide sphere of matrilineal claims that were affected by testamentary disposition along the male line. Instances also occur, however, of dispute on the patrilineal side of the Brew family, due to the fact that actions over property were thought to have been based on too narrow a view of social obligations.

[1] Renner, op. cit. p. 802.
[2] Sarah Wood v. Kwamina Buachee and others, 14 Feb. 1908, H.C.C.C. 323/52. It was this Richard Brew who was interpreter to the Judicial Assessor's Court at Cape Coast; see p. 153 above, also p. 141.
[3] Renner, op. cit. pp. 501, 802–4. The following cases are also relevant: Sarah Wood v. Kwamina Buachee and others, 14 Feb. 1908, H.C.C.C. 323/52; the same v. the same, 11 Dec. 1909, H.C.C.C. 324/52.

One instance was the written will of Samuel Collins Brew, which was drawn up, witnessed and sealed towards the end of his life. By this will, he created a trust for the education of his youngest son and appointed a friend as trustee. The rest of his children were omitted from its benefits. In 1881, after Samuel Collins's death, the will was challenged by an elder son, the attorney James Hutton Brew. Using the argument that this was the act, not of an Englishman but of a native, James Hutton Brew declared that native law prevented his father from excluding as beneficiaries all members of his family save one. He appealed against a judgement that had been given in favour of the trustees, and succeeded in establishing himself as the administrator of his father's estate.[1]

As in lineage and inheritance, Brew practice also reveals interesting trends in the sphere of marriage. There was the choice of literate wives, for instance, once education had reached a small number of women in the coast towns. These unions were formalized, not by customary law but by Christian procedure, and the wife acquired the name 'Mrs. Brew'. In particular the rites of Methodism were adopted, after its introduction on to the Gold Coast in 1835, an event with which Henry Brew, Sam Kanto's elder son, was connected.[2] Henry himself made a second marriage, to a literate wife in Cape Coast, while his two sons, Samuel Henry and Richard Henry, who were the offspring of the first union, a customary law one, were likewise married within the church. In Richard Henry's case, his wife was the niece of an important Anomabu merchant, Samuel Ferguson, contemporary with Samuel Collins Brew. In the next generation, the Brew-Ferguson alliance was repeated when Richard Henry's nephew, Samuel Henry, Junior, also took a Ferguson as wife.[3]

An interesting point is thus raised—the degree of inter-

[1] James H. Brew v. Francis Williams and John Ogoe, 26 May 1881, H.C.C.C. 287/52; In matter of estate of S. C. Brew of Cape Coast and Anomabu, deceased, 10 April 1882, ibid.; Re S. C. Brew's estate, 24 March 1883, H.C.C.C. 205/52.

[2] See p. 188 below.

[3] Brew v. Brew, 30 Oct. 1865, H.C.C.C. 435/52; Mrs. Marian Gordon v. Mrs. Henry Brew, 28 Feb. 1870, H.C.C.C. 278/52; Brew v. Brew, 15 Jan. 1900, H.C.C.C. 310/52; R. H. Brew v. Abimah Aigammah, 6 May 1902, H.C.C.C. 315/52; entry, 29 Nov. 1823 in *Royal Gold Coast Gazette and Commercial Intelligencer, 1822–3*, vol. 50, no. 1, and personal communication. Instances occur where the husband and wife eventually separated.

marriage between western-educated families on the coast from
the mid-nineteenth century, and its social consequences.
Further examples of intermarriage are provided by the daughters of Samuel Collins Brew. One of them, Mary, married the
Reverend de Graft Hayford and became the mother of J. E.
Casely Hayford, while another, Elizabeth, married Edmund
Bannerman of Accra, the friend and political ally of her
brother, James Hutton Brew.[1] It is certainly possible that these
family unions helped to create a sense of cohesion among the
western-educated, which was strong enough by the nineteen-
twenties for them to claim the leadership of society in the
movement for political rights.[2]

Within the Akan lineage system, then, it could be said that
a 'Brew family' emerged displaying western traits—emphasis
on the male line of descent, an individualist strain in property
attitudes, and Christian marriage with literate wives. Status
passed from father to son, associated with education and achievement, while trade, law, and government service opened up the
way to self-acquired property.

But traditional society left its imprint, too, and there was an
admixture of patterns, traceable though the family might be to
male and not female ancestry. Corporate sense was strong,
the kinship network wide—over one hundred and twenty names
appear on a list of members of the Brew family drawn up during
the nineteen-twenties[3]—and attendance at family funerals, in
accordance with Akan custom, was a compelling social obligation. In marriage, the adoption of western forms did not
preclude polygamy and unions contracted by customary law,
and it was not uncommon for the Brews to have domestics or
family dependants as wives. A notable example was Samuel
Collins Brew. He married one wife by church rites, but had
several who were domestics, sometimes acting as his agents in
charge of trading stations along the coast.[4] Nor were marriage
alliances confined to the educated élite. Two of Samuel Collins's wives were from a 'royal' background, while in the
early twentieth century a branch of the Brew family became

---

[1] Personal communication, and see p. 168 above.
[2] See p. 173 above.
[3] I am indebted to Mrs. William Ward Brew for this list.
[4] Personal communication.

established up-country through the marriage of one of James Hutton Brew's nephews and the daughter of an Ashanti chief.[1]

Viewed from the angle of their social behaviour, the Brews must be considered innovators in a number of spheres, none more important than religion. At an early stage they came under the influence of Christianity, which was itself inter-related with western education and affected the family pattern.[2] The Brews' special field of interest was Methodism. Here Henry Brew played a historically significant part. Probably educated at the Castle School in Cape Coast, he belonged to the Bible Study group whose desire for further religious knowledge helped to bring the Methodists to the Gold Coast in 1835.[3]

A new phase of missionary endeavour was introduced then, and embraced several generations of Brews. Henry, for example, became a prominent member of the Methodist Church at Cape Coast and in 1857, along with the Reverend Thomas Birch Freeman, he was co-administrator of a deceased missionary's estate.[4] Two of Henry's great-nephews, the brothers William Ward Brew and James Hutton Brew, Junior, served as local preacher and catechist;[5] after his death in 1943, a tablet to Ward Brew was erected in the church at Cape Coast. Method-ism also had a place in Brew family ritual. When Henry's son, Richard Henry, married in 1858, the ceremony was performed by a minister of that church, and it was in the Methodist Cemetery at Anomabu that Henry's brother, Samuel Collins, was eventually buried.[6]

The new associations on the Gold Coast during the nine-teenth century were secular as well as religious in kind and

[1] One of Samuel Collins's wives was Amba Opanwa from the stool family of Abura Dunkwa, the mother of James Hutton Brew. The other was Adjua Esson from the royal family of Cape Coast; personal communication. James Hutton Brew's nephew was also called James Hutton Brew.
[2] See Williamson, *Akan Religion and the Christian Faith*.
[3] F. Wolfson, *Pageant of Ghana* (London, 1958), p. 15; Kimble, *Political History of Ghana*, p. 63 n. 4 and p. 146 n. 3. The Castle School, of course, owed its existence to the efforts of the Reverend Philip Quaque, Henry Brew's relative; see pp. 22–3 above. For the history of the Methodist Church in Ghana, see F. L. Bartels, *The Roots of Ghana Methodism* (Cambridge, 1965).
[4] T. B. Freeman v. Henry Brew, 30 Oct. 1857, H.C.C.C. 251/52. Freeman, a Methodist missionary of part-African descent, worked for many years in West Africa; he was the first to open up a Methodist connection with Ashanti.
[5] Personal communication.
[6] Brew v. Brew, 30 Oct. 1865, H.C.C.C. 435/52 and see p. 157 above.

ranged from mutual assistance to politics; with these the Brews were again closely linked. Both the lawyer, William Ward Brew, and the civil servant, Ebenezer Annan Brew, were Freemasons; Ward Brew's 'indefatigable' services to the order included the foundation of a 'Scottish Lodge' in Cape Coast. Ebenezer Annan Brew also acted as Grand Master of a Friendly Society, the Patriarchal Order of Oddfellows.[1] Active in matters of an intellectual kind was his brother, Samuel Henry, who read papers to the Gold Coast National Research Association,[2] while in the political sphere, J. E. Casely Hayford and William Ward Brew were among the founder members of the National Congress of British West Africa, which was inaugurated in 1920.[3]

Not only in the associations to which they belonged but in their private manner of life did the Brews display modernist tendencies, although evidence on this subject is necessarily somewhat sparse now. But Sam Kanto Brew, for example, is known to have worn European dress in the early nineteenth century,[4] and a number of western habits on the part of his son, Samuel Collins, can reasonably be assumed. It will be recalled that Samuel Collins had acted very successfully as host to the British traveller, John Duncan, in 1844, and that one of his wives had accompanied them on a local tour[5]—possibly she was the 'Mrs. Brew' who died on 6 October 1851 after a long illness borne with 'Christian fortitude and resignation'. In memory of this wife, a tablet, suitably engraved in European fashion, was laid 'by her bereaved and sorrowing husband'.[6] James Hutton Brew, Samuel Collins's son, undoubtedly adopted a number of western ways, and a photograph shows him in the attire of a Victorian gentleman with a cigar-holder in his hand. At Cape Coast, he embarked on an 'early private experiment' in telephones and tried unsuccessfully, during the eighteen-eighties, to install a line at Brew House, his family residence.[7]

---

[1] Hutchison, *The Pen-Pictures of Modern Africans and African Celebrities*, vol. I, pp. 54–5; E. A. Brew's obituary notice, *The Gold Coast Farmer*, vol. I, no. 2 (June 1932); Kimble, op. cit. p. 147.

[2] See p. 176 above.

[3] See p. 173 above.

[4] Sir Charles Macarthy to Lord Bathurst, 4 Aug. 1823, C.O. 267/58.

[5] See p. 148 above.

[6] The broken tablet can still be seen at the ruins of Samuel Collins Brew's house in Anomabu.

[7] Kimble, op. cit. p. 32 n. 4, and see plate 4.

These signs of westernization, however, should not be interpreted to mean abandonment by the Brews of traditional
attitudes and conduct. On the contrary, the traditional hold remained strong. Christian marriage and burial were paralleled
by polygamy and funeral custom, and it was reported of
Samuel Collins that he believed in the existence at Kormantin,
near Anomabu, of a male child in a state of permanent youth-
fulness since the beginning of the world. When the traveller
Duncan, the source of this information, laughed at his friend's
story, 'it somewhat offended . . . Mr. Brewe, who declared that
he himself and his father had actually seen this infant.'[1]

New associations, furthermore, linked though they might be
with political reform and with techniques such as journalism,
did not lead to the eclipse of African tradition. During the later
nineteenth century, a cultural renaissance began in Fanti. Two
forward-looking political figures, James Hutton Brew and
Casely Hayford, were connected with it, and used the columns
of their newspapers to stress the importance of indigenous custom, language, and dress.[2] Among Casely Hayford's published
works, one—*Gold Coast Native Institutions* (London, 1903)—had
been inspired by opposition to the Crown Lands Bill, and reflected this growing emphasis on the African way of life.[3]

From the foregoing account, it might appear that the Brews
were poised uneasily between two worlds, and that they were
cut off from full participation in Fanti by the degree of European culture they had absorbed. The attitude of contemporaries
towards them and the extent of social cleavage are matters that
do not readily lend themselves now to detailed examination. But
the opinion is advanced here that despite their innovating
activities, in the final analysis, it was the African sphere that
claimed them.

The Brews reveal the consequences of western individualism
which had operated through the channels of trade, education,
and Christianity; some friction between old and new was inevitable. A degree of social mobility had come into existence on
the coast, and even family domestics might acquire trading

---

[1] Duncan, *Travels in Western Africa in 1845 and 1846*, vol. I, p. 51. According to
Sir Charles Macarthy, Sam Kanto Brew—Samuel Collins's father—had combined
European dress and language with 'the very grosest [*sic*] superstition, idolatry and
fetish'; Sir Charles Macarthy to Lord Bathurst, 4 Aug. 1823, C.O. 267/58.

[2] Kimble, op. cit. pp. 517–18.   [3] Kimble, op. cit. p. 350.

wealth, possess dependants of their own and emerge as an
influential branch of the lineage.[1] Also as a result of European
contact, the patrilineal tie, by no means unimportant in Fanti,
received considerably wider emphasis. Yet innovation was
constantly tempered by the old order, displaying its vigour
through chieftaincy, the corporate family, and a socially per-
vasive religion, and from none of these were the Brews dis-
sociated.

For many centuries, European 'stranger communities' on the
seaboard had been affected by the Akan environment. Certain
of the strangers who accepted local responsibilities—and
Richard Brew was one—had been 'adopted' into Fanti,[2] where
their mulatto descendants ultimately enjoyed prestige, both as
members of a lineage and of the educated élite. This was so in
the case of the Brews during the nineteenth and early twentieth
centuries. While further inquiry into the history of western-
educated families is necessary, study of the Brew family suggests
that Akan society on the coast showed no small capacity for the
assimilation of alien cultural traits, and indeed of alien blood.

[1] See p. 184 n. 2 above.
[2] For the Akan practice of adopting strangers, see Otutu Bagyire VI, *Abiriwhene*,
'The Guans: a preliminary note' in *Ghana Notes and Queries*, no. 7 (January 1965),
p. 22.

SELECT BIBLIOGRAPHY

Manuscript Sources

(1) PUBLIC RECORD OFFICE, LONDON
(a) Treasury Records
T. 70 (Records of African Companies) vols. 29–36, 40, 41, 69, 71, 74, 144, 145, 151–3, 986–8, 1022, 1029, 1031, 1035, 1063, 1067, 1130, 1369, 1450, 1454, 1455, 1467, 1476–80, 1482, 1483, 1504, 1516–18, 1520–2, 1530–6.
(b) Colonial Office Records
C.O. 267 (Sierra Leone, Original Correspondence, Secretary of State) vols. 6, 58.
C.O. 388 (Board of Trade, Commercial, Original Correspondence) vols. 45–7, 53.
(c) Board of Trade Records
B.T. 6 (Miscellanea) vol. 2.
(d) Court of Bankruptcy Records
B. 1 (Order Books) vol. 66
B. 4 (Registers of Commissions of Bankruptcy) vol. 21.
(e) Admiralty Records
Adm. 1 (Secretary's Department, Captains' Letters) vols. 1485, 1604.
(f) Privy Council Office Records
P.C. 2 (Privy Council Office Registers) vol. 103.

(2) GHANA NATIONAL ARCHIVES, ACCRA
(a) Records of the High Court, Cape Coast, vols. 197/52, 198/52, 201/52, 202/52, 204/52, 205/52, 246/52, 248/52, 251/52, 256/52, 258/52, 270/52, 271/52, 274/52, 277/52, 278/52, 284/52, 287/52, 296/52, 310/52, 315/52, 320/52, 321/52, 323/52, 324/52, 413/52, 435/52, 499/52.
(b) ADM. 1 (Original Correspondence) vols. 450, 469, 701, 702, 704, 705, 758.
(c) Establishment Files.
(d) Blankson Papers, SC 1.
(e) Bannerman Papers, SC 2.
(f) Freeman Papers, SC 4.

(3) SOCIETY FOR THE PROPAGATION OF THE GOSPEL,
     LONDON

'C' Manuscripts, West Africa. Letters of Philip Quaque, or Kweku,
from Cape Coast Castle, 1765–1811.

(4) BALME LIBRARY, UNIVERSITY OF GHANA

Furley Collection of Notes and Transcripts, particularly W.I.C.
(Archives of the second Dutch West Indies Company, the State
Archives, The Hague) vols. 116, 119, 967, 990.

(5) GENEALOGICAL OFFICE, DUBLIN CASTLE

Molony Collection.

Printed Sources

(1) OFFICIAL PUBLICATIONS

Gold Coast, Department of Agriculture, *Gold Coast Agricultural
Reports*, 1916–20.
Gold Coast, Department of Agriculture, *The Gold Coast Farmer*, vol.
1, no. 2 (June 1932).
Gold Coast Colony Blue Books, 1868–1933.
Gold Coast Government Gazette, 1877–99.
*Journal of the Commissioners for Trade and Plantations from January 1759
to December 1763* (London, 1935).
*Journal of the Commissioners for Trade and Plantations from January 1776
to May 1782* (London, 1938).
Report from Select Committee on the West Coast of Africa, pt. II (London,
1842).
Report of the Deputy Keeper of the Records, 1928 (Belfast, 1929).
Report of the Deputy Keeper of the Records, 1936 (Belfast, 1937).

(2) COLLECTIONS OF DOCUMENTS

Blake, J. W., *Europeans in West Africa, 1450–1560* (Hakluyt Society,
2nd series, vols. 86–7, London, 1942).
Chart, D. A., *Marriage Entries from the Registers of the Parishes of St.
Andrew, St. Anne, St. Audoen and St. Bride, Dublin, 1632–1800*
(Dublin, 1913).
Crooks, J. J., *Records relating to the Gold Coast Settlements, 1750–1874*
(Dublin, 1923).
Donnan, E., *Documents Illustrative of the History of the Slave Trade to
America*, vols. II and III (Washington, D.C., 1931, 1932).
Langman, A. E., *Marriage Entries from the Registers of the Parishes of
St. Marie, St. Luke, St. Catherine and St. Werburgh, Dublin, 1627–1800*
(Dublin, 1915).

Metcalfe, G. E., *Great Britain and Ghana, Documents of Ghana History, 1807–1957* (Ghana, 1964).

Newbury, C. W., *British Policy towards West Africa, Select Documents, 1786–1874* (Oxford, 1965).

Renner, P. A., *Cases in the Courts of the Gold Coast Colony and Nigeria,* vol. I, pts. 1 and 2 (London, 1915).

Wolfson, F., *Pageant of Ghana* (London, 1958).

(3) CONTEMPORARY WORKS

Adams, J., *Remarks on the country extending from Cape Palmas to the River Congo* (London, 1823).

African Merchant, An, *A Treatise upon the Trade from Great Britain to Africa* (London, 1772).

Barbot, J., *A Description of the Coasts of North and South Guinea . . .* (London, 1732).

Bosman, W., *A New and Accurate Description of the Coast of Guinea* (London, 1705).

Bowdich, T. E., *Mission from Cape Coast Castle to Ashantee* (London, 1819).

Cruickshank, B., *Eighteen Years on the Gold Coast of Africa,* 2 vols. (London, 1853).

Duncan, J., *Travels in Western Africa in 1845 and 1846,* 2 vols. (London, 1847).

The Gentleman and Citizen's Almanack (Dublin, 1761, 1762).

Gentleman's Magazine, vols. XIX (1749), XX (1750) and XXXIII (1763).

Gore's Liverpool Directory (Liverpool, 1805).

Hippisley, J., *Essays* (London, 1764).

Lee, R., *Stories of Strange Lands* (London, 1835).

Meredith, H., *An Account of the Gold Coast of Africa* (London, 1812).

Newton, J., *The Journal of a Slave Trader 1750–1754,* ed. B. Martin and M. Spurrell (London, 1962).

Owen, N., *Journal of a Slave Dealer,* ed. E. C. Martin (London, 1930).

Ricketts, H. I., *Narrative of the Ashantee War* (London, 1831).

Royal Gazette and Sierra Leone Advertiser (Freetown), 1817–21, 1822–7.

Royal Gold Coast Gazette and Commercial Intelligencer, 1822–3.

Thompson, T., *An account of Two Missionary Voyages* (facsimile reprint, London, 1937).

(4) LATER WORKS
   (a) Books

Ade Ajayi, J. F. and Espie, I. (ed.), *A Thousand Years of West African History* (Ibadan, 1965).

Bartels, F. L., *The Roots of Ghana Methodism* (Cambridge, 1965).

Bottomore, T. B., *Elites and Society* (London, 1964).

Brown, E. J. P., *Gold Coast and Asianti Reader*, 2 vols. (London, 1929).

Camp, A. J., *Wills and their whereabouts* (Canterbury, 1963).

Christensen, J. B., *Double Descent Among the Fanti* (New Haven, 1954).

Clare, W., *A Simple Guide to Irish Genealogy* (London, 1938).

Claridge, W. W., *A History of the Gold Coast and Ashanti*, 2 vols. (London, 1915).

Coombs, D., *The Gold Coast, Britain and the Netherlands 1850–1874* (London, 1963).

Crowder, M., *The Story of Nigeria* (London, 1962).

Curtin, P. D., *The Image of Africa* (Madison, 1964).

Curtin, P. D. (ed.), *Africa Remembered* (Madison, 1967).

Curtis, E., *A History of Ireland* (London, 1961).

Davies, K. G., *The Royal African Company* (London, 1957).

Dike, K. O., *Trade and Politics in the Niger Delta* (Oxford, 1956).

Evans-Pritchard, E. E., *Essays in Social Anthropology* (London, 1962).

Fage, J. D., *Introduction to the History of West Africa* (Cambridge, 1955).

Foster, P., *Education and Social Change in Ghana* (London, 1965).

Frost, J., *The History and Topography of the County of Clare* (Dublin, 1893).

Gill, C., *Merchants and Mariners of the Eighteenth Century* (London, 1961).

Hancock, W. K., *Survey of British Commonwealth Affairs*, vol. II, pt. 2 (London, 1942).

Hargreaves, J. D., *Life of Sir Samuel Lewis* (London, 1958).

Hayford, J. E. Casely, *Gold Coast Native Institutions* (London, 1903).

Hennessy, J. Pope, *Verandah* (London, 1964).

Hutchison, C. F., *The Pen-Pictures of Modern Africans and African Celebrities*, vol. I (London, n.d.).

Johnson, J. W. de Graft, *Towards Nationhood in West Africa* (London, 1928).

Johnson, J. W. de Graft, *Historical Geography of the Gold Coast* (London, 1929).

Jones, G. I., *The Trading States of the Oil Rivers* (London, 1963).

Kimble, D., *A Political History of Ghana, 1850–1928* (Oxford, 1963).

Lawrence, A. W., *Trade Castles and Forts of West Africa* (London, 1963).

Lloyd, P. C. (ed.), *The New Elites of Tropical Africa* (London, International African Institute, 1966).

MacLysaght, E., *Irish Families; Their Names, Arms and Origins* (Dublin, 1957).

MacLysaght, E., *More Irish Families* (Dublin, 1960).
MacLysaght, E., *Irish Life in the Seventeenth Century* (Cork, 1950).
McPhee, A., *The Economic Revolution in British West Africa* (London, 1926).
Malinowski, B., *The Dynamics of Culture Change*, ed. P. M. Kaberry (New Haven, 1945).
Mannix, D. P. and Cowley, M., *Black Cargoes* (London, 1963).
Martin, E. C., *The British West African Settlements, 1750–1821* (London, 1927).
Metcalfe, G. E., *Maclean of the Gold Coast* (London, 1962).
O'Hart, J., *The Irish and Anglo-Irish Landed Gentry when Cromwell came to Ireland* (Dublin, 1884).
Ponsioen, J. A., *The Analysis of Social Change Reconsidered* ('S-Gravenhage, 1962).
Porter, A. T., *Creoledom: A Study of the Development of Freetown Society* (London, 1963).
Reaney, P. H., *A Dictionary of British Surnames* (London, 1958).
Reindorf, C. C., *History of the Gold Coast and Asante* (Basel, 1895).
Robinson, R. and Gallagher, J., *Africa and the Victorians* (London, 1961).
Sampson, M. J., *Gold Coast Men of Affairs* (London, 1937).
Sarbah, J. M., *Fanti Customary Laws* (London, 1904).
Sarbah, J. M., *Fanti National Constitution* (London, 1906).
Southon, A. E., *Gold Coast Methodism, the First Hundred Years 1835–1935* (Cape Coast and London, 1934).
Vicars, A. (ed.), *Index to the Prerogative Wills of Ireland, 1536–1810* (Dublin, 1897).
Ward, W. E. F., *History of Ghana* (London, 1966).
Williams, B., *The Whig Supremacy, 1714–1760* (Oxford, 1945).
Williamson, S. G., *Akan Religion and the Christian Faith*, ed. K. A. Dickson (Accra, 1965).
Wraith, R. E., *Guggisberg* (London, 1967).
Wyndham, H. A., *The Atlantic and Slavery* (London, 1935).

(b) Articles

Agbodeka, F., 'The Fanti Confederacy, 1865–69' in *Transactions of the Historical Society of Ghana*, vol. VII (1965).
Arhin, K., 'Diffuse Authority among the Coastal Fanti' in *Ghana Notes and Queries*, no. 9 (November 1966).
Bartels, F. L., 'Philip Quaque, 1741–1816' in *Transactions of the Gold Coast and Togoland Historical Society*, vol. I, pt. 5 (1955).
Bevin, H. J., 'The Gold Coast Economy about 1880' in *Transactions of the Gold Coast and Togoland Historical Society*, vol. II, pt. 2 (1956).

Birmingham, D., 'A Note on the Kingdom of Fetu' in *Ghana Notes and Queries*, no. 9 (November 1966).

Boahen, A. A., 'The Origins of the Akan' in *Ghana Notes and Queries*, no. 9 (November 1966).

Brooks Jnr., G. E., 'The Letter Book of Captain Edward Harrington' in *Transactions of the Historical Society of Ghana*, vol. VI (1963).

Collins, E., 'The Panic Element in Nineteenth-Century Relations with Ashanti' in *Transactions of the Historical Society of Ghana*, vol. V, pt. 2 (1962).

Debrunner, H., 'Notable Danish Chaplains on the Gold Coast' in *Transactions of the Gold Coast and Togoland Historical Society*, vol. II, pt. 1 (1956).

Dorjahn, V. R. and Fyfe, C., 'Landlord and Stranger: Change in Tenancy Relations in Sierra Leone' in *Journal of African History*, vol. III, no. 3 (1962).

Fage, J. D., 'The Administration of George Maclean on the Gold Coast, 1830–44' in *Transactions of the Gold Coast and Togoland Historical Society*, vol. I, pt. 4 (1955).

Hallett, R., 'The European Approach to the Interior of Africa in the Eighteenth Century' in *Journal of African History*, vol. IV, no. 2 (1963).

Hargreaves, J. D., 'Assimilation in Eighteenth-Century Senegal' in *Journal of African History*, vol. VI, no. 2 (1965).

History Department, University of Ghana, 'A New Check List of the Forts and Castles of Ghana' in *Transactions of the Historical Society of Ghana*, vol. IV, pt. 1 (1959).

Hyde, F. E., Parkinson, B. B. and Marriner, S., 'The Nature and Profitability of the Liverpool Slave Trade' in *Economic History Review*, 2nd series, vol. V (1953).

Johnson, J. C. de Graft, 'The Fanti Asafu' in *Africa*, vol. V, no. 3 (1932).

Johnson, M., 'The Ounce in Eighteenth-Century West African Trade' in *Journal of African History*, vol. VII, no. 2 (1966).

Little, K. L., 'The Study of "Social Change" in British West Africa' in *Africa*, vol. XXIII, no. 4 (1953).

Matson, J. N., 'The French at Amoku' in *Transactions of the Gold Coast and Togoland Historical Society*, vol. I, pt. 2 (1953).

Otutu Bagyire VI, *Abiriwhene*, 'The Guans: a preliminary note' in *Ghana Notes and Queries*, no. 7 (January 1965).

Polanyi, K., 'Sortings and "Ounce Trade" in the West African Slave Trade' in *Journal of African History*, vol. V, no. 3 (1964).

Priestley, M., 'A Note on Fort William, Anomabu' in *Transactions of the Gold Coast and Togoland Historical Society*, vol. II, pt. I (1956).

Priestley, M., 'Richard Brew: an eighteenth century trader at Anomabu' in *Transactions of the Historical Society of Ghana*, vol. IV, pt. I (1959).

Priestley, M., 'The Ashanti Question and the British: eighteenth century origins' in *Journal of African History*, vol. II, no. 1 (1961).

Priestley, M. and Wilks, I., 'The Ashanti Kings in the Eighteenth Century: a revised chronology' in *Journal of African History*, vol. I, no. 1 (1960).

Sheridan, R. B., 'The Commercial and Financial Organization of the British Slave Trade, 1750–1807' in *Economic History Review*, 2nd series, vol. XI, no. 2 (December 1958).

Skinner, E. P., 'Strangers in West African Societies' in *Africa*, vol. XXXIII, no. 4 (1963).

Swanzy, H., 'A Trading Family in the Nineteenth Century Gold Coast' in *Transactions of the Gold Coast and Togoland Historical Society*, vol. II, pt. 2 (1956).

Wilks, I., 'The Rise of the Akwamu Empire, 1650–1710' in *Transactions of the Historical Society of Ghana*, vol. III, pt. 2 (1957).

Wilks, I., 'Aspects of Bureaucratisation in Ashanti in the nineteenth century' in *Journal of African History*, vol. VII, no. 2 (1966).

APPENDIX

Figure a

NOTE This family tree is not exhaustive. It concentrates on those members of the family mentioned in the text. Dates are given, where known, but the seniority of children cannot always be ascertained.

THE BREW FAMILY

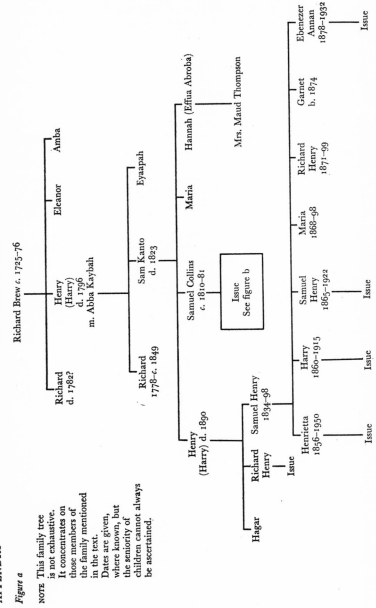

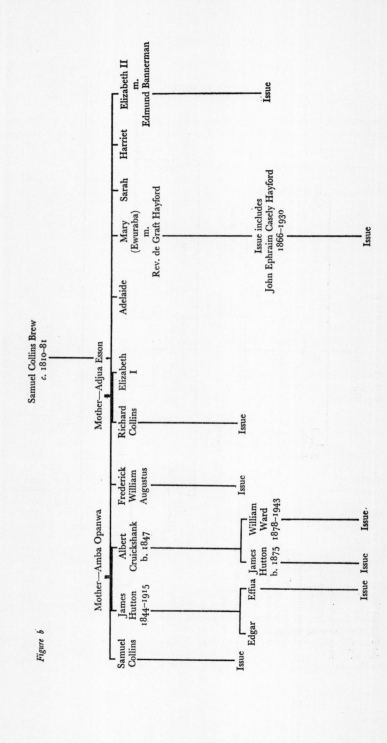

Figure b

INDEX

Names shown in the Brew family tree (Appendix (a) and (b)) are given in capital letters. Where Christian names are identical, the entries are given in generation order.

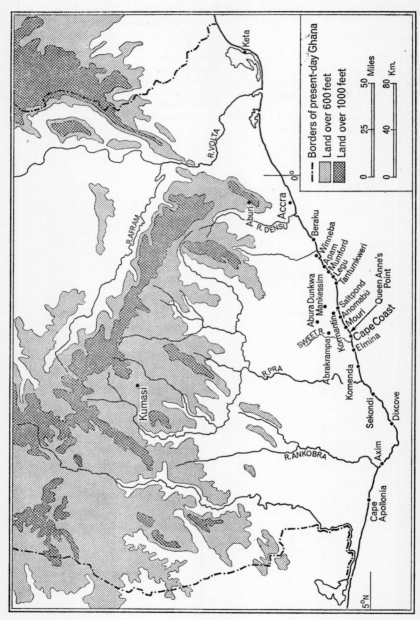

1. THE GOLD COAST, showing places mentioned in the text and main geographical features.

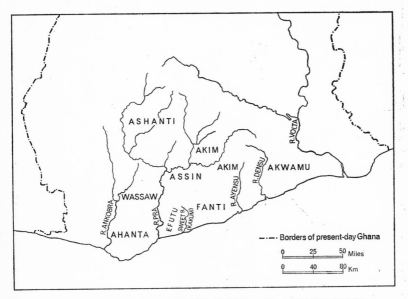

2. EIGHTEENTH-CENTURY GOLD COAST STATES, as
mentioned in the text.

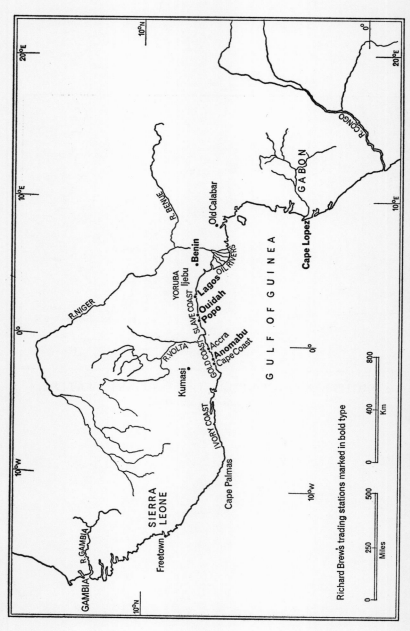

3. WEST AFRICA, showing Richard Brew's trading stations.

Richard Brew's trading stations marked in bold type

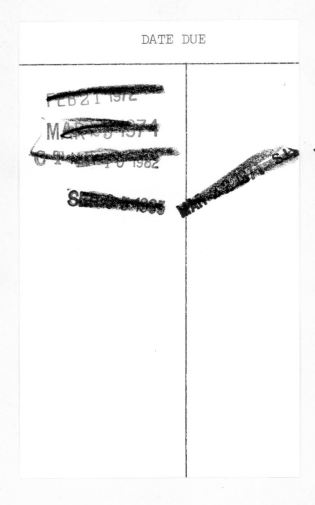